Praise for
ONE MIND

*"Larry Dossey is a pioneer who keeps finding new frontiers. With **One Mind**, his merging of science and wisdom has come full circle, as Dossey makes the case for ancient spiritual teachings about the one and the many. I'm happy to embrace Larry as a kindred spirit."*
—**Deepak Chopra**, author of *Spiritual Solutions*

*"**One Mind** is a magnum opus—delightfully inspiring and exciting—while also satisfying the requirements of rigorous scientific inquiry. Larry Dossey is a master storyteller, physician, and critical thinker. And I love this book."*
—**Christiane Northrup, M.D.**, author of *Women's Bodies, Women's Wisdom*

*"Dr. Larry Dossey's excellent book **One Mind** lays the groundwork for the coming global awakening of consciousness and helps map out the path toward it. Dr. Dossey makes an eloquent case that such consciousness is, indeed, One Consciousness. His is the science of 2012 and beyond"*
—**Eben Alexander, M.D.**, author of *Proof of Heaven:
A Neurosurgeon's Journey into the Afterlife*

"I have lived what Dr. Larry Dossey writes about. I know and can prove consciousness is nonlocal. I have used nonlocal knowing to make diagnoses and help make therapeutic decisions for my patients. I have learned to live by my experience and not by limited beliefs."
—**Bernie Siegel, M.D.**, author of *A Book of Miracles* and *Faith, Hope & Healing*

*"**One Mind** is a compelling, gripping, altogether convincing book about the nature of Mind and Consciousness and the deeply important role they play in our lives and our world. Do yourself a favor and start reading it right away!"*
—**Ken Wilber**, author of *The Integral Vision*

*"This beautifully rendered masterwork from one of our most cherished sages of the spirit makes an eloquent and indisputable case for human consciousness as a singular entity. The sheer weight of mind-boggling evidence and compelling stories—from near-death experience and reincarnation, to creativity, ESP, and crowd intelligence—demolishes the current 'mind equals brain' theory of modern science and expands our perception of how the world works. **One Mind** is Dr. Larry Dossey's boldest and most majestic work to date, with a powerful, lingering message: nature has designed us to stay connected forever."*
—**Lynne McTaggart**, author of *The Field*, *The Intention Experiment*, and *The Bond*

"Larry Dossey is not arguing simply for the existence of psychic phenomena, for which there is now much evidence, but for a deeper linkage we all share to One Mind which underlies our seemingly separate individual minds. This book combines a thought-provoking thesis with remarkable and vivid accounts of personal experiences. Only Larry Dossey could carry this off."
—**Rupert Sheldrake, Ph.D.**, author of *Science Set Free: 10 Paths to New Discovery*

"Contemporary science has long acknowledged that the atoms that make up the human body are the same as those that comprise the galaxies. However, the implications of this insight have never been spelled out with such elegance and clarity as Larry Dossey has described them in **One Mind**. Dossey leaves his readers filled not only with hope but with the determination to play their role in mending the tattered fabric of their lives on planet Earth."
—**Stanley Krippner, Ph.D.**, professor of psychology at Saybrook University and co-author of Personal Mythology

"With characteristic breadth, depth, and clarity, Larry Dossey explores, explains, and illustrates through concrete examples the abundant scientific evidence for the pantheistic hypothesis that our individual minds are included within, and are expressions of, a single One Mind. A joy to read, **One Mind** is highly recommended for both expert and novice alike."
—**Neal Grossman, Ph.D.**, professor emeritus of philosophy, University of Illinois at Chicago and author of Healing the Mind: The Philosophy of Spinoza Adapted for a New Age

"This landmark book is a brilliant synthesis of the hugely significant work that Larry Dossey has undertaken over the last 30 years. It creates an overarching theoretical framework in which a huge variety of experiences make sense. This is important not only for science but also for the future of the planet as we evolve toward a more empathic culture, realizing that we are all deeply interconnected in a greater whole."
—**David Lorimer, M.A., P.G.C.E, F.R.S.A.**, director of The Scientific and Medical Network, editor of the Network Review, and author of Whole in One

"**One Mind** is Larry Dossey's magnum opus—his finest and most lasting contribution since **Recovering the Soul**. Encyclopedic, visionary, and just plain fascinating, this spectacular book is a must-read for anyone interested in the science of human consciousness."
—**Jeff Levin, Ph.D., M.P.H.**, professor of epidemiology and population health at Baylor University

"In Larry Dossey's latest book, he takes us into new territory where we unite in the deepest dimensions of shared humanity. He affirms a global consciousness that unites all hearts and minds, held together by Cosmic Love. It is his finest work to date."
—**Jean Watson, Ph.D., RN, AHN-BC, FAAN**, distinguished professor of nursing, Murchinson-Scoville endowed chair in caring science at the University of Colorado Denver College of Nursing, and founder of the Watson Caring Science Institute

"Is there hope for the future? Dr. Larry Dossey plots a direct course that takes us there NOW filled with love and possibility. Amid the cacophony of doomsayers **One Mind** is our personal invitation to discover a new way to think about common spiritual experiences. This book is an invaluable tool which reaffirms our knowing and demonstrates, again and again, that no one of us is really alone!"
—**Reverend Canon Ted Karpf**, adjunct lecturer of religion, public health, and international development at Boston University School of Theology

"For more than three decades, Larry Dossey has given us the gift of insightful commentary about the nature of our being, who we are, and how we fit in the universe. All expressed in notably elegant prose, **One Mind** is no exception. If you want to know about the nature of consciousness, Dossey should be on your must-read list."
—**Stephan A. Schwartz**, senior fellow at the Samueli Institute and author of Opening to the Infinite

ONE
MIND

ONE MIND

HOW OUR INDIVIDUAL MIND
IS PART OF A GREATER CONSCIOUSNESS
AND WHY IT MATTERS

LARRY DOSSEY, M.D.

HAY HOUSE, INC.
Carlsbad, California • New York City
London • Sydney • Johannesburg
Vancouver • Hong Kong • New Delhi

Published and distributed in the United States by: Hay House, Inc.: www.hayhouse.com® • *Published and distributed in Australia by:* Hay House Australia Pty. Ltd.: www.hayhouse.com.au • *Published and distributed in the United Kingdom by:* Hay House UK, Ltd.: www.hayhouse.co.uk • *Published and distributed in the Republic of South Africa by:* Hay House SA (Pty), Ltd.: www.hayhouse.co.za • *Distributed in Canada by:* Raincoast: www.raincoast.com • *Published in India by:* Hay House Publishers India: www.hayhouse.co.in

Cover design: Angela Moody www.amoodycover.com
Interior design: Pamela Homan

The Universal Spectrum of Love © 2012 Larry Dossey. "What's love got to do with it?" *Alternative Therapies in Health and Medicine.* 1996; 2(3): 8–15.

Reprinted by permission of the translator: "Come, come, whoever you are" by Jalal al-Din Rumi, *Rumi: The Big Red Book,* trans. Coleman Barks, New York: HarperCollins © 2010 by Coleman Barks and "The minute I heard my first love story" by Jalal al-Din Rumi, *Rumi: The Book of Love,* trans. Coleman Barks, New York: HarperCollins © 2003 by Coleman Barks.

Library of Congress Cataloging-in-Publication Data

Dossey, Larry
  One mind : how our individual mind is part of a greater consciousness and why it matters / Larry Dossey, M.D. -- 1st edition.
    pages cm
  Includes bibliographical references and index.
  ISBN 978-1-4019-4315-8 (hardcover : alk. paper) 1. Parapsychology. 2. Consciousness. 3. Extrasensory perception. 4. Mind and body. I. Title.
  BF1031.D67 2013
  299'.93--dc23
                    2013006891

Hardcover ISBN: 978-1-4019-4315-8

16 15 14 13   4 3 2 1
1st edition, October 2013

Printed in the United States of America

SUSTAINABLE FORESTRY INITIATIVE
Certified Chain of Custody
Promoting Sustainable Forestry
www.sfiprogram.org
SFI-01268

SFI label applies to the text stock

As always, for Barbara

CONTENTS

ACKNOWLEDGMENTS

During the final phases of the writing of this book, several events occurred that shed light on whom to acknowledge.

Barbara, my wife, and I live in the foothills of the Sangre de Cristo Mountains in northern New Mexico. As I wrote, coyotes began to visit. This was especially interesting, as it often occurred while I was crafting the section about the connections between the minds of humans and animals. I would look up from my computer to see one, two, or three coyotes peering at me through the windows of my study. As they drilled holes in me with their gaze, I had the feeling they were curious about the manuscript and were making sure I got it right. After a few eye-to-eye moments, they would amble off. They continue to come back occasionally, as if checking on things. This is new. In these parts, coyotes are normally shy creatures. Over the two decades we've lived here, they have never behaved this way.

And then there was the breathtakingly beautiful bobcat that appeared one cold, snowy day just outside my window while I was writing. He plopped down, groomed himself, and looked things over for nearly an hour—another never-before happening. There are also the resident birds and deer, who always seem quite sure they own the place.

I think these creatures have appeared as ambassadors from the greater web of life. They have come calling to remind me that they, too, are part of the One Mind and that they don't want to be left out of this account. I feel that they are signaling for me to acknowledge and extend gratitude to *all* sentient creatures.

And so I do.

I am especially grateful to James Levine, my literary agent, for his generous support, friendship, and advice over many years. I remain on my knees in gratitude to Patricia Gift at Hay House, who gave this book a home, and to editor Peter Guzzardi, whose skills in bringing order to chaos are unparalleled. Working with Patricia and Peter brought the book's title to life, because it has seemed as if we were of one mind. Thanks, too, to my colleagues at *Explore: The Journal of Science and Healing* for their support, and to journal publisher Chris Baumlee and Elsevier for affording me a platform for my editorial rants about any subject I consider important. I also extend gratitude to the Js for their feedback and champagne discussions of early versions of the manuscript, and to Rupert Sheldrake for invaluable advice. Any subsequent blunders are mine, not theirs. Deepest thanks also to readers who continue to send me accounts of nonlocal, beyond-the-body events in their lives, many of whom say they have never before shared these experiences with anyone.

But every time I consider the individuals I should thank, from whom I've drawn information and inspiration, I am simply bewildered. There are far too many to name. And if my theme of the One Mind is valid, acknowledgments present an even deeper problem. For if all individual minds come together in a collective domain of intelligence, how is one to know whom to thank? How can one trace the origin of any idea, contribution, or achievement? In the One Mind, does "origin" even make sense?

The eminent German physicist and philosopher Baron Carl Friedrich von Weizsäcker understood the problem of origins. He said, "[In any great discovery] we find the often disturbing and happy experience: 'It is not I; I have not done this.' Still, in a certain way it is I—yet not the ego . . . but . . . a more comprehensive self."[1] And as the great inventor Thomas Edison said, "People say I have created things. I have never created anything. I get impressions from the Universe at large and work them out, but I am only a plate on a record or a receiving apparatus—what you will. Thoughts are really impressions that we get from outside."[2]

That's what I've experienced. In writing about the One Mind, I've felt that I am part of it. It has often seemed that my thoughts are not my own; they flow from an invisible company of informants, supporters, friends, and ancestors. The stereotype of the lonely, solitary writer struggling with his material does not apply. I have help.

So to each and all in the Great Connect: thank you.

This book would never have been birthed without inspiration from Garry and Bet, my brother and sister—but most of all from Barbara, my wife and my fixed star. My love and gratitude to her are written in invisible ink on every page.

AUTHOR'S NOTE

About *Mind* and *Consciousness*

In the late '80s I had the opportunity to lecture to physicians in New Delhi about the emerging evidence that mind and consciousness can be potent factors in health and illness. In the discussion that followed, an elderly Indian physician stood and said very politely, "Dr. Dossey, can you be more specific about what you mean by mind and consciousness? In my tradition they are not the same. We have many levels of consciousness and states of mind. Now you will tell us which one you mean." I was out of my league and stammered my way through a pathetic nonanswer.

T. S. Eliot once said of Indian philosophers, "Their subtleties make most of the great European philosophers look like schoolboys."[1] In this book, I have deliberately chosen to risk looking like one of those schoolboys, hoping this up-front confession might get me off the hook for sliding over distinctions that are sure to make anyone groan who is acquainted with the sophisticated views of consciousness that have developed in the East. For most Western readers, however, I find that these granular analyses of consciousness can be off-putting. To be told that in Buddhism the Kamaloka, or empirical/worldly plane of consciousness, has 54 states and that the Lokuttara, or transcendental plane, has 40 states makes Western eyes glaze over.[2] If I've done my job, you'll know what I mean by the context in which I use *mind* and *consciousness*. If not, I deserve your censure.

Perhaps it is a mistake to force certain concepts into a locked-on trajectory via a narrow definition. Maybe some terms should be allowed to wander freely and float in deliberate ambiguity if they are to be adequately expressed. An excuse for sloppiness, or wisdom? You, dear reader, can decide.

For those readers who nonetheless want to carry with them an image of consciousness through the pages that follow, I offer the following thoughts from one of India's eminent contemporary philosophers and consciousness researchers, K. Ramakrishna Rao. Many Western scientists and philosophers share Professor Rao's views,[3] as we shall see:

> Consciousness in the Indian tradition is more than an experience of awareness. It is a fundamental principle that underlies all knowing and being. Various forms of manifest awareness are images of consciousness revealed to the person as reflections in her mind. The cognitive structure does not generate consciousness; it simply reflects it; and in the process limits and embellishes it. In a fundamental sense, consciousness is the source of our awareness. In other words, consciousness is not merely awareness as manifest in different forms but it is also what makes awareness possible. It is said in *Kena Upanisad* that consciousness is the ear of the ear, the thought of the thought, the speech of the speech, the breath of the breath and the eye of the eye. . . . Consciousness is the light which illumines the things on which it shines.

Trying to comprehend consciousness with the mind is a fruitless endeavor. As Buddhist scholar Alan Watts said, this effort is like trying to see one's eye *with* one's eye, or trying to bite one's teeth *with* one's teeth—the wrong tool for the job.

This "tool problem" has long been recognized. As Lao Tzu, the Chinese sage of the 6th century B.C.E., said of the Tao, or Way of nature, "The Tao that can be expressed is not the eternal Tao; the name that can be defined is not the unchanging name."[4] As with the Tao, so with the One Mind.[5]

In the spring of 1933, physicists Werner Heisenberg, Carl Friedrich von Weizsäcker, and Niels Bohr met a few friends in a crude mountain hut in Bavaria for a ski holiday. By this time Heisenberg and Bohr were famous on the world stage of physics. As Heisenberg describes in his book *Physics and Beyond*, he engineered the get-together, wanting "just one more happy holiday with old friends." Chores were assigned. Heisenberg became the group cook, and Bohr washed the dishes. Heisenberg reports that Bohr, while washing up after dinner one night, began discussing the shortcomings of language in describing the results of atomic experiments.

"Our washing up is just like our language," Bohr said. "We have dirty water and dirty dishcloths, and yet we manage to get the plates and glasses clean. In language, too, we have to work with unclear concepts and a form of logic whose scope is restricted in an unknown way, and yet we use it to bring some clarity into our understanding of nature."[6]

The problem that Bohr, Heisenberg, and the architects of quantum theory encountered is that there is nothing in human experience comparable to their experimental findings and therefore no language existed to adequately describe them.

Neither can the goal of this book—to describe the unification of individual minds in a unitary, collective One Mind—be satisfactorily accomplished with the writer's tool of language. We are trying to clean the plates and glasses with dirty water and dirty dishcloths. Bohr believed the physicists managed to get their "dishes" reasonably clean nonetheless. But there is a difference between clean and sparkling.

That is why more than words are needed as we go forward, and why I have frequently relied on the experiences of individuals throughout this book. Skeptics who are afflicted by "randomania" or "statisticalitis" often deride people's experiences as "mere anecdotes," but they are essential to grasping the complementarity between individual minds and the One Mind. If a picture is worth a thousand words, an individual's experience can be worth a thousand pictures. The personal, subjective element can never be eliminated from our attempts to know the world, even our scientific attempts. As Max Planck, the principal founder of quantum physics, said, "Science cannot solve the ultimate mystery of nature. And that is because, in the last analysis, we ourselves are part of nature and therefore part of the mystery that we are trying to solve."[7]

So we proceed, dirty dishcloths and all.

INTRODUCTION

Do not believe on the strength of traditions,
even if they have been held in honor for many
generations and in many places;
do not believe anything because many people speak of it;
do not believe on the strength of sages of old times;
do not believe that which you have yourselves imagined,
thinking that a god has inspired you.
Believe nothing which depends only on the
authority of your masters and priests.
After investigation, believe that which you have
yourselves tested and found reasonable and
which is for your good and that of others.

— THE BUDDHA, *THE KALAMA SUTRA*

This book is about the concept of the One Mind—which, evidence suggests, is a collective, unitary domain of intelligence, of which all individual minds are a part. The One Mind is a dimension in which you and I meet, as we are doing even now.

In the 20th century we were introduced to several subdivisions of mind, such as the conscious, the preconscious, the subconscious, the unconscious, the collective conscious, and the collective unconscious. The One Mind is an additional perspective on our mental landscape.

The difference is that the One Mind is not a subdivision. It is the over-arching, inclusive dimension to which all the mental components of all individual minds belong. I capitalize the One Mind to distinguish it from the one mind that is possessed by each individual.

Why the One Mind Is Important

I have written this book because I believe the One Mind is a potential way out of the division, bitterness, selfishness, greed, and destruction that threaten to engulf our world—from which, beyond a certain point, there may be no escape. Identifying with the highest expressions of human consciousness can clear our vision, prevent the hardening of our moral and ethical arteries, and inspire us to action. These are not ordinary times. Boldness is required, including boldness in how we think about who we are, our origins and destiny, and what we are capable of. I do not consider the One Mind as a philosophical plaything. It is not a luxury concept to be contemplated at leisure. Urgency is afoot.

We humans have ingenious ways of ignoring the obvious and deceiving ourselves, even when we are faced with impending trag-edy. One of my dearest patients was a man in his early 30s who was a brilliant classical musician and a member of the city's symphony. He came to me because he could not sleep. This highly intelligent man was a walking textbook of pathology—anxious and driven, obese, diabetic, and a heavy smoker. He disdained exercise of any sort. When I asked him what he did for relaxation, he said, "What do you mean?" His family history was riddled with heart disease and diabetes. Most of the males, including his father, had died of heart attacks in early middle age.

After completing his workup, I described what in all likelihood lay ahead for him—that, statistically, he was headed for disaster unless he made major changes. He did not want to hear this. "My mother lived into her nineties," he protested. "Maybe I've got her genes." He altered nothing. A year later he had a major heart attack but survived. It was his wake-up call. He transformed his lifestyle completely. He lost weight, his diabetes went away, and he gave up smoking. He took up meditation and became a fitness fan. "Overnight my heart attack made me see things in a different way," he said. "Too bad I had to nearly die to learn how to live."

We humans are a lot like my patient. We are staring a variety of impending problems in the face and denying their reality. Must we undergo some planetary version of a heart attack before we come to our senses? Facts and statistics are apparently not sufficient to move us in sensible directions. But there is another way. An existential shift can make it possible for us to see the world in a new way, a way that redefines our relationship to one another and to the earth itself. This shift can radically transform how we choose to live. That's what the One-Mind perspective is all about. I am not saying that awakening to the One Mind is the *only* way out of the dilemmas we face, but it is *a* way, a very potent path that is available to everyone.

How This Book Works

I've constructed this book as a series of stand-alone, bite-size vignettes about the One Mind—what one reader called "subway reading." There is a flow and pattern to them, but each section also stands on its own as a portal, or entry point, to the concept of the One Mind. Each deals with a particular way in which the One Mind leaves its tracks in human affairs. Each could be the subject of an entire book and often has been.

My strategy is to look at a large variety of phenomena so that the concept of the One Mind does not rise or fall on the basis of any single one of them but draws its strength from the whole. As the philosopher F. C. S. Schiller said, "A synthesis which embraces such a multitude of facts does not rest solely on any one set of them, and in a sense grows independent of them all."[1] As the proverb has it, "A single arrow is easily broken, but not ten in a bundle."

I've directed this book to general readers, not to scientists, philosophers, or my peers and colleagues who are involved in consciousness research. It is intended for any layperson who retains the capacity to wonder, to marvel, as we all did as children before we learned that there is a "proper" way to think. Still, some sections are more complex than others. So if some sections are not your cup of tea, skip them. It's the big picture that counts.

As you engage these various viewpoints, you may begin to notice patterns in your own life that seem more comprehensible and coherent from the One-Mind perspective. If this happens, I'd love to hear from you.[2]

Encountering the One Mind

We may experience the One Mind in a variety of ways. Think of the One Mind as a desert spring where we go to drink. We may arrive at the spring alone and have a solitary experience. Or we may meet another individual there, a group of individuals, or perhaps a throng. Just so, when we "drink" of the One Mind, the experience may affect us singly and individually, manifesting as a transcendent moment, an epiphany, or a creative breakthrough. Or we may acquire information inexplicably, as if by revelation, or experience a premonition that proves valid. Alternatively, One-Mind experiences may involve two or more people, such as when spouses, siblings, twins, lovers, or groups of individuals share emotions, thoughts, or feelings at a distance. As we'll see, they can also occur across species. Although One-Mind events are endlessly varied, they have this in common: they involve unbounded, extended awareness.

But how can we be confident that the One Mind exists? There are no meters or gadgets that can calibrate it. This problem applies to many things we believe are real but cannot be measured directly—love, caring, compassion, patriotism, or a preference for peanut butter and jelly sandwiches, to name just a few. In situations like this, we informally set up criteria for proving to ourselves that something exists. For instance, we calculate that if a person is loving, he or she will behave in such-and-such a way. Then if the person behaves in these ways, we presume that he or she is indeed capable of love. In the absence of measurements, we can take the same approach to the One Mind.

What criteria should we set up to show that the One Mind exists? How would interconnected, overlapping minds manifest in daily life? If individual minds are linked with all other minds via the One Mind, what sort of experiences would individuals have? How would they know they are part of a greater mind?

If the One Mind existed we would expect to see the following:

- A person could share thoughts and emotions—and even physical sensations—with a distant individual with whom she has no sensory contact.

- An individual could demonstrate detailed knowledge possessed by a person who has died, which that individual could not have acquired by normal means.

- Distant communication could take place between humans and sentient nonhumans, such as pets.

- Large groups of animals—herds, flocks, schools—could behave in such highly coordinated ways that shared, overlapping minds are suggested.

- A dying or even healthy individual could experience direct contact with a transcendent domain in which it is revealed to her that she is in fact part of a greater mind that is infinite in space and time.

- An individual could find hidden or lost objects through mental means alone, or perceive in detail, without sensory contact, distant scenes that are known to someone else.

As it turns out, none of these possibilities is hypothetical; they are all real, as we shall see. And because they exist we can infer, with solid justification, that the One Mind is also real. We can also take some assurance from the number of creative geniuses in fields of endeavor as varied as theoretical physics, philosophy, and music, who over the centuries have expressed their belief in the One Mind.

Nonlocal Mind

The ultimate argument for the One Mind, however, is the *nonlocality* of consciousness. We will explore the meaning of this term in the pages that follow, but briefly it is this: Individual minds turn out to be not just individual. They are not confined or localized to specific points in space, such as brains or bodies, nor to specific points in time, such as the present. Minds, rather, are *nonlocal* with respect to space and time. This means that the separateness of minds is an illusion, because individual minds cannot be put in a box (or brain) and walled off from one another. In some sense, all minds come together to form a single mind. Throughout history, many individuals, including eminent scientists, have glimpsed this fact. This includes Nobel physicist Erwin Schrödinger, who proclaimed, "There is only one mind," and the distinguished physicist David Bohm, who asserted, "Deep down the consciousness of mankind is one."

I coined the term "nonlocal mind" in 1989 in my book *Recovering the Soul* to express what I believe is a spatially and temporally infinite aspect of our consciousness.[3] Nonlocal mind resembles the age-old concept of the soul, as we'll see.

Survival

Not a week goes by these days without some combustible congressman or febrile journalist warning us that our nation is becoming second rate. Various reasons are cited but a major one, we're told, is our educational system. We are falling behind in the hard sciences, and this imperils us in an increasingly competitive world. We are sternly warned that we must focus in our schools and universities, before it is too late, on the STEM areas—science, technology, engineering, and mathematics.

No one valued the hard sciences more than physician-researcher Lewis Thomas, who for many years directed research at Memorial Sloan-Kettering Cancer Center. But Thomas was also concerned about the headwaters of wisdom that lay upstream from science. He realized that science is not a stopping place for human understanding. He was thus a one-man wrecking crew of the walls separating knowledge into the "hard" and "soft" domains. In his sparkling, wide-ranging essays in the *New England Journal of Medicine*, he tackled anything that struck his fancy. Two of his favorite subjects were Montaigne and Mahler. Nothing was off the table; he even conjectured that consciousness might be recycled after death into a "biospherical nervous system" because, he said, it seems too valuable an entity for nature to waste. This sortie evoked gasps of disbelief and suspicions of woolly-headedness from a few buttoned-up scientists, but Thomas knew what he was doing.

He sensed we were losing our way, and he was not afraid to say so. He believed that the limitations of our minds constitute a kind of planetary emergency. As he put it, "We need to know more. . . . We now know that we cannot do this any longer by searching our minds, for there is not enough there to search. . . . We need science, more and better science, not for its technology, not for leisure, not even for health or longevity, but for *the hope of wisdom* which our kind of culture must acquire *for its survival* [italics added]."[4]

Avoiding extinction. This is a threatening concept our society does not wish to face. Having scraped by the Cold War without a nuclear exchange, many thought smooth sailing lay ahead, but now we know better. The problems we face are systemic and metastatic. They may not be as dramatic as nuclear horror, but they are equally deadly. They involve the gradual degradation and deterioration of our world because of the way we choose to behave, abetted by an unremitting greed, a paralysis of will, the clouding of vision, and a willful ignorance toward the rigorous kind of science that Thomas cherished. As a people, we seem to be seriously impaired. It is as if we have suffered a culturewide stroke that has damaged the higher centers that control our ability to reason and act in rational ways.

What will see us through? There is increasing talk that we must *engineer* our way out of the problems posed by global climate change, environmental destruction, pollution, poverty, hunger, over-population, desertification, water scarcity, species collapse, and so on. Maybe. But as Thomas implied, something beyond today's science is needed: "the hope of wisdom."

What kind of wisdom? Surely it involves the awareness that we are an inseparable part of life on Earth, for without this perception it is unclear whether we can muster the will to make the choices that are required to survive. We know intellectually that we cannot secede from nature. This is hardly news; it has been the keystone message of environmental science for a century. Yet the colossal importance of this insight is broadly denied. It is clear that in addition to factual knowledge, we need something that can stir our blood and connect us with something beyond our me-centered selves. We need more skin in the game.

This is why the One Mind is vital. If all individual minds are united via the One Mind, for which there is impressive evidence, it follows that at some level we are intimately connected with one another and with all sentient life. This realization makes possible a recalibration of the self-oriented Golden Rule, from "Do unto others as you would have them do unto you" to "Be kind to others, because in some sense they *are* you." The task of the great wisdom traditions throughout history has been to transform this awareness from an intellectual concept into a felt certainty that is so real that it makes a difference in how we conduct our lives.

The realization of the One Mind carries us beyond the isolation and frustration of the separate individual struggling against impossible odds. Life becomes more than a wearisome journey from the cradle to the crematorium. A felt unity with all other minds conveys renewed meaning, purpose, and possibility and a sense of the sacredness of all things.

We are nearly there. The "hope of wisdom" that Thomas prized is within our reach, and much of the "more and better science" he called for already exists. It has surfaced in the form of evidence for a unifying, nonlocal, universal form of consciousness, as I shall try to show. Many scientists—*great* scientists—have embraced this concept, as we shall see.

The Collaboratory

The challenges we humans face are so huge, so global, that it can be difficult to see how our individual efforts can make any difference. Consider environmental issues such as pollution and global climate change. Barbara, my wife, and I garden organically and have had a passive solar wall on the entire south side of our house for 20 years. Although these measures make us feel better and represent our commitment to environmental responsibility, they are offset by a recurring sense of futility in the big scheme of things. It's like the Breton Fisherman's Prayer: "O God, thy sea is so great and my boat is so small," a plaque of which President John F. Kennedy kept on his desk.

If Barbara and I multiplied our environmental efforts a thousandfold, they would still be puny.

Environmentalist Carolyn Raffensperger wrote, "I have a hypothesis about the lack of public support for environmental action. I suspect that many people suffer from a sense of moral failure over environmental matters. They know we are in deep trouble, that their actions are part of it, but there is so little they or anyone can do individually."[5] As journalist Anne Karpf, author of *The Human Voice,* wrote in *The Guardian,* "I now recycle everything possible, drive a hybrid car and turn down the heating. Yet somewhere in my marrow I know that this is just a vain attempt to exculpate myself—it wasn't me, guv."[6]

Karpf elaborated:

> Indeed, when I hear apocalyptic warnings about global warming, after a few moments of fear I tune out. In fact I think I might be something worse than a climate-change sceptic—a climate-change ignorer.
>
> The fuse that trips the whole circuit is a sense of helplessness. Whatever steps I take to counter global warming, however well-intentioned my brief bursts of zeal, they invariably end up feeling like too little, too late. The mismatch between the extremely dangerous state of the earth and my own feeble endeavours seems mockingly large.

Karpf found she is not alone. She asked two colleagues about their attitudes toward global warming. One, a 48-year-old man, said he thought about it often and was angry about the role of big business, but as to his own interventions, he said, "I do feel it's like pissing in the wind really—I don't know why I bother." The other, a 57-year-old politically engaged man, admitted that he rarely thought about climate change because it simply didn't interest him. But when pressed he revealed that he recycled, signed petitions to conserve old buildings, and didn't drive, but quickly realized that he couldn't sustain his contention that "I don't harm the environment."

To recognize a problem and act to solve it while knowing that one's actions are inadequate leads to a sense of helplessness. This feeling is not apathy but a moral injury, a soul wound, a profound sense of inadequacy that smothers one's best and truest efforts to make a difference. It is compounded by the realization that we cannot avoid adding to the problem. When our lives are tallied up when we die, almost all of us will be judged to have been a drain on the planet. This realization constitutes what Raffensperger described as "a steady, grinding erosion, a slow-motion relentless sorrow." We can change out our light bulbs and turn down the thermostat all we want, but the fact of our birth and all those years of environmental unawareness cannot be erased.

Isolated individual acts will never be enough. We must act collectively, in concert, bypassing the inexorable sorrow we may experience in private actions.

Enter the One Mind. Its power is revealed when we realize that our combined action within it is not merely additive but exponential. In the One Mind, one plus one no longer make two, but many. This realization diminishes the "slow-motion relentless sorrow" of individual activities. This understanding led Margaret Mead to observe, "Never doubt that a small group of thoughtful, committed individuals can change the world. In fact, it's the only thing that ever has."[7]

As members of the One Mind, we continue to act individually; but as we become more aware of our communal selves, an alchemical process kicks in, in the form of heightened imagination and creativity. We enter a field of knowing that is greater than that of any group member and greater than the sum of a group's members. The result is what Marc Barasch, founder and CEO of Green World Campaign, calls a "collaboratory."[8] Solutions to problems surface that we did not anticipate. We become more imaginative, inventive, inspired, productive, resourceful, and innovative. In the One Mind, pooled neurons outperform individual brains, as we'll see.

We are learning how to reclaim our forgotten citizenship in the One Mind. As author Jeremy Rifkin put it in *The Empathic Civilization*, "A new science is emerging whose operating principles and assumptions are more compatible with network ways of thinking. The old science views nature as objects; the new science views nature as relationships. The old science is characterized by detachment, expropriation, dissection, and reduction; the new science is characterized by engagement, replenishment, integration, and holism. The old science is committed to making nature productive; the new science to making nature sustainable. The old science seeks power over nature; the new science seeks partnership with nature. The old science puts a premium on autonomy from nature; the new science on reparticipation with nature."[9]

The power of the One Mind resides in the fact that it does not need to be created. The collective One Mind does not need to be tweeted or Facebooked into being. It already *is*—an overarching dimension of consciousness of which we are *already* a part. We have simply forgotten our belongingness, trading our oneness for the illusion of isolated individuality, that insidious, erroneous belief that personhood is *all* we are. Once we cease believing that we are a coin with only one side, we shall wonder how we could have deceived ourselves so thoroughly for so long. And we can begin to act accordingly.

Those Embarassing Meteorites

Paradoxically, one of our major challenges is with scientists themselves.

Scientists often decry the science illiteracy of schoolchildren and the public, yet, ironically, a parallel form of science illiteracy exists among scientists. It largely results from doggedly ignoring the empirical evidence for a nonlocal, unified aspect of the mind. Nobel physicist Brian Josephson, of the University of Cambridge, calls this "pathological disbelief."[10]

Pathological disbelief caused learned 18th-century scientists to state, with absolute certainty and in spite of hold-in-your-hand evidence, that meteorites do not exist because "stones cannot fall from the sky," as Antoine Lavoisier, the discoverer of oxygen, assured his colleagues at the French Academy.[11] As a result of this prejudice, some scientists were ashamed of dealing with the subject. Not wishing to be considered old-fashioned and superstitious, they discarded entire collections of meteorites, such as the Imperial Natural History Collection in Vienna. Today there is hardly a single specimen that predates 1790 except for the 280-pound meteorite that fell in Alsace in 1492, now housed in the town hall of Ensisheim in northeastern France. This stone that fell from the sky was simply too heavy for the pathological disbelievers to lift.[12]

Equally dogmatic views persist. Many scientists currently insist that consciousness, our current meteorite equivalent, cannot manifest outside the confines of the brain and body, in spite of hundreds of studies suggesting otherwise. Aggressive, hubristic pathological disbelief has become something of a blood sport among many mind-equals-brain materialists in the scientific community. These individuals seem to vie with one another for who can come up with the cleverest, most satirical putdown of the sort of information we'll examine, in spite of the fact that the odds against a chance explanation for many of these findings is astronomical. This is not only a disgrace to the scientific tradition; it is also a dangerous game because it diminishes the "hope of wisdom" we need for survival.

If the wisdom we need is to grow and make a difference, scientists must walk their talk. This means following empirical findings wherever they lead. So it is not just laypersons who must do their part if we are to survive and thrive. Scientists must do the same by ceasing to sacrifice empirical findings in order to protect their pet notions of how consciousness *ought* to behave. There are distinguished exemplars, as we shall see. Schrödinger, Arthur Eddington, James Jeans, Kurt Gödel, Gregory Bateson, Bohm, and others who have supported a universal, unified view of consciousness have already shown the way.

Einstein clearly saw that our very survival depends on a transition from the sense of the isolated self to an expanded level of awareness that includes all sentient beings. He said, "A human being is part of the whole, called by us 'universe,' a part limited in time and space. He experiences his thoughts and feelings as something separate from the rest—a kind of optical delusion of his consciousness. This delusion is a kind of prison for us, restricting us to our personal decisions and to the affection of a few persons nearest us. Our task must be to free ourselves from this prison by widening our circle of compassion to embrace all living creatures and the whole of nature in its beauty."[13] Failure to do so risks global devastation. As Einstein wrote in a letter to President Truman in 1950, "I do not know with what weapons World War III will be fought, but World War IV will be fought with sticks and stones."[14]

In simpler times it was not greatly important to the overall health of the planet and the future of humanity how any single individual behaved. The natural world contained absorbent buffers capable of neutralizing even massive human stupidity. That time has passed. Our room for error is diminishing. Many scientists believe that irreversible tipping points loom. Unlike previous generations, we can glimpse an end.

The One Mind concept is scientific, philosophical, and spiritual, but it is also enormously practical. It is about survival, the highest form of practicality. It is about summoning the better angels of our nature. It is about saving our own skins and those of future generations as well.

Emerson and I

During the writing of this book, I have often thought about how I came to believe that consciousness is one. Nothing in my upbringing and subsequent university and medical training pointed in this direction. Like most Americans, I was nourished by the belief in *individual* worth and achievement. Yet our culture's emphasis on individuality never quite fit. Something vital, something unspoken, seemed to be missing.

The most profound influence nudging me toward the concept of the One Mind was growing up as an identical twin. My brother and I, from earliest childhood and to this day, have felt linked in consciousness at some fundamental level. This is not unique to us; many identical twins have similar feelings.

When I was 16, a pivotal event occurred, and it remains seared in my memory. I stumbled, quite by accident, onto a paperback copy of Ralph Waldo Emerson's essays. The discovery occurred one evening in Evans Corner Drug, the teen hangout in tiny Groesbeck, Texas, the town nearest our farm. The big draw for teens was the soda fountain. The Emerson book was in one of those revolving wire display racks nearby. Emerson seemed quite out of place among the cheap westerns and mystery novels, but I was somehow drawn to him. Mindlessly opening the book to page one, these words gobsmacked me:

"There is one mind common to all individual men. Every man is an inlet to the same and to all of the same. He that is once admitted to the right of reason is made a freeman of the whole estate. What Plato has thought, he may think; what a saint has felt, he may feel; what at any time has befallen any man, he can understand. Who hath access to this universal mind is a party to all that is or can be done, for this is the only and sovereign agent."[15]

That was just a warm-up. Emerson's essay "The Over-soul" also clobbered me. The Over-soul, Emerson said, is "that Unity . . . within which every man's particular being is contained and made one with all other . . ." He explained, "We live in succession, in division, in parts, in particles. In the meantime within man is the soul of the whole; the wise silence; the universal beauty, to which every part and particle is equally related, the eternal ONE. And this deep power in which we exist and whose beatitude is all accessible to us, is not only self-sufficing and perfect in every hour, but the act of seeing and the thing seen, the seer and the spectacle, the subject and the object, are one. We see the world piece by piece, as the sun, the moon, the animal, the tree; but the whole, of which these are shining parts, is the soul."[16]

That was strong stuff for a Texas teen, but I purchased that little piece of literary dynamite right then and there. It was my private treasure until I lost it somewhere during the many moves that followed in the next few years.

I also lost touch with Emerson during my university, medical school, and postgraduate training. He was drowned out by the materialistic worldview into which I was pulled, as were all the young people of my generation who pursued a career in medicine. No other approaches were tolerated in my heavily scientific education. A smug triumphalism was in the air. Who needed Emerson and Over-souls when Theories of Everything based in physics seemed within reach? Although for several years I gave my heart to those physically based views, I continued to carry Emerson somewhere deep inside. Looking back, I believe my early exposure to him helped immunize me against completely capitulating to materialistic pseudo-explanations of mind and consciousness. The immunity would prove to be lifelong. Not that Emerson was solely responsible for my evolving views; it's just that he was the original irritant in the oyster around which something grew.

The One Mind: Ancient *and* Modern

The concept of the One Mind is ancient, and it remains an honored belief in many wisdom traditions. The esoteric sides of all the major religions recognize that our individual consciousness is subsumed and nourished by an infinite, absolute, divine, or cosmic source and is ultimately one with it.[17] Samkhya, one of the oldest philosophical systems of India, promoted the concept of the Akashic records, a compendium of information and knowledge encoded in a nonphysical plane of existence, which later interpreters likened to the Mind of God.[18] The Upanishads, India's sacred scriptures that date to the middle of the first millennium B.C.E., proclaim *tat tvam asi*, "thou art that": the human and the divine are one. Similarly from the Christian tradition, the words of Jesus: "The kingdom of God is within you,"[19] and Jesus's words, "Is it not written in your law, I said, Ye are gods?"[20] And as the eponymous sage Hermes Trismegistus said centuries earlier, "There is nothing more divine than mind, nothing more potent in its operation, nothing more apt to unite men to gods, and gods to men."[21]

Although the idea of the One Mind has ancient roots, it is becoming increasingly modern as well. For more than a century we have witnessed a steady outpouring of books that, in one way or another, affirm the recognition that consciousness is larger than our individual mind. Examples include pioneering works such as R. M. Bucke's *Cosmic Consciousness*, Emerson's essays on the Over-soul and transcendentalism, William James's *The Varieties of Religious Experience*, Arthur Lovejoy's *The Great Chain of Being*, C. G. Jung's *The Archetypes and the Collective Unconscious*, and Erwin Schrödinger's *My View of the World*, *What Is Life?*, and *Mind and Matter*. More recent contributions include Ken Wilber's *The Spectrum of Consciousness*, Peter Russell's *The Global Brain*, David Lorimer's *Whole in One*, Nick Herbert's *Elemental Mind*, Huston Smith's *Beyond the Post-Modern Mind*, David Bohm's *Wholeness and the Implicate Order*, David Darling's *Soul Search*, Robert G. Jahn and Brenda J. Dunne's *Consciousness and the Source of Reality*, Rupert Sheldrake's *A New Science of Life*, Lynne McTaggart's *The Field*, Ervin

Laszlo's *The Akashic Experience* and *Science and the Akashic Field,* Menas Kafatos and Robert Nadeau's *The Conscious Universe: Parts and Wholes in Physical Reality,* Dean Radin's *The Conscious Universe* and *Entangled Minds,* Stephan A. Schwartz's *Opening to the Infinite,* Charles T. Tart's *The End of Materialism,* Russell Targ's *Limitless Mind* and *The Reality of ESP,* Edward F. Kelly and colleagues' *Irreducible Mind,* and many, many others.

If there are so many books dealing with the One Mind, why do we need another? What can one more voice add to this chorus? I can only say that my approach is that of a physician, which has profoundly influenced my perspective on the ways in which the One Mind manifests in people's lives. For much of my life I have dealt with dying people in hospitals and on battlefields. I have listened to their joys, concerns, fears, and sufferings for decades. Many of these individuals have revealed to me experiences that shattered what I'd been taught about how the mind behaves. Many of these experiences simply don't show up in textbooks of medicine, biology, physics, or psychology.

Moreover, there is something about the doctor-patient relationship that encourages people to share their innermost thoughts and experiences. This often transcends what individuals are willing to share with their favorite physicist, biologist, philosopher, or mathematician, if they happen to have one. So I'm bold enough to think I might add some notes to the chorus that have gone missing or not been full-throated enough.

Of course the unitary, nonlocal One Mind has been a recurring theme among philosophers and poets through the ages. As Plato (427–347 B.C.E.) has Aristophanes say in his *Symposium,* "This becoming one instead of two, was the very expression of [humanity's] ancient need. And the reason is that human nature was originally one and we were a whole, and the desire and pursuit of the whole is called love."[22] William Butler Yeats (1865–1939): "The borders of our minds are ever shifting, and . . . many minds can flow into one another . . . and create or reveal a single mind, a single energy."[23] And as Jack Kerouac (1922–69), the Beat novelist, poet, and author of *On The Road* and *The Dharma Bums,* glimpsed, "Devoid of space/Is the mind of grace."[24]

Neuromythology

The dominant view in science is that the brain somehow makes consciousness, like the liver makes bile.[25] But this is an unproven assumption that has never been explained, can hardly be imagined, and has never been directly observed. The status of this belief is neuromythology, not science. Still the belief persists, just as many mythologies have persisted for long periods in the history of science, such as the belief in the ether; phlogiston; and the absoluteness of matter, energy, space, and time. Our current neuromythology insists that a brain is necessary for consciousness to exist and that consciousness cannot exist outside the brain. Since brains are obviously individual, minds must also be individual, one per person. In order for a One Mind to exist, there would have to be One Brain, which is obviously absurd.

The nature of consciousness, however, remains a mystery. As cognitive scientist Donald D. Hoffman of the University of California at Irvine wrote, "The scientific study of consciousness is in the embarrassing position of having no scientific theory of consciousness."[26] As to how consciousness might arise from a physical system such as the brain—if indeed it does—Harvard University experimental psychologist Steven Pinker confessed, "Beats the heck out of me. I have some prejudices, but no idea of how to begin to look for a defensible answer. And neither does anyone else."[27] Recognizing our ignorance about the origins of consciousness is important, because this opens the door to possibilities such as the One Mind, which a strictly material viewpoint prohibits.

There's no getting around the mystery of it all. So I hope you will be willing to suspend judgment and plunge into the unknown alongside me as we proceed. We've got good company. As novelist and philosopher Aldous Huxley said, "I am entirely on the side of mystery. I mean, any attempts to explain away the mystery is ridiculous. . . . I believe in the *profound and unfathomable mystery of life* . . . which has a . . . divine quality about it."[28]

Lewis Thomas also recognized the importance of admitting our ignorance, mystery's close cousin. Toward the end of the 20th century he wrote, "The only solid piece of scientific truth about which I feel totally confident is that we are profoundly ignorant about nature . . ."[29] He goes on to say, "Only two centuries ago we could explain everything about everything, out of pure reason, and now most of that elaborate and harmonious structure has come apart before our eyes. We are *dumb*."[30]

In his brilliant book *Science Set Free*, British biologist Rupert Sheldrake examined the ways in which Thomas's "dumb" expresses itself in the world of science. He explored areas in which science is being constricted by assumptions that have hardened into dogmas, which not only limit science but are also dangerous for the future of humanity.[31]

What the Hell's Going on Here?

In many areas of science, however, the admission of ignorance has been overshadowed by arrogance. And arrogance—the certainty that we know more than we really do—has created a serious obstacle in our understanding of consciousness. It has prevented a fair hearing for a huge body of research pointing to a nonlocal, beyond-the-body aspect of the mind, out of the haughty insistence that such phenomena simply cannot happen, much like rocks falling from the sky; and since they cannot happen, they don't happen—damn the evidence, case closed. This book reopens the case by examining evidence that challenges the current assumption that consciousness is entirely local—that it is produced by the brain and confined to it.

As a corrective to the hubris that is epidemic in many areas of science, we might take seriously the playful suggestion of Wes Nisker, the Buddhist meditation teacher. "Just imagine how good it would feel," he wrote, "if we all got together once in a while in large public gatherings and admitted that we don't know why we are alive, that nobody knows for sure if there's a higher being who created us, and that nobody really knows what the hell's going on here."[32]

Ignorance and Opportunity

In science, we often know *that* something works before we have a clue about *how* it works. This is particularly true in medicine, my field. Examples are numerous, including aspirin for inflammation and pain, penicillin for infection, cinchona for malaria, colchicine for gout, general anesthetics, and so on. Explanations often come later. While we await them, we do not ignore the efficacy of these interventions out of some pigheaded demand for an explanation of the mechanism involved. I have never seen a patient who needed major surgery refuse a general anesthetic because the anesthesiologist could not explain precisely how it works.

In the same spirit, I believe that the hypothesis of the One Mind must be taken seriously. The concept of the One Mind works not because we know the mechanism, but because it models certain observations as well as or better than other hypotheses about how the mind behaves.

Future generations may one day explain the operations of the One Mind—or maybe not, for the problems are formidable. At present, we cannot even explain individual mind, let alone the One Mind. But, as mentioned, our ignorance is also an opportunity. Knowing so little about consciousness, we can be bold in exploring the possibility of a universal domain of mind.

To some, the One Mind may resemble a crazy aunt hidden in the family attic—too weird to be respectable, too controversial to talk about, too strange to be seen in public. But in view of the evidence we shall examine, she is about to descend the stairs and make a shocking appearance to the guests.

PART ONE

GLIMPSES OF THE ONE MIND

CHAPTER 1

SAVING OTHERS

On January 2, 2007, Wesley Autrey, a 50-year-old African American construction worker and Navy veteran, was waiting for a subway train in Manhattan with his two young daughters at around 12:45 P.M. As Autrey stood there, he was unaware that he was about to become involved in a sequence of events that would change his life, and that would reveal profound truths about the nature of the human mind. He noticed a young man, Cameron Hollopeter, 20, having a seizure. The man managed to get to his feet but stumbled from the platform onto the tracks between the two rails. Autrey saw the lights of an approaching train and made an instant decision. He jumped onto the tracks, thinking he would have time to drag Hollopeter away. Realizing this was impossible, he covered Hollopeter's body with his own and pressed him down in a drainage ditch about a foot deep between the tracks. The train operator tried to stop and the brakes screeched, but by the time he could do so, five cars had passed over the two men. It was a close call; the cars were so close to Autrey that they smudged grease on his blue knit cap. Autrey heard onlookers screaming. "We're okay down here," he yelled back, "but I've got two daughters up there. Let them know their father's okay." Then he heard cries of wonder and applause from the bystanders.

Hollopeter, a student at the New York Film Academy, was taken to the hospital but sustained only bumps and bruises. Autrey refused medical help because, he said, nothing was wrong.

Why did Autrey do it? He told the *New York Times,* "I don't feel like I did something spectacular; I just saw someone who needed help. I did what I felt was right."[1] He said further that, as a construction worker, he was used to working in confined spaces, and that his judgment in this case proved to be "pretty right."

Autrey was extraordinarily modest, but this did not shield him from the public's adulation. He was an overnight celebrity, with appearances on several national morning TV news programs and late-night shows. Gifts poured in—scholarships and computers for his two daughters, a new Jeep Patriot, season tickets to the New Jersey Nets, a one-year free parking pass for use anywhere in New York City, and a year of free subway rides, among other things. *Time* magazine named him as one of the 100 most influential people in the world for 2007.[2] He was named CNN Hero, a title given for making a difference in the world. He was a guest at the 2007 State of the Union Address to the U. S. Congress, where he received a standing ovation.

Why Risk Everything?

Why would one person willingly risk or sacrifice his or her life for another? The answer might seem obvious: he or she simply cares and has empathy or love for the person in need. But that answer is not good enough for evolutionary biologists, who want to know what *purpose* is served by the caring, empathy, and love. What does the individual gain by acting on these feelings?

According to the tenets of evolutionary biology, we are genetically programed to act in ways that ensure our survival and reproduction. Our empathic acts, therefore, might extend to those closest to us who share our genes—our siblings, children, kinship group—because helping them helps us genetically in the long run. Or we might extend empathy toward our tribe or social unit because we might one day need them to reciprocate. In this light, actions like Wesley Autrey's are biological heresy. He was not remotely connected with Cameron Hollopeter—not racially, socially, occupationally, or culturally. Autrey's genes would not have benefited if he died saving the young white man. So, according to evolutionary biology, Wesley Autrey should have stayed on the subway platform and let Cameron Hollopeter fend for himself.

Some might argue that Autrey *did* benefit from saving Hollopeter. He became famous, his daughters got college funds and computers, and he received cash awards and other tangible benefits. Since his action changed his circumstances and made his life and that of his daughters less difficult, perhaps there was a genetic payback in what he did. But he did not know in advance that these things would happen. And in any case, was it worth risking what appeared to be certain death? Surely not. In this dangerous situation, genetic conservation should have kept Autrey on the platform with his daughters, along with all the onlookers who thought it would be suicidal to act as he did.

Becoming Someone Else

Joseph Campbell, the great mythologist, was interested in why people perform selfless acts. Influenced by the views of the German philosopher Arthur Schopenhauer, Campbell observed, "There's [a] wonderful question Schopenhauer asked. How is it that an individual can so participate in the danger and pain of another that, forgetting his own self-protection, he moves spontaneously to the other's rescue, even at the cost of his own life?" Schopenhauer believed that self-sacrifice for another occurs because the rescuer realizes that he or she and the individual in need are one. At the decisive moment, the sense of separation is totally overcome. The danger to the needy person becomes that of the rescuer. The prior sense of separateness is simply a function of the way we experience things in space and time: we may *appear* separate and often *feel* separate, but the separation is not fundamental. Because we experience ourselves as one with the person in need, when we risk our life to save them, we are essentially saving ourselves.

Campbell elaborated, "Now, that spontaneous compassion, I think, would jump culture lines. If you were to see someone of a totally alien world—even a person or a race or nation that you had no sympathy for—the recognition of a common human identity would spark a response. And the ultimate reference of mythology is to that single entity, which is the human being as human."[3]

I have never heard of a rescuer inquiring whether the person in immediate need is a Democrat or Republican, pro-choice or anti-abortion, how he or she stands on global climate change, or whether he or she favors allopathic medicine or homeopathy. The reaction to another human in need leapfrogs these issues in favor of a deeper human response. Schopenhauer realized this. As he wrote in his 1840 book, On the Basis of Morality, "Universal compassion is the only guarantee of morality."[4] He elaborated, "My own true inner being actually exists in every living creature as truly and immediately as known to my consciousness only in myself. This realization, for which the standard formula is in Sanskrit tat tvam asi, is the ground of compassion upon which all true, that is to say unselfish, virtue rests and whose expression is in every good deed."[5]

I'm willing to bet that Wesley Autrey never read a scrap of Campbell or Schopenhauer. He didn't have to. And that's the point. When he sheltered Cameron Hollopeter in the path of an oncoming train, he was defying all instincts for perpetuating his genes. He was in the embrace of the One Mind that binds us all, the unity so clearly glimpsed by luminaries such as Campbell and Schopenhauer. At the decisive moment, from the One-Mind perspective of consciousness, Wesley Autrey was Cameron Hollopeter.

The Downed Chopper

I have long been fascinated by why the Wesley Autreys of the world do what they do. This is not just philosophical curiosity.

I served as a battalion surgeon in Vietnam in 1968 and 1969 in the boonies, beyond anything as fancy as the MASH units popularized in the famous TV series. My world was a sandbag- and barbed-wire-protected primitive aid station with minimal equipment, and helicopter missions to aid wounded troops. I was involved in several Autrey-like moments in which I had to make an immediate decision about putting my life on the line for young men in need.

One day in October 1969, a helicopter crashed not far from my forward battalion aid station. I ran to the crash site. When I arrived, the upside-down chopper was ringed by a group of soldiers standing at a safe distance because of the expectation that it would explode. The pilot was still conscious but was trapped in the wreckage, moaning in pain. Without thinking, I began freeing the door of the inverted aircraft, entered, and cut the seat belts trapping the pilot. One of my medical crew joined me, and we maneuvered the pilot from the wreckage and carried him to safety. To this day the smell of jet fuel pouring from the ruptured fuel tanks remains a vivid memory, but fortunately the aircraft did not explode. I started an I. V. on the pilot, gave him morphine for his pain, and put him on a medevac helicopter that flew him to a medical facility for further attention. This is just one of a number of similar incidents that marked my time in the war.[6]

When I returned to the U. S., I was amazed on looking back. Before going to Vietnam I swore I would never take risks, out of respect for my family and those who cared about me. But whenever instances like the crashed helicopter arose, these resolutions evaporated like morning mist in the jungle. It was as if they never existed. There was no careful deliberation during these decisive moments, no weighing of consequences: just action.

I wondered why I did it. I never considered myself a risk taker. As a physician, I was taught always to be in control to the extent possible, to leave nothing to chance, to apply critical reasoning in every situation. What had happened?

I remember the day, about a year after my return from Vietnam, when in random readings I stumbled onto Schopenhauer's description—how at the crucial moment the rescuer's consciousness fuses with that of the person in need, how separateness dissolves and individuality is set aside, how division is overcome and oneness becomes real. I knew in a heartbeat that this was the explanation for my irrational, risky behavior in the war zone. It was as if a veil had been lifted. This was a revelation of adamantine clarity, an epiphany about a troubling period in my life that I had not been able to fathom. For me, in Vietnam the One Mind had been made flesh. It was a priceless gift for which I still tremble in gratitude.

Author Joseph Chilton Pearce, in his book *Evolution's End,* points out that the word *sacrifice,* like the word *sacrament,* means "to make whole." Sacrifice, however, has taken on negative connotations, such as slaughtering an animal. But the original meaning of the word as wholeness is captured in the experience of giving oneself to another. "To become whole all parts must be left behind," Pearce observed, "for a whole is not the sum of its parts but a different state entirely. [Meister] Eckhart spoke of 'all named objects' being left behind when one enters that unknown. We must go beyond the fragmentation of parts and leave the world of diversity to discover the single unity from which all springs."[7]

But how? Shankara, the 9th-century Indian philosopher, wrote, "Disease is not cured by pronouncing the name of the medicine, but by taking medicine. Deliverance is not achieved by repeating the word 'Brahman,' but by directly experiencing Brahman . . ."[8] It is the same with the principle of oneness. We can read every word of Schopenhauer, Campbell, and a thousand other philosophers who have expounded on this idea, but it will not become real without experience. That is where events like Wesley Autrey's enter. These life-and-death moments in which we completely ally our existence with that of someone else make real the principle that binds all things into unity. These experiences are more persuasive than any spoken or written words. Following these episodes, we can throw away the books, sermons, and teachings—because now we *know.*

If you decide to live dangerously on purpose, with the express intention of awakening to this awareness, forget it; you probably won't be successful and may perish in the process. The humbling fact is that the awareness of oneness most often catches us by surprise, not in perilous situations but in the most mundane settings— listening to music, watching a sunset, hearing a baby's laugh, preparing a meal, or simply doing nothing. The spectrum of trigger experiences is spectacularly varied, and anyone seeking to find a formula that might guarantee the experience will be disappointed. This is the domain where the Law of Reversed Effort kicks in, where paradox reigns. Thus the Buddhist observation:

> It is only when you hunt for it that you lose it;
> You cannot take hold of it, but equally you cannot get rid of it,
> And while you can do neither, it goes on its own way.
> You remain silent and it speaks; you speak, and it is dumb . . .[9]

When we identify so completely with someone that the distinctions between self and other are overcome, we have entered the domain of the One Mind. This prepares us for actions we would not even consider in our self-oriented, everyday frame of mind. Our future depends on our willingness to take this larger view. Today it is not just persons on subway tracks or downed chopper pilots who need our help, but our entire world and all in it. Entry into the One Mind makes this task thinkable. And possible.

CHAPTER 2

THE PATRON SAINT
OF THE ONE MIND

E rwin Schrödinger, the Austrian physicist, was one of the most brilliant scientific minds of the 20th century. In 1933 he was awarded
the Nobel Prize for his discovery of wave mechanics, which lies at the
heart of quantum physics.

Schrödinger believed in the One Mind. As he put it, "Mind is
by its very nature a *singulare tantum*. I should say: the overall number of minds is just one."[1] How did Schrödinger's vision of the One
Mind originate? It is difficult to pinpoint all the vectors that go into
the formation of anyone's personal philosophy, but surely the wan-
ing months of World War I and its immediate aftermath were pivotal for Schrödinger, as Walter Moore, Schrödinger's able biographer,
described.[2]

Starving, Sick, and Brilliant

In January 1918, as the Great War ground to a bloody halt after 16
million deaths, Austria's army was starving and in tatters. The situation
in Vienna, where the Schrödinger family lived, was grim. The family
business was destroyed, and the Schrödingers faced serious financial
difficulties for the first time. Schrödinger's maternal grandmother had
been so involved in the peace movement that she had been arrested
and convicted of treason. His mother was recovering from a major

operation for breast cancer the previous year and was still weak and in pain. Schrödinger, who was 31 years old and unmarried at the time, had health problems of his own. In August 1918 he was diagnosed with inflammation in the apex of one lung. This was almost certainly tuberculosis, for the disease was epidemic among the weakened, malnourished urban population. (In the 1920s Schrödinger would stay several times at a sanatorium in Arosa, Switzerland, where he discovered his wave equation for which he was award the Nobel Prize. He would die of tuberculosis in Vienna at the age of 73.) Food was in such short supply that the family often ate at a community soup kitchen.

In the winter of 1918–19, with the war at an end, things got worse. Food supplies from Hungary were cut off, and the importation of coal from Czechoslovakia was stopped. Thousands of Viennese were starving and freezing. Beggars filled the streets, and maimed ex-soldiers with decorations pinned to their rags were everywhere. Women begged for food in the countryside and foraged for fuel in the Vienna woods, stripping entire hillsides of trees and bushes. Thousands queued overnight for food rations, rushing the distribution point and seizing the goods so that women in the rear were left with nothing. On one occasion, when a horse fell on the street, the mob butchered it within minutes and scurried off with the meat.

During this upheaval, Schrödinger somehow continued his intensive research work in theoretical physics at the University of Vienna's Physics Institute, but with an added interest. As he put it, "I was just now with great enthusiasm becoming familiar with Schopenhauer and, through him, with the doctrine of unity taught by the Upanishads." Schrödinger filled notebook after notebook with commentaries based upon his reading of European and Eastern philosophers. "It was in those dying days of the Danube Empire," Moore wrote, "that he formed the foundations of his philosophy, which was to remain remarkably constant all his life."[3]

Arthur Schopenhauer, whom we met earlier in our discussion of saving others, was known as a philosopher of pessimism, but his views may have come as consolation to Schrödinger amid the suffering and turmoil of four years of senseless war and destruction. The impact of Schopenhauer's philosophy has been immense. This "lone giant" in Western philosophy, as the novelist Arthur Koestler called him, influenced individuals as diverse as Nietzsche, Freud, Mann, and Wagner.[4] Schopenhauer honored the wisdom of the East, especially India's contributions of Vedanta and the Upanishads. He named his faithful dog "Atman," the Hindu term for the spiritual principle of the universe that is inherent in all individuals. At his bedside he kept Hindu scriptures and a gold-leafed statue of the Buddha dressed as a beggar.[5]

Among Schopenhauer's views that may have given comfort to Schrödinger amid the misery of war-ravaged Vienna was Schopenhauer's understanding of the harmony of life. He maintained that not only do all the events of an existence fall into place in one's own trajectory through life, but they simultaneously mesh with the life courses of all other individuals, even though the drama of others' lives may be unknown to her. When viewed in aggregate, multiple lives fit together like a jigsaw puzzle whose overall pattern is so complex it is beyond the comprehension of any particular individual. Said Schopenhauer, "Everything is interrelated and mutually attuned."[6] Schopenhauer saw order in disorder and apparent randomness, offering meaning to Schrödinger's world turned upside down.

Only One Mind

Schrödinger thought deeply about the key teachings he read. He reformulated them in his own words, and they became the pillars that sustained him for the rest of his life.[7] In books such as *My View of the World, What Is Life?,* and *Mind and Matter,* he painstakingly built a concept of a single mind, in which consciousness is transpersonal, universal, collective, and infinite in space and time, therefore immortal and eternal. In adopting a unitary view of human consciousness, Schrödinger recognized what he called the "arithmetical paradox"—that although there are billions of apparently separate minds, the view that humans have of the world is largely coherent. There is only one adequate explanation for this, he wrote, "namely the unification of minds or consciousness. Their multiplicity is only apparent, in truth there is only one mind."[8]

Schrödinger believed we are suffering from a consensus trance, a collective delusion, about the nature of consciousness. As he put it, "We have entirely taken to thinking of the personality of a human being . . . as located in the interior of the body. To learn that it cannot really be found there is so amazing that it meets with doubt and hesitation, we are very loath to admit it. We have got used to localizing the conscious personality inside a person's head—I should say an inch or two behind the midpoint of the eyes. . . . It is very difficult for us to take stock of the fact that the localization of the personality, of the conscious mind, inside the body is only symbolic, just an aid for practical use."[9]

Immortality for the mind was a key feature of Schrödinger's vision. He wrote, "I venture to call it [the mind] indestructible since it has a peculiar time-table, namely mind is always *now*. There is really no before and after for the mind. There is only now that includes memories and expectations. . . ."[10] We may, or so I believe, assert that physical theory in its present stage strongly suggests the indestructibility of Mind by Time."[11]

For many Westerners, the extent of Schrödinger's holism can be shocking. He acknowledged this but did not hold back, maintaining, "[As] inconceivable as it seems to ordinary reason, you—and all other conscious beings as such—are all in all. Hence this life of yours which you are living is not merely a piece of the entire existence, but is in a certain sense the *whole*; only this whole is not so constituted that it can be surveyed in one single glance. This, as we know, is what the Brahmins express in that sacred, mystic formula: *Tat tvam asi*, this is you. Or, again, in such words as 'I am in the east and in the west, I am below and above, *I am this whole world.*'"[12]

For Schrödinger, this vision was no airy-fairy piece of philosophy; it was thoroughly practical. Echoing Schopenhauer, he declared that one's unity with others "underlies all morally valuable activity,"[13] including altruism and heroism. In the embrace of oneness with others, individuals will risk their life for an end they believe to be good, lay down their life to save someone else's, and give to relieve a stranger's suffering even though it may increase their own.

Oneness with the All permeated Schrödinger's workaday life as a scientist. Done properly, scientific work was akin to fathoming the mind of God. He wrote, "Science is a game. . . . The uncertainty is how many of the rules God himself has permanently ordained, and how many apparently are caused by your own mental inertia. . . . This is perhaps the most exciting thing in the game. For here you strive against the imaginary boundary between yourself and the Godhead—a boundary that perhaps does not exist."[14]

Schrödinger saw not conflict but harmony between his interpretation of quantum physics and Vedanta. As his biographer Moore explained, "In 1925, the world view of physics was a model of the universe as a great machine composed of separable interacting material particles. During the next few years, Schrödinger and Heisenberg and their followers created a universe based on the superimposed inseparable waves of probability amplitudes. This view would be entirely consistent with the vedantic concept of the All in One."[15]

But not just with Vedanta. Schrödinger cited with approval Aldous Huxley's magnificent treatise *The Perennial Philosophy*, an anthology of mystical writings from the esoteric side of the world's major religions.[16] This suggests that Schrödinger agreed in principle with the view that "all mystics speak the same language, for they come from the same country."[17] If Vedanta had not existed, he would have found affirmation of his vision in other traditions. The stars don't rise; it is the earth that tilts and spins, causing the stars to come into view. So it is with great truths. Although they are always present, they await *our* movement in order to be seen.

Patron Saint of the One Mind

For all of his insights into Eastern philosophy, Schrödinger was no one's idea of a "spiritual physicist." He made no pretense of being saintly. His personal shortcomings were obvious in his relations with other persons, which were often tumultuous. As Moore delicately put it, "He did not achieve a true integration of his beliefs with his actions." Moore elaborated: "The *Bhagavad-Gita* teaches that there are three paths to salvation: the path of devotion, the path of works, and the path of knowledge. By inborn temperament and by early nurture Erwin was destined to follow the last of these paths. His intellect showed him the way, and throughout his life he expressed in graceful essays his belief in Vedanta, but he remained what the Indians call a *Mahavit*, a person who knows the theory but has failed to achieve a practical realization of it in his own life. From the *Chandogya Upanishad*: 'I am a Mahavit, a knower of the word, and not an Atmavit, a knower of Atman.'"[18]

Well, all right. Schrödinger would no doubt agree that he was not *the* way, he merely *pointed* the way. And for all his imperfections, our world could use more scientists like him.

If there were a patron saint of the One Mind among physicists, it would be Erwin Schrödinger.

Professor Kothari and My Debt to India

A personal note. I, too, owe a debt to India.

In 1988 I was invited to deliver the annual Mahatma Gandhi Memorial Lecture at the Gandhi Peace Foundation in New Delhi. The invitation was brokered by Professor D. S. Kothari, whom I had never met. Kothari was one of the best-known Indian physicists of the 20th century, whose research on statistical thermodynamics and the theory of white dwarf stars brought him an international reputation. The invitation included the opportunity to lecture at Gujarat Vidyapith, the university in Ahmedabad founded in 1920 by Mahatma Gandhi, and also to spend time in New Delhi with Professor Kothari.

Prior to my journey to India, Professor Kothari sent me a copy of his landmark paper "Atom and Self."[19] This paper was enormously helpful in my efforts to dissect the relationships between spirituality, physics, and consciousness. His ideas seemed to flow from a seamless fusion of intellect, intuition, and experience. Clearly, this was a voice speaking from profound personal understanding. His humanity and humor showed when I once asked him, "Professor Kothari, do you meditate?" Then in his 80s, he responded, "Oh, no! But I plan to!"

Professor Kothari related that he had read my 1981 book, *Space, Time & Medicine*,[20] in which I had explored the connections between mind and body, consciousness and healing, and how these phenomena might be linked to new areas of knowledge that were emerging in the physical sciences. But of what interest was all this to the Gandhi Peace Foundation? Kothari explained that Gandhi's belief in *ahimsa*, the doctrine of nonviolence toward all living things, was compatible with my premise that consciousness was a potent factor in health and longevity. Consciousness, he said, could be considered the ultimate nonviolent approach to health, when compared with the relatively violent effects of modern drugs and surgical procedures. Thus the tie-in with the Gandhian perspective.

At the time, I was working on another book, *Recovering the Soul,* in which I asserted that the "nonlocal mind"[21] is *infinite* in space and time, therefore immortal, and thus resembles the age-old concept of the soul. I was tentative about these concepts because no one in medicine, as far as I could determine, had applied the concept of non-locality to the mind. Professor Kothari assured me that I was on firm ground and that he shared the view that consciousness is nonlocal and infinite, therefore immortal, eternal, and one. As we spent many hours exploring these ideas, he gave me the confidence to proceed in my explorations. I owe him a debt I can never repay.

Professor Kothari died peacefully at his home in 1993, with a copy of the *Bhagavad Gita* under his pillow.

CHAPTER 3

ONE-MIND EXPERIENCES

The One Mind is like an invisible, nonphysical cloud-computing platform with infinite storage capacity that is user free. There is no need for linkage, because all minds are *already* connected nonlocally as a unitary whole. Distance and place do not apply. "There is no there there," as Gertrude Stein once remarked about her disappeared childhood home in Oakland, California.[1]

When we experience the One Mind, however, we tend to describe these events in the see-touch-feel language of ordinary three-dimensional life. This is not surprising, for the human brain is not well adapted to understanding transcendent, nonphysical phenomena, and it largely screens out experiences that are not related to biological survival. Thus when we dip into the One Mind and make person-to-person contact with an apparently distant individual, we are wont to label this experience as telepathy, and we typically imagine some sort of squiggly vibration carried by a kind of cosmic Pony Express carrying the mail from one place to another and bridging the gap. When we acquire information about a distant situation, we customarily consider this to be remote viewing, or clairvoyance, that is mediated by *something*. If we insert information into the environment through an act of intention, and it appears as a distant effect—such as, say, remote healing—we tell ourselves that we must have sent something to cause the distant event "out there." But there is no out there out there.

I call these various occurrences beyond-the-brain-and-body happenings. During a national book tour in 2009 for *The Power of Premonitions*, I was showered with people's accounts of these One-Mind experiences. Nearly everyone, I found, has a story. After I spoke at a bookstore event, a cluster of people would typically linger until the crowd had thinned, then come forward and say, "Do you mind if I tell you about an experience of mine?" They'd often say next, "I've never told anyone about this in my life." That's because a stigma is often attached to stories like these, causing many people to hesitate telling them for fear of being thought of as weird. Here are some of the stories I heard.

A String of Numbers

A middle-aged woman living on the East Coast of the United States suddenly developed a powerful feeling that her son, who lived thousands of miles away on the other side of the country, was in serious jeopardy. She tried to ignore the feeling, but it became stronger. Suddenly a string of numbers popped into her mind, whose meaning was utterly obscure. Then she developed an urge to dial the cluster of numbers on her telephone. When she did, she found herself connected with the emergency room of a major hospital in the far-off city where her son lived.

"May I help you?" a nurse asked.

"I have no idea. I'm just worried about my son," the woman stammered.

"Who is he?" She told the nurse her son's name.

"Oh, he was admitted to the ER a couple of hours ago. Dr. Smith has just finished taking care of him. Let me get him—he can give you an update."

Soon Dr. Smith was on the phone. He explained to the bewildered, anxious mother, "Your son was involved in an automobile accident. He was seriously injured, but I'm happy to tell you he's going to be just fine."

A nearly identical story was related to me in another city by a woman who suddenly became concerned about her young daughter for no apparent reason. She also saw a jumble of numbers, dialed them, and was connected with the hospital emergency room where her daughter was undergoing treatment following an automobile accident.

The Insistent Friend

A young engineer flew to South America on a private plane piloted by an acquaintance of his. He planned to visit a friend whom he had not seen since college days. When it came time for the return flight to the United States several days later, his friend came to his hotel room and told him he should not fly back on the plane. He'd had a dream the night before that the plane would crash and everyone on board would be killed. The engineer told his friend his premonition was nonsense, and an argument followed. A fight ensued in which his friend tackled him and physically restrained him. Not until the plane's departure time had passed did he let him go. The engineer was furious; he would now have to fly home on a commercial flight at his own expense. Then word arrived that the private plane had indeed crashed, killing everyone on board.

During my book tour, Air France Flight 447 crashed in the Atlantic Ocean on June 1, 2009, carrying 216 passengers and 12 crewmembers to their deaths. Immediately following the crash, Stefan van Oss, a middle-aged man living near Amsterdam, was interviewed on Dutch television. Van Oss held a reservation on the doomed flight. A close friend of his had a premonition that something bad would happen, and that if van Oss got on the plane he would never return home alive. Van Oss trusted his friend's premonition, canceled his reservation, and lived to tell about it.[2]

The Cancer Is Right Here

A woman had a dream that she had breast cancer. Worried sick, she visited her physician the next morning. She pointed with one finger to a specific spot in her upper left breast where she'd seen the cancer in the dream. "It's right here," she said. She could not feel a lump, however, and neither could her physician. A mammogram was done, which was normal. When the physician reassured her that nothing was wrong and that they should take a wait-and-see approach with frequent exams, she was not satisfied. "This was the most vivid dream I've ever had," she protested. "I'm certain I have breast cancer at this exact spot." When she insisted on going further, the physician, against his better judgment, pressured a surgeon to do a biopsy.

"But where? There's nothing there," the surgeon objected.

"Look, just biopsy where she points," the physician said.

In a few days the pathologist called the original doctor with the report. "This is the most microscopic breast cancer I've seen," he said. "You could not have felt it. There would have been no signs or symptoms. How did you find it?"

"I didn't," he replied. "She did. In a dream."

An Intimation of Doom

In December 1972 an American businessman was visiting Nicaragua. He had been in the capital city of Managua for a week and planned to stay for a week longer. He suddenly experienced an urge to leave the city. This made no sense because leaving early would mean that his business deal would probably collapse. The compulsion became so strong that he knew he must leave as soon as possible, so he gathered his belongings, dashed to the airport, and fled the country on the first available flight. He felt silly doing so until he heard about an event that occurred two hours after he left. On December 23, at 12:29 A.M., an earthquake of magnitude 6.2 occurred beneath the center of the city; and within an hour, two severe aftershocks occurred. Five thousand people were killed, 20,000 were injured, and a quarter million were left homeless. The hotel where the man had been staying was demolished.

The Collapsed Bridge

On August 1, 2007, a middle-aged woman was commuting home from work during evening rush hour in Minneapolis, Minnesota. Her trip was so routine she said she could drive it blindfolded. This time, her boredom was interrupted by an inexplicable compulsion to take another way home. She knew any other route would result in a considerable delay, so she resisted the urge. The feeling grew to such intensity, however, that she found herself veering onto an alternate road. Before she reached home she heard on her car radio that the I-35W Mississippi River bridge, which she regularly traveled twice a day, had collapsed into the river, killing 13 people and injuring 145. She was so shaken she had to stop her vehicle to regain control of her emotions before proceeding.

The Secretary Knows

A young woman who worked as a secretary on a busy medical ward of a large metropolitan hospital began to realize that she knew in advance which patients were going to experience medical emergencies such as cardiac arrest during her shift. She had neither medical training nor any direct contact with patients, however, and she knew that if she went public with her premonitions she would be ridiculed and possibly fired. When she learned that a particular nurse on her shift had an interest in such matters, she made friends with her and eventually opened up to her. At the beginning of each shift, she would covertly tell the nurse which patients required special attention. She was almost never wrong. She and the nurse kept their communication secret for years. Both women are certain that many patients' lives were saved as a result.

The Rogue Wave

In early 1991, Marilyn Winkler of Dandridge, Tennessee, and her husband, David, decided to take a break from parenting and go on a vacation to the island of Saint Lucia in the Caribbean.[3] Her mother-in-law came for a visit to babysit their 15-month-old daughter, Kate.

After they settled into a Marigot Bay hotel on Saint Lucia, the Winklers boarded a water taxi, a 22-foot motorized boat, to take them to the coastal town of Soufrière, where they planned to have lunch. As they hugged the coastline on the 50-minute trip, the weather was perfectly calm and no storms were predicted. Oddly, Winkler started glancing down at the floor of the boat and began picking up small items of debris, such as a rusty nail, and throwing them overboard. This turned into an obsession as she visualized these objects as projectiles if the boat were wrecked. There was no apparent reason for this concern; she was at home on boats, she was a good swimmer, and the weather was ideal.

She found herself continually looking toward the east and surveying the horizon. She looked for other boats and saw none. As they approached Soufrière, Gregory, the local water-taxi helmsman, and Stan, another local crewman, decided to enter Soufrière Bay by sailing through a cut in a reef rather than circling around the reef and entering the bay from farther out to sea. Winkler knew instinctively that it was wrong to enter the cut, and she started yelling at her husband to take the tiller from Gregory and steer them clear of the cut. The men laughed at her and began making chauvinistic remarks. She fought back an urge to seize the tiller herself. Then she started stuffing her personal items into waterproof bags, as if preparing for an emergency. Again she looked around and saw no other boats in the vicinity.

Halfway through the cut, a gigantic wave appeared from nowhere. It lifted their boat onto its 20-foot crest, turned it upside down, rotated it 360 degrees, then slammed it down, smashing it into "toothpicks," as Winkler put it. Winkler and Stan found themselves 30 feet under the surface of the ocean. Then, Winkler remembers, time seemed to stand still. As she saw the beautiful rays of the sun beaming down, she felt complete peace. Her thoughts suddenly turned to Kate, whom she heard yelling "Mommy" as clearly as a bell. Then she felt two hands behind her chest lifting her, pushing her to the surface, and she began to swim. When she popped to the surface, she looked toward the shoreline to orient herself. She saw that all three men had surfaced. She again looked for other boats but saw none. Then out of nowhere an elderly fisherman with a long gray beard appeared a few yards away. He calmly invited the swimmers into his boat and held out his hand to each in turn. He took them into Soufrière, where locals gathered around them and walked with them to a clinic. It must have been a difficult walk because they had to frequently pause to spew water from their lungs. Gregory, the helmsman, had a broken nose, and David had a bleeding scalp laceration that required 20 stitches.

Shaken up and lucky to be alive, the next day they caught a flight and returned home, arriving back in Tennessee late at night. They told her mother-in-law they had been shipwrecked, but before they could explain further, her mother-in-law said that little Kate, while being fed her lunch in her high chair the previous day, had suddenly started saying, "Mommy and Daddy are drowning!" and "Daddy is bleeding from his head." She also said that a shark was in the water. Although Winkler had not seen a shark, it was conceivable in view of all the blood in the water. Winkler states that her daughter could barely talk at this stage in her life, had spent all her 15 months in the Smoky Mountains, had never been to the ocean, and may not even have known what a shark was. But Winkler had no doubt that she really had heard Kate saying "Mommy" while she was in the ocean.

Winkler's premonition of disaster was especially noteworthy on several counts. It was so profound that she spoke to others about it before it happened and started preparing for it. Her toddler, around 2,000 miles away, seemed to know what was happening to her parents, and she seemed to speak to Winkler as she nearly drowned. But what of the hands she felt lifting her up? And the old fisherman who appeared from nowhere to rescue them—why was his boat not wrecked along with theirs?

Anecdotes or Case Histories?

People's lives don't unfold as a series of controlled laboratory experiments. Extraordinary events occur in the course of most lives, and it is foolish to dismiss them because they *are* extraordinary and one of a kind. Skepticism about people's stories can be overdone. As philosopher and consciousness researcher John Beloff, of the University of Edinburgh, stated, "Skepticism is not necessarily a badge of tough-mindedness; it may equally be a sign of intellectual cowardice."[4]

There is an old saying in medicine about people's stories. "If you don't like the story, you call it an anecdote. If you like it, you call it a case history."

Anecdotes or case histories? You decide.

CHAPTER 4

THE ONE MIND IS
NOT AN INFINITE BLOB

If all individual minds are part of a greater mind, what keeps all mental activity from melding into some featureless muddle in the One Mind? What accounts for the specificity and individuality we see in One-Mind, beyond-the-body experiences? How does a concerned mother who senses that her child is in serious difficulty in a faraway city know that it is *her* child who is involved and not some other child somewhere else in the world?

The Picky, Precise One Mind

Psychologist Joseph Chilton Pearce, whom I quote often in this book, has thought deeply about the question of specificity. He firmly opposes the New-Ageisms that are offered as explanations. "To . . . assume that 'all our thoughts are really one, that our separateness is just delusion,' is nonsense," he wrote. "There are levels on which thoughts can, under very special conditions, interchange, and there are levels where they cannot." This is fortunate; it prevents us from being swamped by a continual flood of thoughts from our seven billion fellow earthlings. Drawing a parallel to the discovery of entangled states among subatomic particles once in contact—whereby a change in one particle is correlated with an equal and instantaneous change in a distant particle, no matter how far away—Pearce observed that that there are rules governing these connections; otherwise the world would be a mess. "Particles are not all bonded; that would be just as great a chaos as no particles being bonded.[1] . . . Our intuition of an underlying wholeness shouldn't imply melting into a homogenous mass."[2] Because our minds don't dissolve into sameness, specific and individualized One-Mind events are preserved. The One Mind is picky. A worried mother can connect with *her* child, not all children. Minds can affect *specific* electronic gadgets, not all electronic systems. Remote viewers can connect with *specific* scenes, not the entire planetary landscape.

Whether we call the One Mind the Source, the All, the Whole, the Absolute, Universe, Pure Being, God, Allah, the frequency domain, the collective unconscious, the holographic realm, the Akashic records, or something else, it is not a featureless, infinite blob. It manifests in our lives in unique ways. How could this be?

An image I find useful is that the One Mind is like the stem cells in our body. Stem cells are pluripotent, meaning they can transform into any type of specialized cell in the body. But stem cells don't go off on their own, randomly turning into just any or all cell types. They are on call. When prompted, these uncommitted, undifferentiated cells transform into a *specific* type of cell—cardiac, skin, intestinal, blood, and so on—depending on the body's need.

Like stem cells, the One Mind, the Source, awaits instructions and prompting. This is why information arising from it can be highly individualized, not random. Pattern, specificity, and individuality, therefore, typify the way the One Mind manifests in our lives. It responds to the needs, wishes, desires, and intentions of individuals and situations. The One Mind can spin out the thoughts and knowledge of a savant, a Leonardo, or an Einstein. It can grant the discovery of fire or the invention of the wheel. It can reveal the composition of the *Mona Lisa,* the periodic table of the elements, or the secret of heavier-than-air flight. Its generative possibilities are unlimited.

As we've seen, the One Mind also has a warning function. It can reveal itself as a precognitive dream of a natural disaster or an impending illness. These need-based revelations are quite common, arising as if from a larger frame of knowing.

Author David Grann reported an example in his captivating book *The Lost City of Z,* which details the adventures of the legendary British explorer Percy Fawcett in the Amazon jungles in the early 1900s. There are many ways of perishing in this environment—lethal infections, a variety of predators, starvation, accidents, madness, murder by hostile tribes—yet Fawcett had an uncanny capacity to avoid nearly all of them. His ability to avoid predators was astonishing. On one occasion, after leaping over a pit viper, he wrote in his journal, "What amazed me more than anything was the warning of my subconscious mind, and instant muscular response. . . . I had not seen it till it flashed between my legs, but the 'inner man'—if I can call it that—not only saw it in time, but judged its striking height and distance exactly, and issued commands to the body accordingly!"[3] This sort of knowing is often labeled as a "sixth sense" or "second sight," but to label something is not to explain it. Nonlocal mind or boundless, nonlocal awareness, which leads to the premise of the One Mind, is another point of view.

It is foolish to try to separate stem cells from the body. Their behavior and fate are so intimately integrated with the body that they *are* the body. Just so, it is unwise to separate human consciousness from the information source that is the One Mind. There is no separate source. We are it and it is we. Together we occupy a timeless, spaceless domain.

In the One Mind, all possibilities, all configurations of information, appear to exist *in potentia,* all superimposed on one another, awaiting some prompt in order to transform into an actuality in our world of experience. This is an image that physicists would immediately recognize because it is the one they employ in quantum physics. Most physicists believe that before a measurement is made at the quantum level, a particle exists in all its theoretically possible states. There are no real entities at this stage, only an ensemble of potentials that coexist in an all-at-once "superposition." When a measurement or observation occurs, these potentials undergo a "collapse of the wave function," which is a mathematical description, and manifest as only one of many possible configurations, like the famous cat in Schrödinger's famous thought experiment. Measurement or observation makes the ghostly potentials real.

(There are other interpretations within physics. Some physicists believe that following an observation at the quantum level, *all* possibilities are realized, and that we are aware of only one of them—the so-called many-worlds or parallel universe interpretation of quantum measurement theory.)

In the One Mind, however, it is not *measurement* that produces a transformation of the potential into the actual, but *need.*

Entanglement and Nonlocality

Another promising image that has arisen to explain our intimate connections is entanglement, a concept also drawn from the world of quantum physics.[4] An object is said to be entangled if it cannot be fully described without considering one or more additional objects; it is as if the separate, distant entities comprise a single system. Entanglement has been experimentally verified many times over the past three decades and is accepted by the majority of physicists as a fundamental feature of nature.[5]

Nonlocality is considered to be the mechanism for the effects of entanglement. According to physicist Nick Herbert, "A non-local connection links up one location with another without crossing space, without decay, and without delay." These connections have three identifying characteristics, says Herbert. They are *unmediated* (no connecting signal is involved), *unmitigated* (the strength of the correlations does not fade with increasing distance), and *immediate* (they are instantaneous).[6]

The implications of entanglement and nonlocality are stunning—*so* stunning that some physicists have had great difficulty believing them. This includes Einstein, who ridiculed nonlocal connections as "spooky action at a distance."[7] Einstein was wrong in his objections, however, and the unbelievable has come to pass. As physicist Menas Kafatos and science historian Robert Nadeau said in their book *The Conscious Universe: Parts and Wholes in Physical Reality,* "The universe on a very basic level could be a vast web of particles that remain in contact with one another over any distance in no time in the absence of the transfer of energy or information."[8]

In order for distant particles to demonstrate nonlocal connections and entanglement, they must have once been in contact. According to the Big Bang theory, all the matter in the universe was originally in contact, concentrated in a "very hot dot" of matter-energy that exploded around 14 and a half billion years ago, resulting in the universe we see.[9] So, if the Big Bang theory is valid, a requirement for nonlocal connections—original contact—was met early on.

Only recently, scientists believed entanglement was limited to the microworld of atoms and subatomic particles. Today, however, entanglement has been proven to be a feature of the biology of living creatures, apparently including ourselves, as we shall see later in this first section.[10]

Can entanglement account for the connectedness we see in the One Mind? Consciousness researcher Dean Radin believes it might. In his illuminating book *Entangled Minds,* he shows how entanglement may apply at the mental level, accounting for the various beyond-the-brain, One-Mind experiences we examine in this book.

Holograms

The hologram is another metaphor that helps illustrate the relationship between individual minds and the One Mind. In the 1980s the eminent physicist David Bohm, professor of theoretical physics at Birkbeck College, London, advanced his concept of the "implicate order" in his classic book *Wholeness and the Implicate Order.* Bohm proposed the implicate order as an explanation for universal wholeness. Its essential features are that the whole universe is in some way enfolded in each part, and that each part is enfolded in the whole. Bohm proposed the hologram as "an instrument that can help give a certain immediate perceptual insight into what can be meant by undivided wholeness. . . . "[11] *Hologram* is derived from Greek words meaning "to write the whole." Each part of a hologram contains sufficient information to reconstitute the entire hologram—in effect, "writing the whole."

The hologram is strikingly similar to the metaphor of Indra's net, developed in the 3rd century by the Mahayana school of Buddhism. When Indra fashioned the world, he made it as a net or web, in which there is a glimmering jewel at every knot. The net is infinite in dimension; therefore the jewels are infinite in number. In the glittering surface of every jewel is reflected the image of all the other jewels in the net—an infinite mirroring process, symbolizing the interpenetration, interconnectedness, and simultaneous mutual identity of all phenomena in the universe.[12]

Enfoldment

In addition to the hologram, Bohm uses a simpler example to illustrate the enfoldment of parts and wholes. Consider a transparent container full of a very viscous fluid and equipped with a mechanical rotator that can "stir" the fluid very slowly. If a droplet of insoluble black ink is added to the fluid and the stirring device is activated, the ink is slowly transformed into a thread that extends through the whole fluid, eventually appearing as if it is distributed randomly throughout the fluid as a shade of gray. But if the mechanical stirrer is reversed, turning in the opposite direction, the transformation is reversed and the droplet of black ink suddenly reappears, reconstituted. The ink droplet has retained its individuality, even though it appeared to be randomly dispersed.[13] In the same way, individual minds retain their individuality, even though they are enfolded into the One Mind.

David Bohm was one of the most distinguished physicists of the 20th century. He was known for fearlessly challenging scientific orthodoxy, and his interests spilled into many areas such as philosophy, psychology, religion, biology, and the nature of consciousness. He arrived at his ideas of unitary consciousness through the rigorous path of modern physics, as well as his personal experiences. His dialogues with the spiritual teacher Jiddu Krishnamurti inspired thousands and are still available.[14]

Bohm and I got to know each other a bit, exchanging ideas about the role of meaning and the mind in healing. Once, in a hallway conversation at a small, intimate gathering, I asked him his opinion of the future of humankind. "Do you think we'll make it?" He paused, thinking intently, then said, "Yes. Barely."

Chaos and Fractals

The more alternatives there are, the more uncertain the outcome. The more uncertainty, the greater the potential for information transmission.

—Roy Lachman et al[15]

A model for how individual minds might come together in the One Mind has arisen from a surprising source—an area of mathematics called chaos theory and fractals.

In 1975 the mathematician Benoit Mandelbrot coined the term *fractal* from a Latin term for *broken,* from which *fracture* is derived. In a fractal structure, similar patterns recur at progressively smaller scales. Fractals have been used to describe partially random or chaotic phenomena such as crystal growth, fluid turbulence, and galaxy formation. Fractal patterns have been found at all levels of nature, such as in clouds, coastlines, snowflakes, crystals, blood vessel networks, ocean waves, DNA, heart rhythms, various vegetables such as cauliflower and broccoli, mountain ranges, river networks, and fault lines. Fractal art is now commonplace, as stunningly beautiful patterns are generated on computers by mathematicians and fractal artists.

Mathematician Ralph Abraham of the University of California at Santa Cruz is an expert in chaos theory, which deals with dynamical systems that are extremely sensitive to initial conditions. This means that long-term predictions in how these systems will behave are generally impossible. The best-known example is weather and the "butterfly effect," according to which the flutter of a butterfly's wing in China could conceivably trigger a tornado somewhere in the United States.

Fractals are "a wide, frothy zone" where unlike things come together, says Abraham.[16] He uses the example of a sandy beach to illustrate how fractals show up in nature. On a map, a coastline appears sharply distinct. But when we view the boundary of land and water up close, the crisp distinctions disappear. On the beach there is water in the sand and sand in the water. "The transition from land to sea is a fractal," Abraham says. "It is spatially chaotic. It is Natural. The Milky Way is a sandy beach in the sky. It is Natural also. Nature teaches us fractal geometry and chaos theory."

Abraham believes there are "fractals in [the] mind" and "fractals in the world soul." He suggests that in a normal psyche, the boundaries between the components of the mind, such as waking awareness and the unconscious, are "thick fractals, which permit a kind of porosity between these components of the psyche, and thus, integration"—what he calls the "sandy beach model" of healthy psychological function. In an unhealthy mind, the "boundaries may be like concrete walls or iron curtains." When this happens, isolated components of the mind cannot communicate with one another. The result may be multiple personality disorder, in which mental domains are split off and isolated. Abraham's term for this situation is *multiple personality dischaos,* a chaos deficiency syndrome.

Chaos deficiency—dischaos—can also take place at a societal and global level, Abraham suggests. It can cause disorders at "the collective conscious and unconscious of our society. . . . Thus, boundaries which are too firm (iron curtains) may be involved in world problems."

Abraham maintains that thick, frothy fractal boundaries are a "prerequisite for the stability and longevity of a culture, or the health of an individual." They are required for interconnectivity, communication, and integration both *within* the minds of individuals and *between* the seven billion individual minds on the earth. The alternative is rigid boundaries that forbid fluid communication, tolerance, and understanding, with the resulting disintegration of both individual personalities and global society.

Unfortunately, we seem to be in the process of defractalizing our society by establishing boundaries that are increasingly impermeable. As Abraham notes, "Our culture has devoted excess attention to the walled fortress . . . concrete walls around the town, locks on the doors and houses, electronic motion detectors, video cameras at the bank card machine, and so on." Gated communities separate us from one another in the name of security. *Guns*—a word derived from a Scandinavian term for *war*—are almost as numerous in America as

Americans. The Occupiers and the 99 Percenters feel increasingly estranged from the One Percenters. Comity has virtually disappeared from the halls of Congress. Impermeable, nonporous boundaries have never seemed so prevalent.

Yet there are those who, like Abraham, see ways in which we can link with one another in the Great Connect. Frederick Turner, professor of arts and humanities at the University of Texas at Dallas, sees in fractal science a path through which individual minds may unite in the universal One Mind. In his book *Natural Religion,* he suggests that a visual experience that momentarily fills us with a sense of awe—e.g., a powerful artwork or a jaw-dropping sunset—"stuns the mind into a blur." At such a moment, says Turner, a "delicate attunement or calibration" can take place in the brain, in which the "strange attractor of the divine mind" influences the individual mind to become "a fractal miniature of the universal mind itself."[17]

There are endless ways to "stun the mind." Later we will examine ways in which highly creative people have overcome the dischaotic, defractalizing, numbing effects of habits, ruts, and routines that prevent our awakening to the transcendent One Mind.

Lipstick at Bergen-Belsen

When British troops liberated Bergen-Belsen concentration camp in Germany on April 15, 1945, they encountered 40,000 prisoners in 200 huts. They also discovered 10,000 bodies. The vast majority had died from typhus or starvation. The German guards, fearing infection, had refused to bury them, and the remaining skeletal prisoners lacked the strength to do so, so the bodies had been dumped in piles around the camp and left to rot.

The British soldiers were shocked beyond belief. They began to retch when they reached the wire, overcome by the stench of death. These hardened troops, who had fought the Nazis all across Europe, cried like babies. But they went to work, bulldozing the corpses into a mass grave. Somewhere among them was young Anne Frank, who had recorded in her Amsterdam diary as early as 1942 that Jews were being abducted and gassed.

By April 28 everyone had been buried. Although 500 inmates continued to die every day, at least there were no more corpses lying about, which resulted in a boost in morale. Food was available, and nearly all the inmates had been deloused with DDT powder, their clothes fumigated, their bodies scrubbed clean. Infected huts were being incinerated with flamethrowers.

Nicholas Best, who provided the above description in his book *Five Days That Shocked the World,* described what happened next:

> Some genius had introduced lipstick to the camp. A large consignment had just arrived, enough for every woman at Belsen to paint her lips if she wished. Huge numbers did so, happily recalling that they had once been feminine and might be so again one day. Lipstick had turned out to be an enormous morale booster, making all the difference between life and death for some of the women in the camp.[18]

British Lieutenant Colonel Mervin W. Gonin, commander of the 11th Light Field Ambulance, R.A.M.C., was among the first British soldiers to liberate Bergen-Belsen in 1945. In his diary, he gave a more graphic description of the effect of the lipstick:

> It was shortly after the British Red Cross arrived, though it may have no connection, that a very large quantity of lipstick arrived. This was not at all what we men wanted, we were screaming for hundreds and thousands of other things and I don't know who asked for lipstick. I wish so much that I could discover who did it, it was the action of genius, sheer unadulterated brilliance. I believe nothing did more for those internees than the lipstick. Women lay in bed with no sheets and no nightie but with scarlet red lips, you saw them wandering about with nothing but a blanket over their shoulders, but with scarlet red lips. I saw a woman dead on the post mortem table and clutched in her hand was a piece of lipstick. At last someone had done something to make them individuals again, they were someone, no longer merely the number tattooed on the arm. At last they could take an interest in

their appearance. That lipstick started to give them back their humanity.[19]

How did someone know that lipstick would restore the resolve to live and thereby save lives? Some anonymous individual was able to identify so intimately with the minds of the starving, suffering, dying prisoners that he or she could see beyond the obvious. I suggest that this was a One-Mind event of the first order.

The horror of Bergen-Belsen occurred because the links between humans were severed and "the other" came to be considered less than human. The lipstick event is the kind of breakthrough that can occur when minds unite in the Great Connect. These polar events are a mirror showing both the worst and the best of which we humans are capable—the beastly and the angelic. It reveals the fact that unity, commonality, and a One-Mind consciousness are not philosophical niceties but necessities preventing our descent into depravity. They are mirrors that should never be taken off the wall.

Who's in Charge?

Who or what is in control of the One Mind? Who turns the spigot of information on and off? For Christians, it is God who creates order and form from the undifferentiated void. For Hindus, it is the interplay between Shakti and Shiva that unleashes the creative process of the universe. For physicist Bohm, it is the unseen, invisible "implicate" and "super-implicate" orders that unfold into the visible "explicate" order that we see, touch, hear, and feel.[20] In our quantum-enchanted era, it is the interplay of wave functions and observers that give birth to the visible world of things.

Beyond Words

In our modern market of ideas, there are many models to choose from in describing the operations of consciousness. Everyone seems to be hawking his or her favorite candidate. At some point, however, all talk of mechanism—whether emergence, entanglement, nonlocality, holograms, implicate orders, or any other process—becomes irrelevant. The sages who represent the esoteric side of the great wisdom unanimously maintain that as understanding grows, all forms of the Absolute are eventually transcended. Name and form, which are the keynotes of our everyday existence, become obstructive and no longer hold any importance. Thus Meister Eckhart, Germany's great 14th-century Christian mystic, proclaimed, "Nothing is so like God as silence."[21]

Father Thomas Keating affirmed Eckhart: "Silence is God's first language; everything else is a poor translation."[22] From the Hindu tradition, Swami Vivekananda: "The seeker's silence is the loudest form of prayer."[23] And from Zen Buddhism the aphorism "He who speaks does not know, and he who knows does not speak." But silence means more than simply being mute; a stone can do that. Silence means that a place has been created where a higher form of knowing can enter. The mystics consider this passage into silence a prerequisite for Divine Union—complete absorption into the One Mind, the All, the Absolute, the Source. At this stage, language is simply outgrown and is superseded by being. When neurosurgeon Eben Alexander entered this state during his near-death experience due to near-lethal meningitis, he simply said, "It is indescribable."[24] The wonders he experienced, the wisdom he was granted, were conveyed wordlessly; ordinary language was unnecessary. Or as Meister Eckhart put it, "It is God's nature to be without a nature."[25] No description possible. No description needed.

CHAPTER 5

THE SENSE OF BEING STARED AT

W inston Churchill once remarked about one of his political opponents, "Occasionally he stumbled over the truth, but hastily picked himself up and hurried on as if nothing had happened."[1] Our encounters with One-Mind phenomena are often like that. Although they are real and should give us pause, we often don't pay attention to them.

Here's Looking at You

One example is the sense of being stared at. Most individuals have had this experience and, when glancing or turning around, have met the other person's eyes. British biologist Rupert Sheldrake, who has studied this phenomenon extensively, reports that between 70 and 97 percent of adults and children in Europe and North America have had such experiences.[2] The phenomenon appears to work the other way around as well: people report causing someone else to turn around and meet their gaze by staring at them. These experiences occur most frequently in public places: stopped at a traffic light, on streets, in bars and restaurants, and so on.

Sheldrake designates the ability to detect the remote gaze of a distant person as the "seventh sense." He suggests that the seventh sense also includes telepathy and premonitions. Why "seventh"? The reason, says Sheldrake, is that these abilities seem to be in a different category from the five normal senses, and they also differ from so-called sixth senses such as the ability of animals to detect electrical, magnetic, and thermal stimuli.[3]

Many experiments show that individuals can detect the stare of a distant individual even when the distant person is looking at them via a closed-circuit television setup. The sensation is often correlated by a change in the electrical conductivity of the skin of the stared-at individual. There seems to be a direct mind-to-mind connection between the two individuals—an overlapping of consciousness, a linkage of distant minds, as if the two minds have momentarily become one.

Survival Value, Again

This phenomenon is especially common in war. As a battalion surgeon in Vietnam, I had intimate contact with combat infantrymen, including Special Forces. Many of these soldiers attributed their survival to a keen sense that warned them that they were being observed by enemy soldiers.

Rupert Sheldrake reports the experience of William Carter, who was leading a patrol of Gurkhas on an antiterrorist operation in Malaya in 1951.[4] Carter's patrol came across a freshly abandoned camp. While they were examining the site, Carter experienced an uncanny feeling that he was being watched. This was associated with a profound sense of danger, as if something were gripping the back of his neck. He turned around to see an enemy soldier about 20 yards away, bringing his rifle up to kill Carter, who knew instantly that one of them was going to die. Carter shot him first. He does not doubt the existence of a sense of being stared at, saying, "But for it, I wouldn't be alive today."[5]

The frequent occurrence of a sense of being stared at in life-or-death combat situations suggests that one of the functions of this ability is survival. This makes sense. Any organism endowed with an ability to sense danger would be more likely to survive and produce offspring, our biological imperative.

In a series of interviews with professionals who watch others for a living, such as surveillance personnel and police, Sheldrake found that most of them were convinced that this sense is real. Some people, they reported, seemed to know they were being stared at, even when the watchers were well hidden. Suspects would often turn around and stare at the vehicle the police officers were in. Detectives are sometimes trained not to stare too often or intently at the backs of people they are following, so as not to provoke the individual to turn around. These precautions are often followed even at a distance, such as when suspects are being viewed through binoculars.

One U. S. Marine told Sheldrake about his experiences as a sniper in Bosnia in 1995. When he aimed at known terrorists through the telescopic sight of his rifle, people seemed to know he was aiming at them. "Within one second prior to actual termination, a target would somehow seem to make eye contact with me. I am convinced that these people somehow sensed my presence at distances over one mile. They did so with uncanny accuracy, in effect to stare down my own scope."[6]

Celebrity photographers report similar experiences, says Sheldrake. Celebrities being secretly photographed up to half a mile away often turn around and look down the lens of the camera. Hunters and wildlife photographers report similar happenings: the animal, for unknown reasons, turns toward the telescopic sight or camera, as if reading the mind of the stalker.[7]

During the summer months here in northern New Mexico, I keep a hummingbird feeder outside my office. I keep binoculars on my desk, and when a hummer alights on the feeder I quickly grab the binocs for a close-up view. Nearly always the hummer flies away within a few seconds. But if I glance quickly without the binocs and do not allow my gaze to rest on the bird, she seems to linger at the feeder for much longer periods of time—an unscientific observation, I know, but one I've made repeatedly over several years.

Some pet owners reported to Rupert Sheldrake that they believe they can awaken their sleeping dogs or cats by staring at them.[8] Many believe their pets can sense their gaze, even when the animal cannot see their eyes.[9]

Are these reports "just stories"? They *are* stories, but they are supported by dozens of laboratory studies and experiments showing that people can detect the gaze of a distant individual. All told, these studies provide strong evidence for the conjoining, interaction, and linking of distant minds. Defying the commonly held assumption that individual minds are locked inside the brain, this research supports the concept of an extended mind that is nonlocal in space and time.

The fact that these phenomena occur in both animals and humans is important. If an ability is distributed throughout nature in different species, this greatly increases the "science cred" of the observations, as if one is observing a generalized principle in the natural world and not an isolated phenomenon.

Because we have become progressively divorced from nature, we have increasing difficulty in acknowledging how widespread these phenomena are. Children today are much more likely to watch *Animal Planet* on television than to venture into nature for actual contact with the wild. Contrast this with the experience of our ancestors, who lived in intimate contact with nature and its creatures every living moment. They took for granted the reality of shared consciousness with creatures great and small, a consciousness that knew no spatial or temporal limitations: the One Mind, of which every living thing partakes.

CHAPTER 6

THEY MOVED AS ONE

Every spring and fall they were on the move, vast herds of them stretching as far as the eye could see. No one really knew how many there were, for they were countless and uncountable. Estimates ranged from 50 million to 150 million. Their running created a faint vibration and a deep rumble in the earth that announced their coming to any living thing in their path. They would stop to rest and feed periodically and bed down at night. Then they were up at dawn to renew their journey toward the horizon and to destinations that had beckoned them for millennia. They were *Bison bison,* the magnificent American buffalo.

On cold mornings their breath formed a giant frosty cloud that hung like a halo over the enormous herd, a sign sought by every hunter. The animals moved as a single organism and with a unified will that caused many to die, because there could be no careful testing of danger or weighing of risk by single individuals when the group mind took charge. When they approached a river, the leading animals would venture hesitantly into the water, probing for deep unseen holes and quicksand. But the herd behind them kept coming, pushing and shoving the leaders into the drowning places and quicksand bogs. Thousands might be killed as a result, a sacrifice to the unbending single-mindedness of the colossal herd. Native Americans were bison mind readers. They understood the instincts that molded the masses into a single organism, and they used this knowledge to drive the bison off precipices such as Wyoming's Chugwater bluffs and Montana's Palisades cliffs.[1]

Encounters with their sheer numbers left men speechless. In May 1871, Colonel R. I. Dodge drove a wagon from Fort Zarah to Fort Larned on the Arkansas River in southwestern Kansas. He bumped into one of the greatest gatherings of large animals on earth—the great southern bison herd, migrating north from the Texas panhandle for the summer grass. Of the 34 miles between the forts, 25 were through "an immense dark blanket of buffaloes," wrote author Mari Sandoz in her classic book *The Buffalo Hunters.* From atop Pawnee Rock, Dodge could see a solid, moving mass of animals for up to ten miles in most directions. Others who saw this herd said it was 25 miles wide, probably 50 miles deep, and took five days to pass a given point. Estimates were from 4 million to 12 million animals in this particular herd alone.[2]

The herd was moving leisurely on this occasion. Two months earlier, however, Colonel Dodge's buffalo encounter had been different, and it almost cost him his life. In cold, blustery weather, Dodge's party made camp in the bend of a creek, crowding the tents and wagons close together. When the campfires died out and everyone except the sentinel was asleep, Dodge heard a faint but deep roaring sound. He soon realized its source—a gigantic buffalo herd bearing down fast on the camp. He knew the herd must be split or the camp would be overrun and they would all be trampled into the earth. He summoned the sentinel and three more men, and they stationed themselves between the charging bison and the camp. When the animals were about 30 yards out, they started firing their rifles as fast as possible and yelling. One animal fell dead, but the others kept coming. The men could feel the earth trembling beneath their feet. More animals fell to their gunfire. When it appeared there was no hope, the stampeding mass parted slightly, then more, then swerved to avoid the men. They passed within 30 feet of one flank of the camp and 75 feet of the other. The sleeping men awoke to the thunder of the stampeding animals and the gunfire and were paralyzed with fear, certain they were doomed.

Native Americans considered buffalo on the run to be one of the true perils of the plains. They always had scouts far out from their villages, whether camped or moving. These individuals could ascertain the distance and direction of a stampeding herd by listening intently with an ear to the ground.

As the railroads extended their reach west, railroad men learned of these dangers the hard way. Rampaging herds would charge anything in their way, including locomotives and cars. The leading animals would plunge head-on into them, pushed from behind, and although many would be killed the train would suffer as well. After trains were derailed twice in one week by charging bison, the trainmen learned to stop at a safe distance and let the animals pass.[3]

The bison's herd behavior is of course not an isolated pattern. Highly coordinated movements are known to occur in the famous wildebeest migrations in Africa, as well as with other quadrupeds. Nor are these patterns limited to large mammals.

Early white settlers in America reported highly organized group behavior in passenger pigeons (*Ectopistes migratorius*). The bird's name is derived from the French *passager*, meaning "to pass by." At the time of Columbus's arrival, it was estimated that of the three billion to five billion birds in what would become the United States, one in four was a passenger pigeon. Huge flocks, numbering in the millions, showered enough excrement when flying over settlements that people were forced indoors. As author Charles C. Mann reports in his book *1491*, the birds fed on mast—acorns and various wild nuts. But they also loved grains such as wheat, oats, and maize, and they destroyed fields so often that the bishop of Quebec formally excommunicated the species in 1703. The pigeons seemed not to notice and the sanction didn't take.

During the first part of the 19th century, passenger pigeons were so numerous that few people imagined they *could* be exterminated. By 1850, however, there were noticeably fewer passenger pigeons to be found. A few conservationists saw a tragedy unfolding, but their attempts to prevent it failed. The last known passenger pigeon, Martha, named after Martha Washington, expired on September 1, 1914, in the Cincinnati Zoo. Her body was frozen in a block of ice and shipped to the Smithsonian Institution, where it was skinned and mounted. Martha is in the museum's archives and is not on public display.

The centennial of the extinction of the passenger pigeon is 2014. Certain organizations, such as Project Passenger Pigeon, are gearing up to commemorate the event "through a wide range of local and international programs, exhibits, teaching curriculum, and other fun activities for people of all ages."[4] The group's main goal is to awaken people to how such a catastrophe might be prevented in the future.

One of the birds most adept at group behavior is the starling, whose acrobatic movements in huge flocks are a kind of aerial ballet. In England during the winter months, thousands of starlings return toward evening from foraging to Otmoor, a 400-acre grassy wetland in southeast England. Small flocks merge into larger flocks called murmurations, at which point they begin to wheel and gyre in arrays that are among the most elegant in nature.[5]

Enormous schools of fish such as herring also demonstrate similar group behavior, wheeling in breathtaking unison, particularly when chased by predators.

When creatures demonstrate group behavior, are they acting unthinkingly and blindly or is something more involved?

When an elephant dies, the herd often gathers around the dead animal and may linger for days, behaving as if they are experiencing genuine grief and mourning. They have been known to bury the dead animal before moving on and may revisit the death site at later dates and fondle the bones. Behaviors have also been observed in dogs, horses, and gorillas that impress ethologists as authentic mourning experiences, described by David Alderton in his book *Animal Grief: How Animals Mourn*.

In one report of a "magpie funeral," a flock of around 40 of the birds gathered around a magpie that had been killed on a road. When the auto that had killed the bird returned, the magpies swarmed it and almost forced it off the road.[6]

In a similar instance, a man shot a crow that had been stealing eggs. Within days his house was under siege by around 30 crows that circled it for days. The man gave up hunting permanently.[7]

Swarm Intelligence

How do masses of individual animals, birds, and fish manage to act in concerted, coordinated ways, as if the group is a single entity? The best-known idea is "swarm intelligence" or "swarm theory," introduced in the 1980s by researchers in artificial intelligence and robotics. According to this concept, the individual units in a group interact locally with one another and with their environment. Although there is no centralized controlling influence dictating how the individuals should behave, the local and often random interactions between the individuals somehow lead to the emergence of intelligent group behavior. In other words, the individual isn't particularly clever but the group is. Swarm theory has been applied to naturally occurring phenomena such as animal herding, bird flocking, fish schooling, ant and termite colonies, beehives, and bacterial growth.[8] Swarm theory has practical applications. It has been used to determine how best to ticket and board passengers onto commercial aircraft, assign aircraft arrivals to airport gates, and route trucks in the most efficient way possible. Scientists have developed software for groups or "swarms" of robots, using simple rules that mimic the behavior of insect swarms. The goal is to use robots to intelligently perform dangerous minesweeping and search-and-rescue operations that would place human first responders at risk. Some day, scientists predict, robotic swarms might explore the surface of Mars.[9]

When animals, birds, fish, or insects swarm, how do they do it? If none of the herring in the school grasps the big picture, how do they change direction in a flash, like a single entity? One key, say swarm theorists, is that no one is in charge. There is no "general" giving orders, which would take time to disseminate throughout the herd, flock, school, or hive. Instead of orders from the top, complex behavior is coordinated by relatively simple rules.

In 1986, Craig Reynolds, a computer graphics researcher, created a simple program he called "boids" in order to explore what these rules might be. In his simulation, generic birdlike objects, the boids, were each given three instructions: (1) don't crowd nearby boids, (2) fly in the average direction of nearby boids, and (3) stay close to nearby boids. When he set the program in motion on a computer screen, there was a striking simulation of the unpredictable and life-like movements seen in flocking.[10]

But why do creatures follow these rules, and why do they form immense herds, flocks, schools, or hives in the first place? The standard answer from biology is that there is a survival advantage in doing so. A big group of animals, birds, or fish has more eyes with which to spot predators. When attacked, they can confuse a predator by coordinated mass movements. A mass of individuals has an advantage in locating a mate, finding food, or following a migration route. As a group member, each individual is more likely to stay alive and reproduce than if isolated and alone.

Ah, if it were all so simple. Even among the scientists involved in swarm intelligence, these events still "seem miraculous even to the biologists who know them best," says *National Geographic* writer Peter Miller. Biologists who live in the wild for long periods and observe creatures up close often have a gnawing suspicion that the neat formulations of swarm theory leave something out.

For five months in 2003, wildlife biologists Karsten Heuer and his wife, Leanne Allison, trailed the Porcupine caribou herd of 123,000 animals for more than a thousand miles in their migration from their winter range in Canada's northern Yukon Territory to calving grounds in Alaska's National Wildlife Refuge.[11] "It's difficult to describe in words, but when the herd was on the move it looked very much like a cloud shadow passing over the landscape, or a mass of dominoes toppling over at the same time and changing directions," Heuer said. One domino hitting the next in line, a succession of falling dominos one after the other: classical cause and effect? Not exactly. Heuer elaborated: "It was as though every animal knew what its neighbor was going to do, and the neighbor beside that and beside that. There was no anticipation or reaction. No cause and effect. It just was."[12]

This sort of talk makes biologists crazy. There is no room in classical biology for "just knowing" that bypasses cause and effect. The closest biologists come to "just knowing" is in the concept of instincts, the inherent inclinations of a living organism toward a particular behavior. These fixed-action patterns are not based on learning but are inherited. Most theorists believe the information guiding instinctual behavior is hardwired in the nervous system of the individual, is stored in parents' DNA, and is passed from parent to offspring. DNA is the cause; instinctual behavior is the effect.

Swarm intelligence and instincts make sense until you start examining the niggling little exceptions that don't fit in, such as the "no-cause-and-effect" observations of ethologists such as Heuer and Allison. I'm suggesting the possibility of collective intelligence—a proto–One Mind that is not dependent on sensory information—that may operate in herds of animals, flocks of birds, and schools of fish.

Group Mind?

Biologists, as we've seen, have tried to explain the group behavior of flocks, herds, packs, and schools as sensory information picked up by one animal from its immediate neighbor and this process extending throughout the entire group. Such an explanation eliminates the need for any sort of group intelligence, or so it is said. But there are are problems with computerized models such as Reynolds's boids. As British biologist Rupert Sheldrake states, what happens on a flat computer screen bears little relation to the behavior of real, three-dimensional flocks of birds. The two-dimensional models, says Sheldrake, are "biologically naïve."[13]

In 1984 biologist Wayne Potts of the University of Utah filmed the banking movements of large flocks of dunlins, small shore-wading birds, over Puget Sound, Washington.[14] When the rapid exposures were slowed down, he found that neighbor-to-neighbor changes in behavior could occur in 15 thousandths of a second. These changes could be originated either by single birds or small groups anywhere in the flock, and spread as a near-simultaneous wave throughout. Potts then tested dunlins in the laboratory to see how quickly they could respond to a stimulus. He found that, on average, it required 38 thousandths of a second for a bird to initiate a startle response to a flash of light. This meant that they could not rely on visual cues from their neighbors to change directions in flight much quicker than their experimentally proven reaction time. Potts nonetheless concluded that the individual birds were indeed responding visually—not to their neighbors, however, but to what he called a "maneuver wave" passing through the flock as a whole. As Potts explained, "These propagation speeds appear to be achieved in much the same way as they are in a human chorus line: individuals observe the approaching manoeuvre wave and time their own execution to coincide with its arrival." Unlikely, says Sheldrake. Members of a chorus line view things that are in front or to the side of them, not what is occurring behind them. For the chorus line model to work in a flock, a bird would need nearly constant, 360-degree visual attention, which they do not possess. How could they be reacting almost instantaneously to waves approaching them from behind? They would need eyes in the backs of their heads. No birds, says Sheldrake, have 360-degree vision, whether they have their eyes at the front like owls, or at the side of the head like geese, ducks, dunlins, and starlings.

What else might be going on? "For decades a number of naturalists have speculated that changes in direction of flying flocks take place so rapidly that they seem to depend on 'collective thinking' or telepathy," says Sheldrake. "My own hypothesis is that flocks of birds are indeed organized telepathically through flock fields, the morphic fields of flocks."[15] Sheldrake discusses the nature of morphic fields in his groundbreaking books *A New Science of Life, The Presence of the Past,* and *The Sense of Being Stared At.* Morphic fields, he hypothesizes, are extended fields of influence that shape behavior and thought. They operate non-locally, unimpeded by space or time. They have been shaped during the long course of evolution and natural selection. Morphic fields do not exclude the importance of vision or any other physical sense in the flocking of birds or the group behavior of any other creatures; it's just that vision alone, or any other physical sense, cannot explain the coordination of the flock's movements.

Two-dimensional, boidlike computer models have also been developed to explain the coordinated movements of schools of fish, which at a distance resemble a single organism. Their most spectacular behavior is the so-called flash expansion, in which the school explodes outward when attacked by a predator, each fish darting away from the center. The entire expansion, Sheldrake notes, can occur in as little as 20 milliseconds. Again, there is no simple sensory explanation for this because it happens too fast for nerve impulses to move from the fish's eye to its brain and then to its muscles.

And fish exhibit schooling at night, so vision cannot be essential. Even when fish have been temporarily blinded by being fitted with opaque contact lenses in laboratory experiments, they remain capable of joining the school and maintaining their position in it. Computer models have also employed pressure changes in the water. Pressure variations are detected by pressure-sensitive organs known as lateral lines, which run along the length of a fish's body. Even when the lateral lines have been severed at the level of the gills, fish continue to school normally.

Sheldrake finds evidence suggesting that fieldlike, nonsensory, group intelligence is required to explain the organized behaviors of not only flocks of birds and schools of fish, but also social insects such as termites, wasps, and bees; herds fleeing from danger; wolves on hunting expeditions; and human crowds, football teams, or family groups. Morphic fields, he suggests, have evolved over eons as a way for members of the group to communicate over and above the regular senses.

"It is in the morphic fields of social groups that we find the evolutionary basis for telepathy," Sheldrake notes. Telepathy may evoke giggles of derision from die-hard materialists, but in Sheldrake's view there is nothing spooky about it. Indeed, it might be predictable. Nonsensory communication is an ability that any creature might develop in a hostile world because, quite simply, it has survival value. Because it aids survival and therefore procreation, it might be incorporated into a creature's genetic structure so that, in time, it might operate throughout the entire species. Such an ability would almost certainly evolve at an unconscious level, because conscious analysis and decision making require valuable time, which could be fatal in predator avoidance. This suggests that telepathy or nonlocal awareness might by now be present unconsciously in nearly all humans to some degree. Even in skeptics.

Sheldrake's morphic fields lend structure and specificity to the One Mind. Morphic fields can be species specific because they evolved through evolutionary pressures to fit the needs of certain creatures and not others. Thus the morphic fields of flocks of starlings are different from those of schooling fish. Social insects such as termites have their own morphic fields. They know how to build elaborate nests up to ten feet tall, with galleries and chambers and ventilation shafts of enormous complexity. Even though the overall plan of the structure could hardly be grasped by any single termite, the colony as a whole knows. Swarms of wasps and bees build structures that are also complex but in different ways, perhaps guided by not just a generalized "insect" morphic field but by a more specific "wasp" or "bee" morphic field.

But the One Mind is not entirely species specific; information can "jump species," as it were. Overlaps are common. Thus we see not only the nonlocal exchange of thoughts and intentions between parents and children, twins, lovers, therapists and clients, but also between vastly different creatures, as when, for example, lost animals return to their human owners across vast unfamiliar distances and incredible obstacles, inexplicable by sensory cues or memory.

Empathy, compassion, caring, and love are often the lubricants in humans for distant communication, and perhaps in other creatures as well. As Sheldrake puts it, "Telepathy is an aspect of the seventh sense that enables members of groups to respond to the movements and activities of others, and respond to their emotions, needs and intentions. Feelings communicated telepathically include fear, alarm, excitement, calls for help, calls to go to a particular place, anticipations of arrivals or departures, and distress and dying," notes Sheldrake.[16]

As an example of apparent distant, cross-species communication, Sheldrake mentions Queen Elizabeth, a renowned animal lover. Training her gun dogs at Sandringham, her estate in Norfolk, is one of her favorite hobbies. The staff at Sandringham say they do not need to be told when the queen is about to arrive because the dogs tell them. "All the dogs in the kennels start barking the moment she reaches the gate—and that is half a mile away," said Bill Meldrum, the head gamekeeper. "We don't know how they can tell and they don't do it with anyone else."[17]

This leads us directly into an exploration of the seventh-sense connection between animals and humans.

CHAPTER 7

THE ONE MIND OF ANIMALS AND HUMANS

Can the minds of humans and animals unite in the One Mind? Lyall Watson, the South African biologist, ethologist, and adventurer, whose books have nourished me for years, wrote:

> I think that there may well be a flow of pattern or instruction which crosses species lines and allows even radically different organisms to borrow each other's ideas. . . . As a biologist, I am aware at times—especially when steeped in some natural cycle—of a kind of consciousness that is timeless, unlimited by space or by the confines of my own identity. In this condition, I perceive things very clearly and am able to acquire information almost by a process of osmosis. I find myself, at these times, with knowledge that comes directly from being part of something very much larger, a sort of global ecology of mind. And the experience of it is literally wonderful.[1]

There is considerable evidence that Watson is correct: where consciousness is concerned, the lines between species are not fundamental.

Bobbie the Collie

During the 1920s, a two-year-old dog named Bobbie, mostly collie with a bit of English sheep dog, became a national sensation. His owners, Mr. and Mrs. Frank Brazier, restaurant owners who lived in Silverton, Oregon, were vacationing in Indiana when Bobbie got lost. Despite intense efforts to locate the dog, the Braziers finally despaired of finding him. Brokenhearted, they resumed their trip westward, never expecting to see him again. Six months later Bobbie showed up, emaciated, at the family restaurant in Oregon. He made his way up to the second-floor living quarters and jumped on the bed, awakening Frank Brazier by licking his face.

No one could believe it. When the *Silverton Appeal* published the story, it quickly spread to newspapers across the country. The Oregon Humane Society launched an investigation into the Braziers' claims. By interviewing people they reconstructed Bobbie's route home, which they estimated was around 2,800 miles, much of which took place in the dead of winter. Bobbie did not follow his owners' route back to Oregon, but traveled an indirect course over terrain he had never seen nor could have been familiar with. This was no look-alike dog; his owners were able to confirm his identity by several unique marks and scars.

Celebrity followed. Bobbie received medals, a gold collar, and gifts from England, France, Australia, and America. He was given a key to the city of Vancouver, British Columbia. The Portland Board of Realtors gave him a fully appointed miniature bungalow for his home. Author Charles Alexander wrote a book about him—*Bobbie: A Great Collie,* published by Dodd, Mead, and Company in 1926.[2] Bobbie played himself in a silent movie, *The Call of the West,* a reel of which is in the archives of the Oregon Historical Society Research Library. When Bobbie died in 1927, he was buried with honors at the Oregon Humane Society. Portland's mayor gave the eulogy. A week later, Rin Tin Tin, the German shepherd who starred in 23 Hollywood movies, laid a wreath at his grave, dog to dog.[3]

I've had the opportunity to discuss distant, nonlocal knowing with many audiences over the years, and I often use returning animals as examples. I find that critics' most frequent explanation for

Bobbie and similar instances is a highly developed sense of smell. This cropped up in a lecture I gave at the Smithsonian Institution in Washington, D.C., where I was interrupted by a comment from a man in the audience. "Pheromones!" he confidently announced. "The dog sensed pheromones coming from his owners in Oregon. The prevailing winds blow west to east. The dog merely followed this chemical signal all the way to Oregon." Pheromones are chemicals produced by mammals and insects, released in minute concentrations into the environment, which play a role in sexual attraction between members of the same species.

"Nearly three thousand miles?" I asked. "And between members of different species? They'd get pretty diluted over three thousand miles, don't you think?" Another man in the audience chimed in with another explanation. "Pure chance!" he said, without a hint of irony. "The dog found the home in Oregon by dumb luck." "There are a lot of houses to the west of Indiana," I offered. "The odds against finding the right house by chance are pretty high." Both men were supremely confident in their suggestions and were unmoved by my comments. It was a reminder to me that many individuals prefer *any* explanation rather than mind-to-mind communication, no matter how implausible or statistically unlikely their alternative ideas may be.

How *did* Bobbie find his way home across 2,800 miles of unfamiliar terrain? The hypothesis of the One Mind suggests that the mind of the animal and that of his owners were part of a larger mind that permitted a sharing of information between them. If Bobbie's owner knew the way home, that knowledge was available to Bobbie as well. There were not two separate minds communicating one to the other, but in essence a single mind. This sharing of knowledge, whether between humans or between animals and humans, is nearly always associated with love, caring, and compassion. This process allowed Bobbie to "home" much like the way an airliner follows a radio signal to a distant airport—the differences being that no electronic signal was involved in Bobbie's case and there is no requirement for emotional mediation in the case of the airliner and the airport.

Bobbie's case is not unique. Instances abound that suggest the existence of a human-animal bond that operates across space and time, a connection that is difficult to break, even when people try. Minosch, a German cat, reportedly traveled 1,500 miles in 61 days to return home after being separated from its vacationing family.[4] Thousands of similar cases have been reported. No doubt some can be dismissed as involving look-alike animals, but not all; often the returning animal has its original collar and name tag, and can be further identified by distinguishing marks.

Particularly fascinating are those cases in which the returning animal appears to be responding to the physical and emotional needs of some remote person. An example is that of an Irish soldier in World War I, whose wife and small dog, Prince, took up residence in 1914 in Hammersmith, London, while he was sent with one of the earliest contingents to the battlefields of France. After a period of service he was granted leave to visit his family, but after the furlough ended Prince was utterly disconsolate and refused all food. Then the dog disappeared. For ten days the wife tried desperately to trace him, to no avail. Finally she decided to break the news in a letter to her husband.

She was astonished when she heard from him that the dog had joined him in the trenches at Armentières, under heavy bombardment. Somehow Prince had made his way through the streets of London and 70 miles of English countryside, hitched a ride across the English Channel, traveled over 60 miles of French soil, and then "smelt his master out amongst an army of half a million Englishmen and this despite the fact that the last mile or so of intervening ground was reeking with bursting shells, many of them charged with tear-gas."[5]

Beyond Coincidence

The classic study of Bobbie-like cases was that of Drs. J. B. Rhine and Sally Rhine Feather, then at Duke University.[6] They described five categories of animal behavior that suggest some kind of distant, nonlocal knowing:

1. Reaction to impending danger to itself or its master

2. Reaction to the death of its master at a distance

3. Anticipation of a master's return

4. Homing

5. Trailing (finding its owner over unfamiliar terrain and sometimes to a previously unknown location)

Of these categories, perhaps the most amazing is trailing. In order to document that trailing had occurred, four major criteria were used:

1. The reliability of the witnesses

2. Positive identification of the animal, such as by a deformity, scar, or name tag

3. How credible and consistent the details of the case are

4. Corroborative evidence, such as other witnesses

Rhine and Feather found 54 cases of dogs, cats, and birds that met these criteria.

Some feats of animals are so astonishing that this is almost a guarantee that they will be ignored by skeptics of beyond-the-brain forms of consciousness. Consider what happened during a pigeon race in Europe in June 1995. A female pigeon belonging to David Dougal of Northumberland, England, was supposed to have flown to his home from Veau Vois, France. Instead she headed southwest to the coast of North Africa, settling into a pigeon loft in Morocco owned by Essoli Mohamed. In October, a second bird, a nephew of the first, also set off from Dougal's home and flew the 1600 miles to join his aunt. "I couldn't believe it when I got another letter from Essoli," Dougal said. "When the first bird went missing we weren't really too surprised, because it was awful weather for the race and that affects the bird's homing instincts. But there is no explanation we can come up with for the nephew. He was only a few weeks old and had just learnt to fly." Dougal was so astonished that the second bird was able to single out his aunt's adopted home from all the other pigeon lofts in the world that he let both birds remain in Morocco.[7]

The legendary J. B. Rhine observed that this sort of thing requires far greater psi powers than have ever been exhibited by human beings.[8] It's also the sort of thing that makes skeptics scurry toward "coincidence" with the desperation of drowning men clutching at straws.

Homing Owners

Sometimes it is the owner who is homing, not the animal. Sheldrake has compellingly demonstrated that pets seem to know when their owners are returning. He spent five years doing meticulous experiments that document what many pet owners believe—that there is a human-animal bond that operates at a distance in both space and time. Even when the experimenter tried to fake out the dogs by varying the time the owner returns, or varying the means of transportation such as returning by taxi, the dogs still seem to know and go on the alert by standing at a door or window minutes before the owner shows up. This occurs even when no one at home knows of the time of the owner's return. Sheldrake's findings are the subject of his provocative book *Dogs That Know When Their Owners Are Coming Home: And Other Unexplained Powers of Animals.*[9]

Dogs may also know when their owners are *not* coming home. In their book *The Haunting of the Presidents,* Joel Martin and William J. Birnes report that just before President Abraham Lincoln was assassinated at Ford's Theatre in Washington, D.C., on the evening of April 14, 1865, the Lincoln dog became frantic "at about the same time as the curtain was rising at Ford's. . . . The usually quiet and gentle pet inexplicably started barking uncontrollably as if seized by a sudden fear for its life, and began running around the family quarters in a frenzy, looking for its master, the president." There was no quieting the dog; none of the White House staff could calm the animal. The dog continued running through the hallways until it stopped, threw its head back, and began to wail. The thought on everyone's mind was that something terrible had gone wrong and that the President was in danger.

Ecological Validity

Animals are often studied in laboratories but the laboratory is not their natural habitat. It's not surprising, therefore, that laboratories may inhibit or extinguish One-Mind manifestations in animals.

As Susan J. Armstrong, professor of philosophy and women's studies at Humboldt State University in California, who has written extensively about animal psi, said, "Psi may in fact be repressed by tightly controlled, sterile, analytic settings."[10] *Ecological validity* is a term that is often used to describe Armstrong's point. It means performing research in a way that does not distort how the phenomenon being investigated occurs in real life.

Armstrong believes in the value of not only formal experiments but also simple observations and case reports. "Experimental and non-experimental evidence can support each other," she wrote. "The very abundance of such reports is striking. This abundance can be seen as mitigating the deficiencies in individual reports."[11]

Armstrong described a personal example of how emotional links between humans and other species can operate at a distance. In the late 1970s she had a pet cocker spaniel and two parakeets. Her practice was to allow the parakeets to fly freely around the living room, since there was never any evidence that the dog would harm them. One afternoon, however, when she went outside to do some gardening, she suddenly felt an incredibly violent feeling, an emotion that was impossible to put into words. She raced inside to discover that her dog had just killed one of the parakeets and was pulling off its feathers in preparation for eating it.[12]

Shared Thoughts?

Dog and cat owners commonly report that their pets can detect their moods. Many pet owners go further and claim that their pets can sometimes detect their thoughts and intentions. A survey by Rupert Sheldrake of pet owners in northwest England found that 53 percent of dog owners and 33 percent of cat owners thought their pet responded to their thoughts or silent commands, and similar percentages believed their pet was sometimes telepathic with them.[13] An example is the Dutch documentary filmmaker Renée Scheltema. In her award-winning documentary *Something Unknown Is Doing We Don't Know What,* she described how her cat ran away and hid every morning on which a visit to the veterinarian was scheduled, even though Scheltema could detect no cues that might prompt the cat's behavior.[14]

Implications for Research

These observations have serious implications for research involving animals. If the One Mind envelops humans and other species, might the animal detect the mood of the experimenter and alter its behavior accordingly? Sheldrake's experiments on dogs who know when their owners are coming home is a case in point. Sheldrake is open to the idea of an extended awareness in pets and the ability of humans and animals to communicate nonlocally, at a distance. His careful experiments to test this possibility consistently yield positive results. One particular debunker of these findings, who is a dedicated skeptic, claims he cannot replicate them.[15] The One Mind hypothesis makes this understandable. If I were a dog, I would not cooperate with him either. It's the sort of thing President Woodrow Wilson had in mind when he remarked, "If a dog will not come to you after having looked you in the face, you should go home and examine your conscience."[16]

Matters of Life and Death

There are thousands of reported cases in which "man rescues dog" and "dog rescues man." We care a lot about our dogs, and they return the favor. Many of these instances have life-and-death consequences; the rescuer does not always survive, whether it's the dog or the human. Earlier we asked why one human would risk her life to rescue another person who was in extreme danger, sometimes sacrificing herself in the process. Mythologist Joseph Campbell and philosopher Arthur Schopenhauer proposed, as we saw, that at the critical moment the minds of the two individuals are fused into a single mind; the two separate individuals have become one. This implies that, from the perspective of consciousness, the rescuer is not rescuing another individual—she is rescuing herself. The frequency of animal-to-human and human-to-animal rescues suggests that the same process may be at work. The One Mind unites not just humans to one another but to their beloved pets as well.

Sometimes the intimate connections between the minds of pets and their owners appear literal, such as the experience of Sir Henry Rider Haggard, the British novelist who authored *King Solomon's Mines*. Haggard's case involved Bob, his black retriever.

Shortly after midnight on July 10, 1904, Rider Haggard cried out in his sleep, gasping and struggling for breath. He was moaning and emitting inarticulate sounds like a wounded animal when his wife awakened him from a dream. He told her it began with a feeling of depression and evolved into a sense that he was fighting for his life. The vividness of the dream increased, and he felt he was trapped inside the body of his beloved retriever Bob. "I saw good old Bob lying on his side among brushwood by water," he said. "My own personality seemed to be arising in some mysterious manner from the body of the dog, who lifted up his head at an unnatural angle against my face. Bob was trying to speak to me, and not being able to make himself understood by sounds, transmitted to my mind in an undefined fashion the knowledge that he was dying."

Rider Haggard described to his wife a marshy area near their home. Four days later he found Bob's body about a mile from the house, floating in the Waverly River. He had been horribly injured with a skull fracture and broken front legs. A veterinarian estimated he had been in the water more than three days, probably since the night of July 9. Two railroad workers suggested that the dog had probably been struck by a train. They calculated that a train had struck the dog on the bridge at about the same time as Rider Haggard's dream.[17]

There is a vast literature on the opposite phenomenon—on animals that mourn the death of their owner. One of the most famous cases is that of Greyfriars Bobby, a Skye terrier who became a symbol of loyalty in Britain. When his policeman–night watchman owner, John Gray, died of tuberculosis in 1858, he was buried without a gravestone in Greyfriars Kirkyard, in Edinburgh's Old Town. Bobby reportedly spent the next 14 years guarding the grave and leaving only for food. According to one account, the graveyard watchman befriended him and gave him food; others said he was fed at a nearby restaurant by adoring fans. When Bobby died in 1872, he could not be buried within the cemetery itself, as it was consecrated ground, so he was buried instead just inside the gate of the main south entrance of Greyfriars Kirkyard, not far from John Gray's grave. Bobby had become famous. In 1873 following his death, an aristocrat, Baroness Angela Burdett-Coutts, had a life-size statue and fountain erected in his honor at the southern end of Edinburgh's George IV Bridge. It originally had an upper part from which humans could drink, and a lower part for dogs.

The "three Bobs"—Bobbie the collie, Rider Haggard's Bob, and Greyfriars Bobby—illustrate in different ways that the minds of humans and animals may come together in the One Mind. The oneness manifests in different ways. For Bobbie, his master's knowledge of the way home over vast distances appeared to be shared and comprehended by the animal. Henry Rider Haggard seemed to *be* Bob, his retriever, when Bob was injured and killed. Greyfriars Bobby seemed indissolubly connected with his deceased owner, mourning his absence at his graveside for 14 years. "We know that we feel terrible when a beloved pet dies, and it seems our pets feel the same way when somebody they love passes away," said journalist Naomi Kane, a Canadian dog breeder. Writing for dogsincanada.com, a website dedicated to "dogs and their Canadians," she continued, "The human/animal bond is a two-way street: Our dogs don't just have behaviors we interpret as affection because we are needy human beings; our dogs truly do reciprocate our love and feel the joy and sorrow of true friendship."[18]

Jim Harrison's Leg Up

Jim Harrison, the acclaimed author and poet, has a way with dogs. While in New York City on a work assignment, he called his wife at their home in Michigan. She was upset because a neighbor's English setter bird dogs had gone missing all day in a Midwestern blizzard. Harrison had hunted with these "glorious creatures," as he calls them, and was especially concerned about them. They were not accustomed to spending the night outdoors in subzero temperatures, and his friend Nick, the owner, feared for their lives. That night in New York City, Harrison had an extraordinarily vivid dream about the path the three dogs took. This included crossing the grave of a friend, then heading over a marsh and a frozen creek to a dense woods bordering Lake Michigan.

The next morning Harrison dismissed the dream as nonsense, an example of the mind wishing it knew where the dogs had gone. He departed LaGuardia Airport and reached home in midafternoon. On rechecking, he found that the dogs were still lost. He dressed warmly, then drove eight miles to the cemetery he had seen in his dream. He was amazed to see three sets of tracks crossing the grave of his deceased friend. Then he drove two miles further to the destination he had dreamed. He saw nothing. But when he beeped the car horn, the three dogs popped up from behind a large snowdrift where they had evidently buried themselves in an attempt to stay warm. "They were pleased to see me, but got in the car without comment," said Harrison.[19]

Harrison conceded that "these kinds of experiences are what scientists call 'anecdotal,' hence unreliable, perhaps specious, but then I have a leg up because I don't care if they are. I'm more inclined to believe the wonderful Acoma Pueblo poet Simon Ortiz, who said, 'There are no truths, only stories.'"[20]

Good Samaritans in All Species

If the One Mind encompasses not just humans but all creatures, we would predict that selfless acts of rescue would involve every combination of sentient beings, not just dogs. That is exactly what happens. These interspecies rescues are so common that they suggest that compassionate behaviors jump not just cultures, as mythologist Joseph Campbell said, but species as well.

Animals Saving Animals. In March 2008 two sperm whales, a mother and her calf, stranded themselves on Mahia Beach on the eastern side of New Zealand's North Island. For an hour and a half rescuers attempted to return them to the water but failed. The whales became disoriented and stranded themselves four more times on a sandbar. Both the rescuers and the whales became exhausted, and the rescuers began to believe it would be necessary to euthanize the whales to prevent their suffering a slow, prolonged death. Then Moko, a bottlenose dolphin well known to swimmers in this area, appeared.

She approached the whales and led them 200 yards through the shallow waters along the beach to a channel that led to the open sea. After rescuing the two sperm whales, Moko returned to the beach to play with the human swimmers.

"I don't speak whale and I don't speak dolphin," said conservation officer Malcolm Smith, "but there was obviously something that went on because the two whales changed their attitude from being quite distressed to following the dolphin quite willingly and directly along the beach and straight out to sea. The dolphin did what we had failed to do. It was all over in a matter of minutes." He added, "I shouldn't do this, I know, but I actually went into the water with the dolphin and gave it a pat afterwards because she really did save the day."[21]

On Marco Island, Florida, in March 2011, a Doberman named Turbo fell over the edge of a concrete wall into a canal. The dog had no chance of getting back up by himself. Turbo struggled for 15 hours and was eventually exhausted and hypothermic, at which time dolphins arrived. They created such a racket that they attracted the attention of a nearby couple, Sam and Audrey D'Alessandro, who were loading up their boat. Sam jumped in the water and buoyed the animal. "They were really putting up a ruckus, almost beaching themselves on the sandbar over there," he said. "If it wasn't for the dolphins, I would have never seen the dog." The couple called 911. Firefighters arrived and helped lift the heavy animal out of the cold water, eventually uniting him with his owner.[22]

Animals Saving Humans. Accounts of dolphins protecting humans go back to ancient Greece, and they're still at it.

On August 28, 2007, surfer Todd Endris, 24, was attacked by a 12- to 18-foot great white shark off of the Marina State Beach near Monterey, California. Without warning, the shark hit him three times, mauling his right leg and shredding his back. Suddenly a pod of bottlenose dolphins appeared and formed a protective ring around him, keeping the shark at bay, providing time for Endris to get to shore. First aid by a friend kept Endris alive until he was evacuated by helicopter to a hospital, where a surgeon stitched him back together. Six weeks later, although still in rehab, Endris was back in the water. He credits the dolphins with saving his life.[23]

Similar events have been reported from all over the world, such as Ocean Beach near Whangerei, New Zealand, in October 2004. Veteran lifeguard Rob Howes, 47, and three female lifeguards were on a training swim 100 meters from shore when a pod of seven bottlenose dolphins swam rapidly toward them and herded them together. The dolphins began behaving "really weird," Howes said, "turning tight circles on us, and slapping the water with their tails." When Howes drifted away from the group, he saw a ten-foot-long great white shark a short distance away.

When the shark started moving toward two of the young women, one of whom was Howe's daughter Niccy, 15, the dolphins circled protectively around the the four lifeguards for another 40 minutes, creating a screen of confusion around them—"just a mass of fins, backs and human heads," Howe reported. The furious activity attracted the attention of a rescue boat. As it neared the swimmers, the shark left. "Dolphins are known for helping helpless things," said Dr. Rochelle Constantine of the University of Auckland School of Biological Science. "It is an altruistic response and bottlenose dolphins in particular are known for it."[24]

A similar incident that captured international attention took place during a free-diving contest in July 2009 at Polarland in Harbin, northeast China. Divers competed to hold their breath as long as possible without breathing equipment in a 20-foot-deep pool containing beluga whales. The water had been chilled to Arctic temperatures. Diver Yang Yun, 26, was perfectly fine during her dive, but when she tried to kick her way to the surface, her legs cramped up from the freezing cold and wouldn't respond. Yun was sinking and about to drown. Yun said, "I began to choke and sank even lower and I thought that was it for me—I was dead. Until I felt this incredible force under me driving me to the surface."[25] A beluga whale named Mila came to her rescue. The whale, who was very familiar with humans, took Yun's leg in her mouth and swam to the surface, lifting her to safety and saving her life.

These incidents are not limited to marine creatures. In August 2007, Fiona Boyd, 40, a farmer in Chapmanton, Scotland, was trying to lead a calf toward a shed when its mother heard its cries and attacked. "The first thing I knew I was just lying on the ground—I thought I was dead," Boyd reported. "Every time I tried to crawl away, the cow just slammed into me again. Nobody was there to help me. I was terrified and I thought the other cows would join in, which can happen sometimes." Sure she would be trampled to death, Boyd rolled up in a ball to protect herself from the cow's hooves. Suddenly her horse Kerry, grazing nearby, charged the cow, scaring the angry animal away and giving Boyd time to scramble to safety. She credits the 15-year-old horse with saving her life.[26]

Binti Jua, an eight-year-old female western lowland gorilla, rocketed to international acclaim in August 1996 when a video camera captured her rescue of a three-year-old boy in a zoo in Brookfield, a Chicago suberb. The youngster had run ahead of his mother, leaned too far over a concrete cliff, and fallen, screaming, 18 feet into the primate enclosure. Binti Jua, whose name means "Daughter of Sunshine" in Swahili, and who was carrying her own infant on her back, ambled over to the unconscious boy, scooped him up, and tenderly deposited him near a door where zookeepers and paramedics retrieved him. Then she turned around as if to shield the child from the other gorillas.

Rushed to Loyola University Medical Center in critical condition, the youngster eventually recovered. Reporters and TV crews from around the world swarmed to Brookfield. Rewards of money and bananas followed. Politicians joined in. First Lady Hillary Rodham Clinton invoked Binti Jua's name in a speech at the Democratic National Convention in Chicago, saying, "Binti is a typical Chicagoan. Tough on the outside but with a heart of gold underneath."[27]

Telling the Bees

Bees are among the most venerated creatures in human history. In the ancient Near East and Aegean cultures, the bee was considered a sacred insect that bridged the natural world to the underworld. Bees appeared in tomb decorations, and sometimes tombs were even shaped like beehives. The Delphic priestess was often referred to as a bee, and Apollo's gift of prophecy is said to have come to him from three bee maidens. In Egyptian mythology, when the tears of the sun god Ra fell onto the desert sand, bees grew from them. The bowstring of Kamadeva, the Hindu love god, is made of honeybees. Bees are associated with altered states of consciousness: mead, the fermented honey drink, was an old Cretan intoxicant, older even than wine. To the Merovingians, honeybees signified immortality and resurrection.[28]

At some point the ancient custom of "telling the bees" arose, which involved letting bees know when their beekeeper had died. It is reported that when King George VI died, "beekeepers went, scarf on head for respect, to inform the bees of his death."[29] Sometimes the hives were draped with black crepe. In a variation, the bees in the hive are believed to die following the death of their keeper, unless the hives are moved to another location; in another version, the hives need only be turned around. The custom is still widely followed.

In 1961, when Sam Rogers, a cobbler and postman of the Shropshire village of Myddle, England, died, his children walked around his 14 hives and told the bees of his death. According to the Associated Press in April 1961, shortly after Rogers's relatives gathered at his gravesite, thousands of bees from his hives, which were more than a mile away, came and settled on and about the coffin, ignoring the flowering trees nearby. After half an hour they flew back to the hives.[30]

One is reminded of the elegiac poem "Telling the Bees" by John Greenleaf Whitter (1807–92):

> . . . For I knew she was telling the bees of one
> Gone on the journey we all must go!
>
> . . . The old man sat; and the chore-girl still
> Sung to the bees stealing out and in.
>
> And the song she was singing ever since
> In my ear sounds on: —
> "Stay at home, pretty bees, fly not hence!
> Mistress Mary is dead and gone!"[31]

In 2005 an anonymous beekeeper posted on the Internet his experience with "telling the bees." In an old folklore book, he read that you must tell bees about significant events such as births, deaths, and marriages that occur within a family—or suffer the consequences. He initially didn't take this warning seriously, and on returning from his mother's funeral found that his bees had swarmed and gone elsewhere, leaving empty hives.

A friend gave him more bees (you must not buy them, according to folklore), and for many years this friend came periodically to harvest the honey. Then the friend became ill and died. The beekeeper attended his funeral and, as with his mother's death years before, neglected to tell the bees about this important event in his life. And as happened in the earlier event, he found his hives empty once again.

This time he was rescued by yet another friend who became his bee partner for a couple of years until this partner, too, died suddenly in his sleep. This time the man "got it" and fully intended to tell his bees of his partner's death, but in the rush of events around the funeral he simply could not find the time. Again the bees deserted his hives.

"But what happened next convinced me like nothing else ever could," he wrote. A dear friend of his lost her three-year-old son to a deadly virus and the family was overwhelmed with grief. The funeral was tragic for all involved. As the service was coming to an end, a bee flew into the church. In full view of all the mourners, it flew to the coffin. For a couple of minutes it buzzed around the flowers draping the coffin. By now everyone's eyes were focused on it. It made larger and larger circles around the casket and then, very slowly, flew over to the three bereaved family members and circled their heads, lingering over the five-year-old sister of the deceased boy, who was especially upset about her little brother's death. Unafraid, she looked up at the bee as it flew to about a foot from her face and hovered again. She seemed hypnotized by it. Then the bee flew out of the church.

"Some cultures in olden days," wrote the anonymous beekeeper, "said that bees were a young person's soul and they flew from the mouth of the deceased upon his death. All cultures treated them with respect and awe and in some cases worshiped them. I know I love bees and miss them [though] I no longer live in the country. . . . One wonders what J. K. Rowling was thinking when she named the Headmaster of Hogwarts, Dumbledore. Dumbledore is an old English name for a bee."[32]

The intimate connections between humans and animals of all kinds, and the love and affection we share with them, have led many individuals to hope that these bonds will continue even after death. This is not far-fetched; if genuinely nonlocal, they are unlimited in time. As the American humorist Will Rogers said, "If there are no dogs in Heaven, then when I die I want to go where they went."[33] And Mark Twain said this: "The dog is a gentleman; I hope to go to his heaven not man's."[34] Animals, some people are convinced, occupy a pure, guileless state that we humans have lost. Charles de Gaulle said, "The better I get to know men, the more I find myself loving dogs."[35] Or as cartoonist Charles M. Schulz, who gave us *Peanuts,* put it, "All his life he tried to be a good person. Many times, however, he failed. For after all, he was only human. He wasn't a dog."[36] Others have hinted that our pets can be gateways to the nonlocal domain. Novelist Milan Kundera wrote, "Dogs are our link to paradise. They don't know evil or jealousy or discontent. To sit with a dog on a hillside on a glorious afternoon is to be back in Eden, where doing nothing was not boring—it was peace."[37]

Cat lovers, don't despair. Although dogs grab the headlines, there are plenty of accounts of cats coming to the rescue. They have saved humans from fires, poisonous snakes, and other predators as well as dangerously low blood sugar and diabetic coma. Some cats can predict epileptic fits. A wheelchair-bound man in Ohio taught his cat Tommy to speed-dial 911—which the cat did on one occasion, saving the man's life.[38] Oscar, a pet cat in a nursing and rehabilitation center in Rhode Island, predicts the death of patients with unfailing accuracy by curling up on their bed up to six hours before their death.[39]

Mark Twain said, "Of all of God's creatures, there is only one that cannot be made slave of the leash. That one is the cat. If man could be crossed with the cat it would improve the man, but it would deteriorate the cat."[40] And to Leonardo da Vinci we give the last word: "The smallest feline is a masterpiece."[41]

CHAPTER 8

ATOMS AND RATS

Nobel physicist Richard P. Feynman once asserted, "Every thing that animals do, atoms do."[1] This dictum is usually taken to mean that animal behavior is ultimately driven by atoms, molecules, DNA, and genes. Rather than affirming materialism, however, Feynman's observation may paradoxically affirm a beyond-the-brain side of consciousness, for now we know that subatomic particles, the constituents of atoms, demonstrate a weird property called entanglement. This is a behavior in which particles, once in contact, remain linked thereafter, no matter how far they are separated. The linkage is astonishingly intimate; a change in one is correlated with a change in the other, instantly, and to the same degree.

Some researchers believe that the entangled behaviors of subatomic particles may in some way underlie these distant connections in humans. This possibility is explored at length in the pioneering book *Entangled Minds* by Dean Radin, chief scientist at California's Institute of Noetic Sciences. Radin suggests that we "take seriously the possibility that our minds are physically entangled with the universe . . ."[2] Radin reviews hundreds of experiments that compellingly suggest that entanglement is more than a metaphor for how minds are linked at the human level. So, if Feynman is correct—if everything animals do, atoms do—he is offering, without realizing it, an indirect explanation of the mechanism underlying an infinite, unitary image of mind.

Standard physics textbooks haven't caught up with contemporary knowledge. They continue to say that the midsize world of bricks, brains, and beasts and the colossal world of planets, stars, and galaxies are the domains of classical physics as described by Newton's laws and Einstein's theories of relativity. But when we descend in scale to subatomic particles and atoms, we cross an invisible boundary where classical physics gives way to the strangeness of quantum behavior, governed by the framework provided by quantum mechanics.

How things change! The June 2011 cover of the journal *Scientific American* displays a human head made of tiny particles and the caption "Living in a quantum world: small-scale physics has a 'spooky' power over the world at large." In his lead article, Oxford physicist Vlatko Vedral explained what this fuss is all about:

> Over the past several years experimentalists have seen quantum effects in a growing number of macroscopic systems. The quintessential quantum effect, entanglement, can occur in large systems as well as warm ones—including living organisms—even though molecular jiggling might be expected to disrupt entanglement. . . . Until the past decade, experimentalists had not confirmed that quantum behavior persists on a macroscopic scale. Today, however, they routinely do. These effects are more pervasive than anyone ever suspected. They may operate in the cells of our body. . . . We can't simply write [quantum effects] off as mere details that matter only on the very smallest scales. . . . The entanglements are primary.[3]

There are apparently no limits to the extent of entanglement. As physicist N. David Mermin has shown, quantum entanglement grows exponentially with the number of particles involved in the original quantum state, and there is no theoretical limit on the number of these entangled particles.[4] "If this is the case," say physicist Menas Kafatos and science historian Robert Nadeau in their book *The Conscious Universe: Parts and Wholes in Physical Reality*, "the universe on a very basic level could be a vast web of particles that remain in contact with one another over any distance in no time in the absence of the transfer of energy or information."[5]

Something Unknown Is Doing We Don't Know What

No one knows if the various beyond-the-brain-and-body phenomena we are exploring in this book will eventually be explained by entanglement at the quantum level. Currently this is what we know: (1) Subatomic particles are entangled; once in contact and then separated, a change in one is correlated with a change in the other, instantly and to the same degree, no matter how far apart. These distant, nonlocal correlations are not in doubt; they have been demonstrated in a series of experiments and are accepted as part of the canon of modern physics.[6] (2) Humans also behave as if they are entangled; they can share thoughts, feelings, and even physical changes when far apart, even at global distances. These phenomena have been documented in hundreds of experiments over many decades.[7]

But we must be careful. Since we don't really know whether quantum entanglement is the same thing as human entanglement, we can't yet say that quantum entanglement *causes* human entanglement. We may be dealing with accidental correlations of language. However, we know that (3) the old prohibition against entanglement in biological, living systems is flat-out wrong.[8] So the tired warnings of skeptics that beyond-the-brain-and-body phenomena are impossible because they "violate the laws of nature" may be dismissed without further ado.

In the meantime, we are free to wonder. It may turn out that the quantum entanglement of subatomic particles is a primitive, elemental foreshadowing of the unity that finds its most majestic expression in the Great Connect, the One Mind. Sir Arthur Eddington, the British astrophysicist, in speaking about the uncertainty principle in modern physics, said, "Something unknown is doing we don't know what."[9] That's an excellent motto as we explore beyond-the-brain-and-body phenomena and the One Mind they point to. It expresses not just humility but also awe and wonder. And wonder, Socrates said, is the beginning of wisdom. "And," he further observed, probably with a twinkle in his eye, "in knowing that you know nothing that makes you the smartest person of all."[10]

Rodent Empathy

Evolutionary biologist Richard Dawkins's influential manifesto *The Selfish Gene,* first published in 1976, became a bestseller worldwide and continues to be widely read. Dawkins's basic premise is that whether we realize it or not, all living creatures, from microbes to humans, are in service to our genes, whose sole purpose is to survive and reproduce themselves.[11] These genes are sneaky con artists. All the higher emotions we experience, such as altruism, compassion, and love, are selfishness in disguise. They are backdoor expressions of "the gene's law of universal ruthless selfishness," [12] as Dawkins puts it. If we think we see genuinely unselfish behaviors in others or experience them ourselves, Dawkins counsels, we should not be fooled. All instances of *apparent* altruism will fall into one or more of three categories that reveal an underlying selfishness: kin selection, reciprocal altruism, or group selection. This is not the place to unpack these subjects in detail. Oxford scholar Charles Foster does so in plain language in his excellent book *The Selfless Gene,* which is a strong counterargument to many of the directions Dawkins takes in *The Selfish Gene.*

The bottom line for Dawkins is that the better angels of our nature are not angelic at all; they are greedy, self-centered biological forces that will stop at nothing to survive and reproduce themselves. The implications for society are serious. "Be warned that if you wish, as I do," says Dawkins, "to build a society in which individuals cooperate generously and unselfishly towards a common good, you can expect little help from biological nature."[13]

Is that all of the story?

I got off to a rocky start with lab rats in my university training. I was severely bitten by a particularly rebellious specimen in an experiment, even though I was wearing protective gloves and was handling him gently. At the time I quite liked rats, but following the attack I was soured on rat experiments. Oh, I managed some degree of rodent forgiveness, but every time I looked at the scar on my index finger my antirat feelings were reinforced. My animal-rights friends always give me a serves-you-right smile when I tell them this story. They always take the rat's side and are certain justice was served. They are right.

But more recently I've rehabilitated my relationship with lab rats. It happened unexpectedly, like a sudden, spontaneous remission of a serious illness. My fondness for rats returned when I read an experiment in the prestigious journal *Science* in December 2011. The study pokes a finger in biologist Dawkins's eye by providing strong evidence for innate, indwelling empathy. The experiment suggests that in the mammalian genetic soup there must be one or more genes that are not selfish.

The experiment was conducted by a team of neuroscientists and psychologists at the University of Chicago.[14] Their goal was to determine whether genuine empathic behavior exists in nonprimate mammals, in this case pairs of white lab rats. The researchers placed a free rat in an arena with a cagemate that was restrained in a clear plastic tube. The tube had at one end a door that could be opened from the outside. The free rat behaved in a more agitated way when its cagemate was restrained, compared to its activity when placed in the arena with an empty restrainer. After several daily sessions, the free rat learned how to open the restrainer door and free its cagemate. Opening the door was not a simple task, but the free rat kept at it until it had mastered the technique. After discovering how to open the door, the free rat thereafter would do so almost immediately upon being placed in the arena with the restrained cagemate.

One of the researchers explained, "We are not training these rats in any way. [They] are learning because they are motivated by something internal. We're not showing them how to open the door, they don't get any previous exposure on opening the door, and it's hard to open the door. But they keep trying and trying, and it eventually works."[15]

Pure empathy appeared to be involved. For example, the free rats did not bother to open the door when a toy rat was placed in the clear plastic restrainer. And they opened it even if it released their companion into a separate area, which showed they were not just looking for company. Moreover, when the free rat was offered two restraining tubes to open, one of which contained its companion cagemate and the other a pile of chocolate chips, one of their favorite foods, they were as likely to free the restrained rat first as to open the chocolate chip–containing tube first. There were also instances in which the free rat retrieved the chocolate chips first but didn't eat them until after freeing the other rat and sharing the chocolate with him.

"That was very compelling," said neurobiology professor Peggy Mason. "It said to us that essentially helping their cagemate is on a par with chocolate. He can hog the entire chocolate stash if he wanted to, and he does not. We were shocked."[16]

The University of Chicago team uploaded a video of the rats in action to YouTube, where it has been viewed by thousands. It is fascinating to watch the free rat try determinedly to liberate his cagemate, and to see them delight in each other's company after the trapped rat is set free by nuzzling, touching, and playing. You can view the video, "Empathy and Pro-Social Behavior in Rats," at http://www.youtube.com/watch?v=WzEOliAzr-8.

PART TWO

WORKING WITH THE ONE MIND

CHAPTER 9

MIND BEYOND BRAIN

The brain does not generate thought . . . any more than the wire generates electric current.[1]

—PAUL BRUNTON

The brain breathes mind like the lungs breathe air.

—HUSTON SMITH

The main objection to the One Mind is the engrained belief that consciousness is somehow produced by the brain and is therefore confined to it. Brains stay put in the cranium and so, too, must minds. How much scientific support is there for this belief?

Karl Lashley, an American behavioral psychologist, trained rats to perform specific tasks such as seeking a food reward. Then he created lesions in specific brain areas to see their effect on the persistence of the behavior. After hundreds of such experiments in rats, Lashley failed to find a single locus of memory. He summed up his findings: "It is not possible to demonstrate the isolated localization of a memory trace anywhere within the nervous system."[2] Lashley concluded that memory is not localized to specific regions in the rat's brain but is distributed throughout the cerebral cortex. This led to the paradoxical conclusion that "memory is both everywhere and nowhere in particular" in the rat's brain.

How Necessary Is Your Brain?

Hundreds of experiments such as Lashley's raise the more fundamental question of not just the brain's relationship to memory but its relationship to consciousness in general. Some of the challenges are really serious. In an article provocatively titled "Is Your Brain Really Necessary?" British neurologist John Lorber questioned whether an intact cerebral cortex is needed for normal mentation.[3] Lorber did CT scans on hundreds of individuals with hydrocephalus (excess fluid in the brain leading to pressure) and found that many of them had normal or above-normal intellectual function.

To even question the role of the brain is still blasphemy within conventional science. Consciousness is considered an emergent property of the brain, produced by its workings, pure and simple. But what do we really know about the origins of consciousness? Many respected philosophers and scientists suggest we are in the dark about these questions. Nobel Prize–winning neurophysiologist Roger Sperry took a similar position, saying, "Those centermost processes of the brain with which consciousness is presumably associated are simply not understood. They are so far beyond our comprehension at present that no one I know of has been able even to imagine their nature."[4] Nobel Prize–winning physicist Eugene Wigner agreed, stating, "We have at present not even the vaguest idea how to connect the physico-chemical processes with the state of mind."[5] And Sir John Maddox, former editor of the prestigious journal *Nature*, wrote "What consciousness consists of . . . is . . . a puzzle. Despite the marvelous successes of neuroscience in the past century . . . we seem as far from understanding cognitive process as we were a century ago."[6]

In view of these great unknowns, the widespread assumption that the brain makes the mind and that the mind is confined to it is open to question, which opens the door to alternative scenarios.

The Brain as a Receiver of Consciousness

There are many reasons why scientists have assumed that the mind and brain are one and the same. When the brain is damaged through physical trauma or stroke, mental function can be deranged as a result. Vitamin deficiencies and malnutrition can cause impairment of thought processes, as can various environmental toxins. Brain tumors and infections can wreak havoc with mentation. In view of these effects, it has seemed reasonable to assume that mind and brain are essentially identical.

But none of these observations *prove* that the brain produces the mind or that the mind is confined to the brain. Consider your television set. Although you can damage it physically and destroy the picture on the screen, this does not prove that the TV set actually makes the picture. We know, rather, that the picture is due to electromagnetic signals originating outside the set itself and that the TV set receives, amplifies, and displays the signals; it does not produce them.

The basic concept that the brain functions as an intermediary for the mind—but is not its cause—is ancient. Two millennia ago, Hippocrates, in his essay "On the Sacred Disease," described the brain as "the messenger to consciousness" and as "the interpreter for consciousness."[7]

Ferdinand C. S. Schiller, the Oxford philosopher, proposed in the 1890s that "matter is admirably calculated machinery for regulating, limiting and restraining the consciousness which it encases." He argued further, "Matter is not what *produces* consciousness but what *limits* it and confines its intensity within certain limits . . ." In cases of brain trauma, Schiller suggested that the manifestation of consciousness has been affected, but consciousness itself has not been extinguished. He further proposed that it is forgetfulness, not memory, that is in the greater need of an explanation. If it were not for the limitations of the brain, he believed, total recall would be possible.[8]

Henri-Louis Bergson, the French philosopher who won the 1927 Nobel Prize in Literature, believed the brain canalizes and limits the mind, excluding factors not required for survival and procreation. The brain, in his view, is both "the organ of attention to life" and an obstacle to wider awareness.[9] Like Schiller, he suggested that memories lie outside the brain and are mostly screened out for practical purposes, as they are not crucial for the biological needs of the organism.[10] He suggested that impairments of memory that result from diseases of the brain may indicate only that we need a healthy brain in order to locate and communicate memories; but the impairments are not evidence that memories exist only in the brain.[11]

Psychologist William James held views about consciousness similar to those of Schiller and Bergson. In his 1898 Ingersoll Lecture at Harvard University, he acknowledged that physical insults to the brain—trauma, stimulants, poisons, arrested development—can abolish memory or consciousness and scramble the quality of one's ideas, but this is not necessarily evidence of a productive function of the brain. There are other possible functional relationships between the brain and the mind, he argued. There might be a permissive function, as found in the trigger of a crossbow, and the transmissive function, as with a lens, a prism, or the keys of a piano. "My thesis now is this," James said, "that, when we think of the law that thought is a function of the brain, we are not required to think of productive function only; *we are entitled also to consider permissive or transmissive function*. And this, the ordinary psychophysiologist leaves out of his account."[12]

Playing devil's advocate, James raised an objection: isn't the production hypothesis simpler and more scientifically rigorous? From the standpoint of empirical science, James answered that this objection carries no weight whatsoever. All we ever observe is the concomitant variations or correlations between states of the brain and states of the mind. James is stating that venerable maxim of science that "correlation is not causation." Night always follows day; the correlation is 100 percent; but that does not mean that day causes night.

Many scientists boast of not believing in miracles. But, James said, if consciousness is indeed produced by the brain, this would count, "as far as our understanding goes, as great a miracle as if we said, thought is 'spontaneously generated,' or 'created out of nothing.'" He continued:

> The theory of production is therefore not a jot more simple or credible in itself than any other conceivable theory. It is

only a little more popular. All that one need do, therefore, if the ordinary materialist should challenge one to explain how the brain *can* be an organ for limiting and determining to a certain form a consciousness elsewhere produced, is to . . . [ask] him in turn to explain how it can be an organ for producing consciousness out of whole cloth. For polemic purposes, the two theories are thus exactly on a par.[13]

Aldous Huxley, who wrote about the nature of consciousness in 1954 in *The Doors of Perception,* affirmed the idea that the function of the nervous system is "eliminative" rather than productive, in that it protects us by eliminating the useless and irrelevant information we continually encounter in our daily existence. Otherwise, there is no reason in principle why each person is not capable of remembering everything in the universe.

"Each one of us is potentially Mind at Large," Huxley states. "But in so far as we are animals, our business is at all costs to survive. To make biological survival possible, Mind at Large has to be funneled through the reducing valve of the brain and nervous system. What comes out at the other end is a measly trickle of the kind of consciousness which will help us stay alive on the surface of this particular planet." Certain individuals throughout history have learned to defy the reducing-valve function of the brain to some degree, Huxley noted, through spiritual exercises, hypnosis, or drugs, as he himself learned to do.[14]

Neuropsychiatrist Peter Fenwick is Britain's leading clinical authority on near-death experiences. He and his wife Elizabeth obtained the details of 350 near-death experiences from people all over England, Scotland, and Wales. Their findings are reported in their book *The Truth in the Light,* a compelling work written through the eyes of an expert neurologist who knows a great deal about consciousness and the workings of the brain.

After methodically tackling the various hypotheses put forward to account for NDEs—drugs, oxygen starvation, buildup of carbon dioxide, or endorphins—Fenwick concluded that all these mechanisms fall short. He wrote:

Clearly there must be brain structures which mediate the NDE and they are probably the same structure that mediates any mystical experience. . . . But the major question still remains unanswered. How is it that this coherent, highly structured experience sometimes occurs during unconsciousness, when it is impossible to postulate an organised sequence of events in a disordered brain? One is forced to the conclusion that either science is missing a fundamental link which would explain how organised experiences can arise in a disorganised brain, or that some forms of experience are transpersonal—that is, they depend on a mind which is not inextricably bound up with a brain.[15]

Fenwick gives serious consideration to the hypothesis that the brain somehow transmits but does not produce consciousness. Underlying the transmission theory is the supposition, as we've noted, that there is a form of consciousness that is external to the brain. The brain is in contact with this source, receiving and modifying information from it. Fenwick proposes that although memories are held partly in the brain, a large part of memory is stored external to the brain. This off-site repository of consciousness would survive the death of the brain and body. It may also help explain why many people feel that they are part of a larger whole.

Fenwick acknowledges the problems with this sort of model. He states, "We come up against the difficulty that at present there is no known mechanism which would link brain to mind in this way, or which would allow memory to be stored outside the brain."[16] Another weakness of transmission theories in general, Fenwick adds, "is that even if they are correct, they are difficult to test. A transmission theory would argue that as mind is transmitted through the brain, disturbances in brain function will produce disorders of mind because their transmission is interrupted. But a similar argument can equally well be used if it is argued that mind is located in and is a function of the brain. Then too a disorder of brain function will produce a disorder of mind. There is no experiment which can easily distinguish between these two possibilities."[17]

Even though all theories of consciousness are speculative, transmission theories have a distinct advantage. They can accommodate the empirical data affirming our ability to acquire information at a distance and without mediation by the physical senses. With a bit of tinkering, they are compatible with the One Mind.

What kind of tinkering? For one thing, transmission theories of consciousness are misnamed. *Transmission* comes from Latin words meaning to "send over or across." There is no evidence that anything is actually transmitted or sent during remote, nonlocal experiences, and there are good reasons why. If consciousness is genuinely nonlocal, as the evidence suggests, it is infinite or omnipresent in space and time. There is, therefore, no place consciousness is not, which means that there is no necessity for anything to be transmitted from point A to point B: it's already there. Moreover, if the mind is genuinely nonlocal, the idea of an off-site, outside-the-brain storage depot for consciousness is meaningless. To store something is to confine it, and the essence of nonlocality is *un*confinement or absence of localization. In a nonlocal model of consciousness, therefore, there is no need to agonize over how consciousness is transmitted and where an extracranial repository of memory may be located, because nonlocality renders these sorts of questions superfluous.

"Transmission," then, is a concept drawn from the classical, mechanical view of the world. When applied to nonlocal phenomena, it gives a misleading impression about the nature of consciousness. Still, transmission theories are an improvement over the brain-based images of consciousness, because they release consciousness from its enslavement to the brain. One day, when we learn to think and speak with ease about nonlocal phenomena, we will create a vocabulary that can stand on its own without being contaminated by inappropriate terms drafted from the classical world view. Until then, perhaps we should keep "transmission" in quotes in order to emphasize its tentative, qualified usage.

If we are to have a ghost of a chance of understanding the One Mind and the relationship between mind and brain, we are going to have to learn to think nonlocally, not locally. Otherwise we will be forever chasing problems that simply don't apply in a nonlocal world.

CHAPTER 10

IMMORTALITY AND
NEAR-DEATH EXPERIENCES

How can you fear personal death if you are really part of God?

—V. S. RAMACHANDRAN[1], DIRECTOR, CENTER FOR BRAIN
AND COGNITION, UNIVERSITY OF CALIFORNIA AT SAN DIEGO

The only secret people keep
Is Immortality.

—EMILY DICKINSON[2]

M ellen-Thomas Benedict, a young stained-glass artist, experienced near-death in 1982. Benedict was dying from an inop-
erable brain tumor. He was offered chemotherapy but declined,
wanting to maintain as high a quality of life as possible in the time
he had left. Having no health insurance, he entered hospice care,
which lasted for about 18 months. He woke up one morning at
around 4:30 A.M. and knew this was the day he would die. He told his
hospice nurse, and they agreed that she would leave his dead body
undisturbed for at least six hours, because he had read that "all kinds

of interesting things happen when you die."[3] Suddenly he experienced being outside his body. He had a sense of panoramic vision and saw a magnificent shining light, the most beautiful thing he had ever seen. It seemed to be a conduit to the Source or the Higher Self. "I just went into it," he said later, "and it was just overwhelming. It was like all the love you've ever wanted, and it was the kind of love that cures, heals, regenerates."[4] Then the light turned into an exquisitely gorgeous mandala of human souls.

Benedict felt all his negative judgments and cynical attitudes about his fellow human beings giving way toward a view that was equally hopeful and positive. He conversed with the Great Light. He rode a stream of consciousness through the galaxy and glimpsed the entire universe. He felt he was in precreation before the Big Bang. His consciousness expanded to infinity. It was revealed to him that there is no death, only immortality. With this assurance, the entire process then reversed itself, and he returned to his body.[5]

His hospice nurse found him without vital signs. She could not detect any blood pressure or heart sounds, even with an amplified stethoscope. His cardiac monitor was flat-lined. She honored his agreement and left his body alone. It began to stiffen. Then he suddenly awakened. On seeing the light outside, he tried to get up and go to it, falling out of bed. The nurse heard a clunk and found him on the floor.

Within three days he was feeling normal, yet different than he had ever felt in his life. He was discharged from hospice. Three months later, a friend suggested he return to his physician to be tested again. Follow-up brain scans were done. As his physician looked at the before-and-after scans, he said, "Well, there is nothing here now." Benedict responded happily, "Really, it must be a miracle?" "No," the unimpressed doctor said, "these things happen. They are called spontaneous remission." "But here was a miracle," Benedict said later, "and I was impressed, even if no one else was."[6]

The Decisive Question

Benedict's absorption into the Source or Higher Self, where he saw an exquisite collection of other human souls, is a recurring motif among individuals who undergo near-death experiences. The pattern is ancient. Fragmentary reports have appeared in the art and literature of all ages, such as the legend of Er in Plato's *The Republic*, written around 300 B.C.E. In Plato's report, a warrior named Er dies in battle. When the bodies of the dead are collected ten days later, Er's body has not decomposed. He awakens two days later on his funeral pyre and describes his journey into the sky in the afterlife. Accompanied by many companions, he experienced wondrous feelings, saw a rainbow shaft of light brighter than anything he had ever seen, and met many deities.[7]

The concept of a Source, a Soul, and a Higher Self that often form part of the near-death experience is an affirmation of the One Mind. As Jung put it, "In addition to our immediate consciousness, which is of a thoroughly personal nature . . . there exists a second psychic system of *a collective, universal, and impersonal nature which is identical in all individuals*" (emphasis added).[8]

In our materialistic culture, the belief in a soul that survives physical death is often considered a cowardly comfort for those who fear death and annihilation. But there are two major reasons to look beyond this criticism.

First, for many people, this general belief is important for healthy function. Thus Jung said, "As a doctor, I make every effort to strengthen the belief in immortality."[9] And, "The decisive question for man is, is he related to something infinite or not. That is the telling question of life. Only if we know that the thing that truly matters is the infinite can we avoid fixing our attention upon futilities and upon all kinds of goals which are not of real importance . . ."[10] George Orwell, author of the chilling book *1984*, agreed, saying, "The major problem of our time is the decay of belief in personal immortality."[11]

Second, the opinion within science is shifting. The idea that consciousness is exterminated at death is no longer taken for granted. As the eminent physicist David Bohm said, "Ultimately all the moments are really one, . . . therefore now is eternity. . . . Everything, including me, is dying every moment into eternity and being born again."[12] The respected French physicist Olivier Costa de Beauregard finds evidence in mathematics and physics that is cordial to "the existence of an all-pervading 'collective unconscious,'" which is suspiciously akin to a timeless, immortal One Mind.[13]

Psychiatrist Ian Stevenson of the University of Virginia reported thousands of cases of children who remembered past lives, whose descriptions of previous existences checked out on investigation, and that strongly suggested reincarnation.[14] And as British astronomer and author David Darling says in his courageous book *Soul Search,* "Death awaits us, but no longer with the threat of extinction. Death may mean the end of body and brain and self. But, precisely because of that, it marks the return to a wider, timeless consciousness. In the light of this knowledge all fear dissolves. Since self is an illusion, its loss amounts to nothing."[15] And, not least, there is the evidence favoring survival in near-death experiences, which are being reported by a significant proportion of the American population. These trends are compellingly described by philosopher Chris Carter in his book *Science and the Near-Death Experience* and by cardiologist Pim van Lommel in his book *Consciousness Beyond Life: The Science of the Near-Death Experience,* as well as many others.

Immortality Allergy

Although the possibility of immortality seen in near-death experiences brings consolation and hope to many persons, it infuriates others. An example is a neurologist at a leading medical school who has strenuously attempted to debunk near-death experiences as nothing more than physical processes occurring in certain areas of the brain. He thinks it is unethical to speak of survival following death, saying:

> People like to say that these experiences are proof that consciousness can exist outside the brain, like a soul that lives after death. I hope that is true, but it is a matter of faith; there is no evidence for that. People who claim otherwise are using false science to engender false hope and I think that is misleading and ultimately cruel.[16]

But where does the cruelty lie? I believe it is cruel to assure people that there is complete annihilation with physical death, when copious evidence suggests otherwise. The cruelty lies in denying the substantial evidence that the mind can operate with enormous precision when the brain is severely compromised. Cruelty arises every time a supposed authority ignores the abundant research by careful investigators that consciousness operates nonlocally, beyond the constraints of space and time, implying temporal infinitude and therefore immortality. The cruelty exists not in giving false hope, as this neurologist charges, but in stripping hope and promoting unnecessary suffering and fear by misreading the scientific record.

In 2011 I received a letter from parents who were seeking solace after their beloved 19-year-old daughter died. She had a congenital heart defect and had undergone several surgeries and endured much suffering during her short life. They had read a book by a leading debunker of near-death experiences and had written him to find out if he held out any hope at all for their daughter's survival following her death. He responded, saying, "I can't offer much hope. I have only a few years left myself."

The couple wanted to know what I thought about his dismal response. I told them I consider it a virtual certainty that some aspect of human consciousness is infinite in space and time, that it is indestructible and immortal. I told them I believed the consciousness of their daughter still exists and will exist throughout eternity. I asked them not to take my word; they should read the scientific evidence of numerous investigators that forms the basis for my conclusions. I referred them to several of the sources I mention throughout this book. I did this because the evidence is *so* abundant for a nonlocal, infinite dimension of consciousness that I knew they would have no difficulty in forming their own conclusion, and that it would likely be the opposite of the gloomy verdict of the debunker they had consulted. They were smart people—he a computer expert, she an attorney; they could judge for themselves without taking anyone's judgment as their own, including mine.

There will probably always be people who consider it an intellectual weakness to believe in anything resembling the soul. As the late Lord Bertrand Russell once mordantly said, "I believe that when I die I shall rot, and nothing of my ego shall survive."[17] I think Russell was correct; his body surely did rot, and nothing of his ego remained. But that is hardly the end of the story. We are more than a physical body and ego. An element of our consciousness is temporally infinite and part of something larger: the One Mind.

Thanks to *E. Coli:* Proof of Heaven?

We may be about to rediscover that dying
is not such a bad thing to do after all.[18]

—LEWIS THOMAS, M.D.

Dr. Eben Alexander, author of the bestseller *Proof of Heaven: A Neurosurgeon's Journey into the Afterlife,* would agree.[19] An academic neurosurgeon for the past 25 years, with appointments at Harvard Medical School and its affiliate hospitals, he is the author of two text-books and nearly 200 scientific papers and is a recognized expert on the workings of the brain. He has dealt with hundreds of patients rendered comatose from trauma, infections, brain tumors, stroke, and ruptured aneurysms. None of this prepared him for what hap-pened in the early hours of November 10, 2008, when he became comatose, was placed on a ventilator, and was begun on multiple intravenous antibiotics. The problem was a rare form of meningitis caused by *E. coli,* the bacterium associated with outbreaks of food poisoning in recent years. Alexander deteriorated fast. His physician team expected him to die and held out little hope to his wife and two sons. Contrary to expectations, he survived. On day seven, when his breathing tube was removed, he said "Thank you." But some-thing had happened between November 10 and 17 that changed his life. During this interval he underwent a near-death experience that demolished everything he thought he knew about the human brain and consciousness.[20]

Alexander's NDE was "hyper-real and extremely crisp and vivid," more so than ordinary waking awareness. He considers it so "shock-ing" and real that it is "indescribable." The experience involved sev-eral phases. The initial vision was "just murky and gross," with a face appearing now and then. Then a "spinning melody" appeared that was "beautiful, beautiful." Alexander became "a speck on a butterfly's wing, among millions of other gorgeous butterflies." Beside him on the wing was "an absolutely beautiful girl" dressed in "a kind of peasant garb . . . kind of a peach/orange and a powder blue, just really beautiful." Although she never spoke in words, she conveyed the thought that "You are loved. You are cherished forever. There's nothing you can do wrong. You have nothing to worry about. You will be taken care of." Included in the message was the realization that he could not stay in this place; he would have to return to his earthly existence.

Alexander was aware of "a Divine presence," a kind of "super-power of divinity." He says, "I was far beyond . . . any kind of human consciousness. [There was] really just one consciousness." Alexander had entered the One Mind. He experienced time as infinite temporal duration. "We always try to sequence things and put them in linear form and description. That just really doesn't work," he said.[21]

Following his NDE, Alexander plunged into the literature surrounding these events, trying to understand what had happened to him. He was impatient with the perennial arguments skeptics use to dismiss these happenings. "That hyper-reality that people describe . . . is not something that is going to be explained by [this] little simplistic kind of talking about CO_2 and oxygen levels. That just won't work. I promise you that won't work." He adds, "It's totally unlike any drug experience. A lot of people have come up to me and said, 'Oh that sounds like a DMT experience,' or 'That sounds like ketamine.' Not at all. That is not even in the right ballpark."

Dr. Alexander is an impeccably credentialed scientist at the top of his game. He values the right kind of skepticism but not the sort that is burdened with preformed prejudice. He acknowledges, "Scientists are as prone to addiction to imposed dogma and faith as [a] religious zealot. So one has to be very careful to really step back and want to know the truth. . . . There's something going on . . . about consciousness that our primitive models don't get. It's far more profound than I ever realized before."

Thanks to *E. coli*, Dr. Alexander walked through a door through which he can never return. "My experience showed me very clearly," he says, "that incredibly powerful consciousness far beyond what I'm trapped in here in the earthly realm begins to emerge as you get rid of the filtering mechanism of the brain. It is really astonishing. And that is what we need to explain. Thousands or millions of near-death experiencers have talked about this."

NDEs, however, are only one way to pass through the eye of the needle. "People don't . . . have to go to a near-death situation," Dr. Alexander says. "There are plenty of mystical experiences that have occurred over millennia that are part of the same mechanism." He's correct, as we'll soon see.

It's all been said before in thousands of books, articles, and interviews since NDE experiences burst on the cultural scene in 1975 with the publication of *Life After Life* by psychiatrist Raymond Moody.[22] What's new about Dr. Alexander's account is Alexander. It is not often that a leading neurosurgeon and expert on the workings of the brain steps forward to defend a beyond-the-brain-and-body event, and to passionately declare that consciousness exists independently of the human brain. Will his arguments carry the day? For some, yes, but not all. Some of his physicians have already said dismissively, "Oh, yes—well, you were very, very sick."

No matter. What counts as "proven" is always shifting. Even physicist Max Planck suggested that science changes funeral by funeral. It isn't necessary to convince everyone. Eighteen percent of Americans continue to believe the sun revolves around the earth,[23] and a few remain convinced that the earth is flat,[24] but that doesn't change the facts. Alexander is optimistic. "I think [the new view of consciousness] is going to change this world in wonderful ways" he says. "I'm very hopeful that science and spirituality will come together hand-in-hand . . . and help people to understand the true nature of our existence. A side effect will be that humanity and the grace and harmony that we will see around this world will expand tremendously as we move forward . . ."

Nearly Dead by the Millions

Surveys taken in the U. S., Australia, and Germany suggest that 4 to 15 percent of the population have had NDEs.[25] A large study conducted in the Netherlands showed that 18 percent of people who suffered a cardiac arrest and were clinically dead reported having an NDE.[26] A Gallup Poll in the 1980s estimated that approximately 13 million Americans had experienced an NDE.[27] One study found that, statistically, every day in the U. S. nearly 800 people have an NDE.[28]

The fallback position of those who doubt the validity of these experiences is that they are the last gasp of a sick, dying, oxygen-starved, dysfunctional, broken brain. In recent years, however, this "explanation" has become increasingly untenable because of the discovery that these experiences occur in healthy individuals as well as in those near death.

In 1992, the International Association for Near-Death Studies (IANDS) sent out a questionnaire to its members asking how they came to their experience. They received 229 responses. They found that 23 percent experienced the near-death phenomena while clinically dying; 40 percent during serious illness or severe physical trauma; and 37 percent without coming close to death or undergoing illness or trauma. The *lowest* percentage of the near-death experience in this survey was in those who were on death's doorstep.[29]

But are the near-death-like experiences of healthy people the same as those who are nearly dead or seriously ill? Psychologist Kenneth Ring of the University of Connecticut believes the answer is yes. Ring is one of the most respected researchers in the near-death field. He says, "One doesn't have to be near death to have the kind of spiritual insights that are typical of near-death experiences. . . . Furthermore, the transformations that follow them . . . can also occur without coming close to death. . . . The trigger or releaser for the experience is irrelevant. What happens to you during the experience is what matters, not what brings you into it."[30]

Nancy Clark should know. She graduated from Women's Medical College of Pennsylvania as a cytologist (cytology is the study of cells), and she taught cytology and did cancer research at a major university before retiring to devote her life to writing and lecturing about near-death experiences. Clark is at home in science and reveres the scientific method; she is hardly the sort of individual who would go looking for what happened to her.

In the early 1960s, long before Raymond Moody alerted Western culture to the near-death experience in *Life After Life,*[31] Clark was believed to have died while giving birth to her son. The problem was eclampsia of pregnancy, characterized by severe high blood pressure, edema, and convulsions. She lost consciousness yet remained aware of what was going on. She saw her physical body below; saw a light source streaming toward her; and felt bliss, peace, and love saturating her entire being. All the while she saw the delivery nurse pounding on her chest saying, "Come back, Nancy, come back!" The nurse soon added, "You have a son." Clark decided to return to her physical body.

It was too late. She regained consciousness in the morgue, lying on a cold metal surface with a sheet over her face. She pulled the sheet away and saw another body on a gurney beside her, also covered with a sheet. Then she lost consciousness again. The next time she awoke she was in a hospital room.

She was mystified. She'd never heard of NDEs. No one spoke about them; the term had not yet been coined. She feared that if she told her physician what she'd experienced she might wind up in the mental ward, so she kept quiet. Her physician refused to discuss with her what had gone wrong. Patting her on the shoulder, he urged her to "move forward with your life and don't look back. Forget what happened." She complied and didn't tell a soul until, at age 38, while perfectly healthy and teaching and doing cancer research, she had an almost identical experience. She was standing at a podium delivering a eulogy for a friend who had died, when the light appeared again. Although her physical body continued to perform normally and the eulogy went off without a hitch, at the same time she had the sensation of leaving her physical body into another dimension she calls "the Light of God." She experienced great beauty, ecstasy, and bliss. Unconditional love poured in, the likes of which she had never felt. She experienced a review of her life.

Clark "felt the illusion of my separate self simply melt away. I loved everyone and everything with an immense transformed consciousness." She "merged into Oneness with the Light of God, [and] communication took place telepathically." She saw her deceased friend, for whom she was delivering the eulogy, standing beside her, holding her hand, letting her know that he was all right and very happy, and that there was no reason to grieve. She had no desire to go back into the body of Nancy at the podium. She did so, however, because she knew she had been given a mission to convey to others what she had experienced. She felt equipped to do so because she sensed she'd been given access to "ultimate knowledge." As she put it, "I knew everything there was to know, past, present, and future. Every word and every thought that was or ever will be spoken or written down was made known to me." She later understood, however, that she was not permitted to remember all of that knowledge, only parts of it. "This is what all near-death experiencers report as well," she wrote. "This is one of the classic, across-the-board similarities in over thirty years of scientific research, revealing this common thread among researchers."[32]

Clark had entered the domain of the One Mind, where all intelligence and information meet and where all knowledge may be accessed. Her experience is identical to Emerson's insight, which we saw in the Introduction: "There is one mind common to all individual men. Every man is an inlet to the same and to all of the same . . . What Plato has thought, he may think; what a saint has felt, he may feel; what at any time has befallen any man, he can understand. Who hath access to this universal mind is a party to all that is or can be done . . ."[33]

After 15 minutes in this ecstatic, idyllic state, Clark returned to her physical body, which was still delivering the euology. When the memorial service was over, several people told her that while she was speaking they witnessed a white glow all over the outline of her body.

Although inspired to convey her experience to others, Clark encountered great obstacles. She lost all her friends because they thought she was crazy. Her own family did not believe her. She was mocked when she related what had happened. A fundamentalist Protestant minister forbade her to talk about what had happened because Satan, he said, could be disguised as an angel of light and was undoubtedly working through her. "To be honest," she says, "I don't think I would have believed someone who told this story, either." But she was undeterred by critics. "The skeptics and naysayers will one day enter that transcendent realm," she says, "and they will find out for themselves what I tried to tell them was true after all."[34]

The inability to communicate what one has experienced during these transcendent experiences sometimes creates serious conflicts. As one woman reported to Clark, "At first I didn't tell many people about the experience and now tell only people I feel are ready to hear it. My husband, at the time of my experience, divorced me. He used to say, 'You are not the same person I married.'"[35] Another woman related that following her near-death-like experience, "Not everything was smooth sailing. My husband thought I was psychotic, or maybe that was just his excuse for wanting a divorce and freedom."[36]

As Clark lectured and wrote about what she'd experienced, she collected 102 reports from people who had undergone experiences similar to her podium event. These individuals were healthy and nowhere near death when they had their transformative experience. They were aged 22 to 93. Some were religious, some were spiritual but not religious, and some were agnostic or atheist. Their experiences erupted spontaneously and without warning. Among the situations that preceded them were being at rest, at work, or play; praying or meditating; driving a car; having a dream; watching television; flying in an airplane; and talking on the phone. Like Clark, they emerged from these experiences with renewed purpose and meaning in life, and with a sense of connection and unconditional love for everyone. They typically described this experience as the most important event of their life.[37]

Clark believes the term *near-death experience* can be misleading, because she is living proof that the experience can also happen to people who are perfectly healthy. She is in a good position to defend this view, since she underwent identical experiences when clinically dead as well as when she was healthy and functioning as a cytology professor and cancer researcher. She says bluntly, "There is no difference" in these experiences.

Researchers agree. In recent years, they have subdivided NDEs. In addition to the *near-death experience* such as Clark experienced during childbirth, there is the *near-death-like* event she experienced at the podium. Another variant is the *fear-death experience,* which is associated with the acute fear of imminent death. These are reported by individuals who face a seemingly inevitable demise, such as when falling during mountain climbing or being involved in a horrific auto accident. Another category is the *nearing-death experience,* which may occur during the gradual, drawn-out process of dying, as from a lingering, lethal illness.[38]

Clark merits our attention. Her experiences have spanned five decades. She underwent clinical death and a classic NDE long before the term was introduced, which rules out the possibility that suggestion and expectation colored her experience. Two decades later she had an identical experience as a well person while speaking at a memorial service. She has seen Western cultures transition from denial of these events to the recognition that millions of Americans have experienced some kind of NDE.[39]

"The Last Person I'd Ever Tell"

Physicians still have difficulty coming to terms with these reports. Consequently, like Nancy Clark, many NDErs remain reluctant to reveal their experiences to their doctors. That is one reason why these events are almost certainly underreported.

Pim van Lommel, the distinguished Dutch cardiologist, in his best-selling book *Consciousness Beyond Life: The Science of the Near-Death Experience,* discussed why most patients remain silent about these events.[40] He described a 1994 conference on NDEs at a university hospital in the United States that was attended by around 300 people. Following a few presentations and a personal story, a physician stood up and said, "I've worked as a cardiologist for 25 years now, and I've never come across such absurd stories in my practice. I think this is all complete nonsense; I don't believe a word of it." Then another man stood and said, "I'm one of your patients. A couple of years ago I survived a cardiac arrest and had an NDE, and you would be the last person I'd ever tell."[41]

The breakdown of communication between physicians and their patients over NDEs is lamentable. But it's not just physicians who close the door. As we saw, Clark's close family refused to believe her, and she lost all her friends when she spoke about her NDE during childbirth. They all thought she was deranged.

Here is an example of what might be gained if these reports were acknowledged. A 97-year-old woman contacted Clark by phone after reading a newspaper article that Clark had written about her NDE. The elderly woman told Clark she, too, had experienced an NDE during childbirth and that she had never told anyone about it. She had been afraid to do so. Through tears, she told Clark about her transformative experience, as Clark wept with her. Clark reports, "She told me that after all these years of keeping the experience to herself, she could now close her eyes for eternity with the peace she now felt after telling me about it. Bless her heart. I will never forget her or the validation she received in knowing that others experienced what she did, and that she was finally able to tell another human being about it without being judged crazy."[42]

Shared-Death Experiences

Similar to the near-death-like experience in healthy people is the *shared-death experience.*

In his book *Paranormal: My Life in Pursuit of the Afterlife,* psychiatrist Raymond Moody says, "Shared-death experiences are like near-death experiences, but they happen, not to people who are dying, but to people who are in the proximity of a loved one who is dying. These spiritual experiences can happen to more than one person and are remarkably like near-death experiences."[43]

The first time Moody heard of these events was in the 1970s from a Dr. Jamieson, a female faculty member at the Medical College of Georgia. Jamieson was visiting her mother when she, the mother, had a cardiac arrest. Dr. Jamieson performed CPR to no avail. As Jamieson, now stunned, realized that her mother had died, she was amazed to find herself outside her body looking down on the CPR scene as if from a balcony. Looking to her left, Jamieson saw her mother hovering beside her. Then she saw light pouring into the room, as if from "a breach in the universe." Within the light were friends of her mother's, all of whom had died in years past. As Jamieson watched, her mother drifted into the light and was reunited with her friends. Then the light disappeared as the breach closed. Jamieson then found herself beside her dead mother, completely puzzled about what had just happened. After hearing Jamieson's account, Moody gave it a name: "the shared-death experience."

Moody heard no more experiences like this until the early 1980s, when people everywhere began to talk freely about NDEs. Individuals began to tell him about being with their dying loved ones and seeing a mystical light pour into the room. The geometric shape of the room would also appear to change. Some individuals experienced being swept into a tunnel of light along with the dying person and would participate in their life review. These experiences would occasionally involve groups of people. "It was as though the living were having near-death experiences," Moody says.

A longtime friend of mine, author Joan Borysenko, related such an episode to me. Dr. Borysenko is a former cancer cell biologist at Harvard, where she underwent a major career change and became a pioneer researcher in mind-body medicine. She and her son Justin, 20, were attending to her dying mother in a hospital room. They had said their good-byes to her around midnight, at which time she had gone to sleep. They knew her death was imminent. Borysenko and Justin were sitting quietly on opposite sides of the bed. She was praying and meditating with her eyes closed. All of a sudden, around three in the morning, she opened her eyes to see that the entire room seemed to be made out of light. "I know that might be hard to understand, but it was like everything was made of particles of light: my mother and the bed and the ceiling. Everything was so beautiful." Borysenko looked across the bed and saw Justin weeping. Tears were streaming down his face and he appeared awestruck. Justin said, "Mom, the room is filled with light. Can you see it?" "Yeah, I see it. I see the light," she responded. Then Justin added, "It's Grandma. Grandma is holding open the door to eternity for us, so that we can catch a glimpse."[44]

It got personal for Moody, too. When his mother lay dying, his two sisters, their husbands, and Moody and his wife were gathered at her hospital bedside. She had been comatose for two days. Shortly before she died, however, she awoke and told the group that she loved them all very much. Moody's sister Kay asked her to say it once more. Pushing the oxygen mask from her face, she said once again, "I love you all very much." As everyone was holding hands, the world changed. The room seemed to change shape. Four of the six felt as if they were being lifted from the ground. Moody sensed a strong force like a riptide pulling him upward. One of his sisters pointed to a spot near the end of the bed, saying, "Look. Dad's here. He's come back to get her!" All six reported that the light in the room changed, becoming soft and fuzzy. Everyone felt joyful. One of Moody's brothers-in-law described leaving his physical body and going into another plane with his dying mother-in-law. It was like nothing any of them had ever experienced, and they spent the next several days trying to assemble all the details into a coherent picture.

The impact on Moody was profound. By this time he was internationally famous as the person who brought the near-death experience to the attention of the world. Following the death of his mother, he knew he had found the next phase of his life's work: the shared-death experience.

As Moody lectured around the world about NDEs, he inquired of his audiences whether they had ever experienced events such as he and his siblings had undergone. Cases poured in. Moody interviewed many individuals in private and in great detail. As word spread, shared-death experiences were reported to other NDE researchers as well.

Everyone realized that this was a devastating rebuttal to skeptics, because these extraordinary events happened to people who were not ill.

A consistent picture has emerged. The shared-death experiences contain most of the traditional elements of the NDE, such as tunnel experiences, seeing a bright mystical light, out-of-the-body sensations, a life review, and so on. Moody emphasizes four features that are usually present. They include music that is often heard by all the individuals attending the dying person. They often say that the music is the most intricate and beautiful they have ever heard. There are also geometric changes in the immediate environment, as if the square room has "shifted" or "collapsed and expanded at the same time." Then there is the shared sensation of seeing an otherworldly light that seems palpable and is experienced as purity, love, and peace.

"This shared sensation of a mystical light by several healthy people who are not ill or dying," says Moody, "does a lot to demolish the skeptics' argument that the light seen by those who have near-death experiences is nothing more than the dying brain shorting out. If a number of people who are not ill or dying share a mystical experience of light, then the light can't be caused by the dying brain of just one of them."[45] A fourth characteristic that sets shared-death experiences apart from NDEs is the emission of an apparent mist from the dying person, often described by onlookers as steam, fog, or white smoke, which often assumes a human shape. Many doctors, nurses, and hospice workers have reported to Moody and other researchers that they have seen this mysterious mist. Although he has found this to be the most consistent element reported in shared-death experiences, Moody does not know how to interpret it.

Shared-death experiences have been occurring under the radar for some time, long before Moody bumped into them. An example is that of the grandmother of psychologist Ryan Rominger, Ph.D., of California's Institute of Transpersonal Psychology. Rominger's grandfather was dying from cancer and had been bedridden for two years. He was in the hospital receiving supportive services. On the day of his death, his wife, Rominger's grandmother, was in his room and had a feeling that something was about to happen. She got up, walked to the bedside, and suddenly found herself walking along a trail with her husband in an otherworldly place—semimountainous, lush, and green. He appeared much younger to her, was wearing his old red hunting cap, and no longer had a tracheotomy. He was smiling as they walked hand in hand.

When they came to a fork in the road, he said, without moving his lips, "Come with me." She replied that she could not, and they parted hands. He walked down the path, over a small hill, and toward a town. She watched him go, then walked down the other path. Then she abruptly regained enough awareness to know she was back in the hospital room and that her husband had just died. Nurses were shutting down the machines and gadgets that had been keeping him alive. A minister and her son had entered the room to be with her. The minister was shaking her, calling her by her first name, and saying, "Come back, come back. It isn't your time to go yet." She had come to during his shaking to realize what had happened.[46]

It is unlikely that die-hard skeptics of the near-death experience will be convinced by shared-death experiences. Their bolt-hole is "group hallucinations" or "group fantasy," in which a number of emotionally stressed, gullible, grieving people see what they want to see. But these criticisms are hard to sustain, as we can see in a collective fear-death experience involving a group of individuals not known for their gullibility: a tough, courageous, elite team of wilderness firefighters.

In 1989, 20-person "Hotshot" crews were inserted by helicopter onto a mountain ridge to control a fire burning below them in thick ponderosa timber and scrub-oak undergrowth. As they were establishing a firebreak, to their horror the wind changed directions and the inferno came raging uphill toward them with explosive force. Soon they were surrounded by fire. The conflagration sucked the oxygen from the air at ground level. As the firefighters struggled to breathe, they were reduced to crawling on their hands and knees. One by one the firefighters fell to the ground, suffocating from lack of oxygen.

Jake, the crew boss, thought, *This is it. I am going to die.* Then he found himself above his body, looking down on it as it lay in a trench. In spite of the raging inferno, Jake felt completely at peace. He looked around and saw other crew members hovering above the scene nearby, looking down on their own bodies. One of them was Jose, who had a defective foot. "Look, Jose, your foot is straight," Jake remarked. Then a bright light appeared, which Jake described as "fantastic." Although it was exceedingly brilliant, he could look at it without hurting his eyes. "When I was there, everything was so perfect, and my spirit body, it . . . was so free. It felt like everything was limitless," he said later.

Jake saw his deceased great-grandfather standing in the light. Other ancestors also appeared. His great-grandfather guided him throughout the entire experience and conveyed to him, through thought alone, that he had a choice of returning to his body or remaining in the peaceful, beatific place in which he had found himself. Jake conveyed to his great-grandfather that it would be devastating to return to a badly burned body. He was informed that he should not worry; neither he nor any other crewmember would suffer ill effects from the fire if they chose to return.

Jake chose to return to his physical body. On doing so, he saw that some of the metal tools he and his crew had used were now melted. Although the fire was still raging, he was somehow able to walk up the steep slope to safety, as if enclosed in a protective bubble that shut out the noise and turbulence of the conflagration. On reaching the ridgetop, he found all the other crew members there. None of them could believe they had escaped certain death. The only damage was a few singed hairs.

They compared notes and discovered that each of them had undergone his own near-death experience, sometimes appearing in each other's NDE. Like Jake, they had met other family members and were given a choice of returning to their physical bodies. As they worked together throughout the summer fire season, they continued to discuss their overlapping experiences and their miraculous deliverance.[47]

Critics have responded by saying that the Hotshots' collective fear-death experiences prove their point: they were oxygen deprived at ground level and their brains were misbehaving. But as we have seen, normal, healthy people who are not oxygen starved report identical out-of-body, transcendent, joyful, life-changing near-death-like experiences that often occur spontaneously. And healthy people also have shared-death experiences with their loved ones. No physical explanation has ever been offered that can explain this full array as the result of malfunctioning brains.

Skeptics might take a lesson from one of the harshest critics Moody ever encountered: his father. Moody's dad was a World War II ex–military officer and a domineering, no-nonsense surgeon. He was so adamantly opposed to Moody's work that he once had Moody committed to a psychiatric hospital against his will. Nearing death, his father was in a coma from which his physicians said he would never regain consciousness. Unexpectedly, however, his breathing became more vigorous and he suddenly opened his eyes. Wearing a beatific smile, he looked into his sons' puzzled faces and announced, "I have been to a beautiful place. Everything is okay. I'll see everybody again. I'll miss you, but we will be together again." "With that proclamation," Moody states, "he died. Dad's deathbed experience made him a believer."[48]

The experience of Moody's nonbelieving father suggests a caution for skeptics: if you do not wish to believe in NDEs, make sure you don't have one.

Erasing Boundaries—for Good

Near-death experiences are an immersion in the unitary, undivided One Mind. In NDEs and the variants that occur in healthy people—fear-death experiences, near-death-like events, and shared-death experiences—there is dissolution of the boundaries that operate in ordinary waking life.

Individuals uniformly experience a profound sense of unity with all there is. "[I was] one with everything [I] saw, heard, felt, sensed, believed, and thought," one man said following his spontaneous, near-death-like experience.[49] They want to share this sense of connectedness with others. "I have come away from my experience wanting nothing else but to help people to better understand the unity of all life," said a healthy woman described her near-death-like experience.[50]

The deep sense of love that invariably accompanies the sense of unity is not restricted to those known in life but is unconditionally generalized to all creatures. Following her near-death experience from an almost fatal laboratory accident, a young female researcher described "a distinctive and immediate change in my behavior . . . an inability to kill even the smallest of creatures, scooping up ants and taking them to the garden. Gratitude abounds for fruits and vegetables as well as meats who had given their lives for my sustenance."[51]

The sense of access to all knowledge is frequent, accompanied by the experience of omniscience—the abolition of boundaries within knowledge. As one healthy individual described his near-death-like experience, "I knew all things past, present and future, and I was enlightened to origins, unity, and purpose though not a word was spoken."[52] Following her unprompted near-death-like experience, a young woman reported, "I immediately had knowledge about the natural world, of how everything worked together—like going to sleep not knowing about mechanics and waking up knowing in detail how all engines work. . . . I experienced a unity with everything and understood everything."[53] During a near-death-like experience that occurred spontaneously during meditation, another man was shown "how all knowledge is available here." He reported that a human/spirit presence then "opens something, and I see all the centuries' accumulated knowledge: history, science, art, architecture, religion, medicine, mathematics. I am absorbing it all very easily, and it is limitless, and the human/spirit presence says to me, 'See, this knowledge is available to you when you come here.'" But he was also shown that he would not retain all the knowledge he had gained when he returned.[54] A woman reported, "Reams of information seemed to be exploding in my brain, like an empty library suddenly being realized . . . in the Oneness of it all."[55]

The "conversation" that takes place during these events is usually described as occurring by thought alone. This, too, suggests that individual minds unite as a single mind, making possible extraordinarily intimate forms of discourse that no longer depend on speech and hearing.

The erasure of boundaries persists on returning to ordinary awareness. For instance, from 55 to 89 percent of NDErs report an increase in psychic phenomena or healing abilities following their NDE, further evidence that the assumed separations between individuals in waking life are not fundamental.[56]

Through all these experiences flows an ineffable sense of perfection, love, and bliss that is invariably transformative. And with this transformation comes the confidence that these events are previews of what lies ahead for perhaps everyone.

Before concluding this chapter, here's one last account of how minds appear to be linked beyond death.

In 1985, at age 18, Dawn Wanzo was a guitarist working toward her goal of becoming a recording artist. One night she had a vivid dream that her close friend Lisa was killed in a car wreck. She awoke extremely disturbed. Later that day she told Lisa about her dream but withheld the fact that she had died in the accident. A week later Lisa was killed in a horrible auto crash. When Dawn saw the demolished car, it looked exactly as she had seen it in her dream.

Dawn was devastated. For 15 years she tried to block out Lisa's death and her failure to fully warn her by staying busy playing, writing, and recording music. Then in 2000, Lisa began to appear to Dawn in very vivid dreams. She began to devise ways of convincing Dawn she really existed, because this seemed important in helping Dawn have closure with her death.

During a particular meditation, Dawn saw herself and Lisa sitting at a table on which food was spread—steak cut into small cubes, a baked potato, corn cut from the cob, and a champagne glass filled with water. "Why the food?" Dawn asked. "You don't need it anymore where you are." Lisa conveyed that it would be a validation that she really existed, and that Dawn was actually with her in another realm.

When Dawn came home later that day, her sister was in the kitchen preparing a plate for her. This was strange, because she never did so. On the plate there was steak cut into small cubes, a baked potato, and corn shaved from the cob. Dawn asked her why she had picked this combination of food and why she was preparing a plate for her in the first place. Her sister said she did not know why; she just felt like it. As Dawn sat down at the table, her sister placed a champagne glass filled with water beside her plate.

The event proved to be a pivotal point in Dawn's closure with Lisa's death. "I wanted nothing more than to help others to realize that we are still connected with our loved ones in spirit," she said afterward, "and that there is no separation."[57]

CHAPTER 11

REINCARNATION

It is not more surprising to be born twice than once.
—VOLTAIRE[1]

*While this may seem to be an astounding statement—that memories,
emotions, and physical injuries can carry over from one
life to the next—the evidence, I think, leads us to that conclusion.*
—JIM B. TUCKER, M.D.,[2] UNIVERSITY OF VIRGINIA HEALTH SYSTEM,
LIFE BEFORE LIFE: CHILDREN'S MEMORIES OF PREVIOUS LIVES

*Were an Asiatic to ask me for a definition of Europe, I should be
forced to answer him: It is that part of the world which is haunted by
the incredible delusion that man was created out of nothing, and that
his present birth is his first entrance into life.*

—ARTHUR SCHOPENHAUER[3]

In 2009, a Pew Research Center survey found that 24 percent of
Americans overall say they believe in reincarnation—that people
will be reborn in this world again and again.[4] This is not just a New

Age belief, but involves mainstream religions and all racial groups. The survey found that 22 percent of Christians, 34 percent of blacks, and 29 percent of Hispanics share this belief.

In reincarnation-type cases, the newly born person often displays the memories, personality, and behaviors of the deceased person who is purported to be reincarnated. In the interval prior to rebirth—which may be weeks, months, or years—what happens to the consciousness of the deceased individual? Where does it hang out before it takes up residence in the newly born individual? I suggest it "goes home" to the One Mind. But first let's look at what we know about reincarnation by examining specific cases.

Children Who Remember Past Lives

In the field of research that deals with the possibility of reincarnation and past lives, one name towers above all others—Ian Stevenson, M.D. (1918–2007), who was Carlson professor of psychiatry and director of the Division of Personality Studies (now Division of Perceptual Studies) at the Health Sciences Center at the University of Virginia. No one else has researched this area with the scholarship, thoroughness, and dogged devotion to detail as he. Stevenson combed the planet, from the back roads of Burma and the remote villages of India to the largest cities on earth. He devoted decades to scouring every continent except Antarctica, investigating always the same quarry—children who appear to remember a past life. The scope of his work is breathtakingly universal, and even skeptics are generally awed by the thousands of cases he has amassed.

These cases occur in every culture including our own and demonstrate a strong internal consistency. Typically, a child between the ages of two and four will begin to speak about experiences he or she had in a previous life, usually with intense emotions. This usually makes no sense to the parents. Nearly always the child describes his or her death in the previous life, which is often violent. This is one reason, Stevenson states, why remembering a previous life is almost never a pleasant experience for a child. In addition, he says, "Too often the children are troubled by confusion regarding their identity, and this becomes even more severe in those children who, conscious of being in a small body, can remember having been in an adult one, or who remember a life as a member of the opposite sex. To these tormenting awarenesses may be added a tearing division of loyalties between present and previous families."[5] Between the ages of five and eight, as memories fade, the child generally ceases to speak about a remembered life.

An example is Lekh Pal Jatav, born in December 1971 in the village of Nagla Devi in the Mainpuri District of Uttar Pradesh, India. Lekh Pal was born without the fingers of his right hand, which were mere stubs. Shortly after he began to talk, he mentioned a few words about a previous life and continually repeated the word "Tal, Tal," which made no sense to his family. In due course a woman from the village of Nagla Tal, about eight kilometers away, came to Nagla Devi and noticed Lekh Pal in his mother's arms. This prompted her to relate that a child in Nagla Tal had had his fingers cut off in an accident, resulting in a deformity resembling Lekh Pal's birth defect.

Lekh Pal began to speak about the life of Hukum, the child from Nagla Tal who, at about three and a half years of age, stuck a hand in the blades of a fodder-chopping machine while his father was not looking and had his fingers cut off. He said he had a father and mother, as well as an older sister and a younger brother in "Tal." Eventually Lekh Pal's parents took him to Nagla Tal and the distant families got together.

Were Lekh Pal's memories and birth defect evidence that Hukum had reincarnated in his body? In view of thousands of similar cases, Stevenson thinks reincarnation is the best explanation for these events, but he concedes it is not the only one. Although wildly improbable, the sequence of events could be due to chance, "just one of those things."

In his book *Where Reincarnation and Biology Intersect,* Stevenson reports 35 cases, including photographs. They show a wide spectrum of physical deformities and birthmarks that seem to be transmitted from one life to another. In addition to the above case, there are malformed fingers corresponding to the amputation of fingers from a sword in a remembered lifetime; birthmarks corresponding to the entry and exit wounds of bullets in the remembered personality; congenital constriction rings in the legs of an individual who recalled being bound by ropes in a previous existence; the congenital absence of the lower leg corresponding to an accidental amputation of the leg in the previous personality; and birthmarks corresponding to burns, knife wounds, and various other traumas occurring in the remembered individual's life.

In addition to memories, birth defects, and birthmarks, Stevenson believes that behaviors may be carried over from life to life. For example, children often experience phobias consistent with the mode of death of the remembered personality. A child remembering a life that ended in drowning may be afraid of being immersed in water. One who recalls a life terminated by a shooting may demonstrate a phobia of guns and loud noises. If death involved an auto accident, the child may be phobic of cars, trucks, and buses. These phobias often begin before the child can speak, and there may be no model for them in the family that might explain them.

Philias, or unusual attractions, also occur. These may take the form of a desire for particular foods not eaten in the subject's family or for clothes that are entirely different from those worn by family members. There may be craving for tobacco, alcohol, and other drugs the previous personality was known to use.

Some subjects show skills they have not been taught or have not witnessed, which the remembered personality was known to possess.

Children sometimes remember a past life of a person of the opposite sex. Such children almost invariably show traits of the sex of the remembered person such as cross-dressing, playing games of the opposite sex, and displaying attitudes typical of that sex. As with phobias, these preferences attenuate as the child grows older, but a few children remain intransigently fixed on them, and in one case the child became homosexual.[6]

"I do not expect my readers to accept readily the idea that the mind of a dead person can influence the form of a later-born baby," Stevenson conceded.[7] To overcome this obstacle, he described a variety of ways in which the images in the mind of a living person may create changes in that person's own body and sometimes in the body of another living person. He singled out stigmata and the physical phenomena associated with hypnosis as evidence that the thoughts of an individual can create demonstrable, visible effects on their own bodies. He discussed "telepathic impressions" through which consciousness bridges between individuals at a distance.[8] (We call these happenings "telesomatic events.") He described "maternal impressions," the possibility that a pregnant woman's thoughts and emotions may create birth defects and birthmarks in her newborn. He documented how most medical journals published such cases well into this century, until this idea was eclipsed by the rising prominence of genetics and developmental embryology—not altogether convincingly, he believed.

"I believe it is better to learn what is probable about important matters than to be certain about trivial ones," Stevenson once said.[9] Just so, it is not important whether or not Stevenson is correct in every single detail of his interpretation. It is the broad strokes that count. If he is anywhere near the target, then some of the deepest assumptions of modern biology need to be reexamined—particularly the unproven belief that consciousness is derived from the brain, is confined to it, and perishes with bodily death.

Stevenson is not trying to dismantle science. He honors the role of genetic and environmental influences; he introduces reincarnation not as a replacement for them but as a "third factor" to account for some of the yawning chasms that biology and environmental influences have not bridged.[10]

Some individuals may not understand the need for a third factor to help explain birth defects and birthmarks. They may believe that current science can do the job. But Stevenson states that only 30 percent to 50 percent of birth defects can currently be explained by genetic abnormalities, teratogens such as thalidomide and alcohol, and infections such as rubella. This leaves 50 percent to 70 percent in the "cause unknown" category. Moreover, geneticists can't tell us why one fetus and not another is affected, nor why a birth defect takes a particular form, nor why a birthmark occurs at a particular place. Reincarnation, in contrast, provides a reason why a particular defect or birthmark occurs in one individual and not another, where it occurs on the body, and the shape it takes.[11]

Why *not* consider nongenetic explanations for birth defects and birthmarks? Genes, in Stevenson's view, are being asked to explain far more than they are capable of. They provide instructions for the production of the ingredients of proteins, yet they give us almost no knowledge about how proteins and other metabolites become organized into cells and the complex organs that make up our bodies. These limitations are not widely admitted. "Some geneticists are not modest in assuring us that they will in due course supply all the information we need to understand embryology and morphology," Stevenson notes. But "this amounts to a promissory note with no immediate cash value, and in the meantime we are free to consider the possibility of other contributory factors"—such as reincarnation.[12]

What difference would it make if reincarnation were accepted? The most important consequence, Stevenson believed, would be the recognition of the duality of mind and body. "We cannot imagine reincarnation without the corollary belief that minds are associated with bodies during our familiar life, but are also independent of bodies to the extent of being fully separable from them and surviving the death of their associated body [and at some later time becoming associated with another body]."[13]

In saying this, Stevenson declared himself to be a proponent of interactional dualism, an idea about the mind that has an ancient history. Two of its most lustrous recent proponents were William James, the father of American psychology, and the philosopher Henri-Louis Bergson. The main idea of interactional dualism is that the brain and consciousness interact but are not the same. The brain processes sensory stimuli and affects the content of consciousness, like a transmitter or receiver, but it does not "make" consciousness. How mind and brain actually interface with one another remains a mystery and, said Stevenson, "is part of the agenda for future research; but that is equally true of the claims confidently made by many neuroscientists who assert that minds are reducible to brain activity."[14]

Between Lives

Lewis Thomas, for many years director of research at Memorial Sloan-Kettering Cancer Center, has never been accused of "going mystic." Nonetheless, he wondered what happens to consciousness at death, writing, "There is still that permanent vanishing of consciousness to be accounted for. Are we to be stuck forever with the problem? Where on Earth does it go? Is it simply stopped dead in its tracks, lost in humus, wasted? Considering the tendency of nature to find uses for complex and intricate mechanisms, this seems to me unnatural. I prefer to think of it somehow as separated off at the filaments of its attachment, and then drawn like an easy breath back into the membrane of its origin, a fresh memory for a biospherical nervous system . . ."[15]

Ian Stevenson hypothesized a similar process. "I believe that we are obliged to imagine a mental space that, necessarily, differs from the physical space with which we are ordinarily familiar," he said.[16] "I think that introspection can show that our thoughts occupy a mental space distinguishable from physical space, even while we are alive. . . . [This] mental space where discarnate personalities might exist . . . has already been . . . described in considerable detail by several philosophers familiar with the evidence of the phenomena now called paranormal."[17]

Stevenson believed that thoughts and mental images might abound in this space, and some might be reincarnated. These *diathanatic* (carried through death) qualities, as he called them, might include cognitive information about the events of a previous life, a variety of likes and dislikes, and, in some cases, residues of physical injuries or other markings of the previous body. The intermediate vehicle carrying these qualities he called the *psychophore,* which he derived from Greek words meaning "soul bearing" or "mind carrying."[18] Stevenson's "psychophore," Thomas's "biospherical nervous system," and the One Mind appear similar, if not identical—a vehicle for consciousness in a spaceless, timeless dimension.

The information that is carried over, however, does not come through in its original detail but is much attenuated, Stevenson found. This is true not just of thoughts but of physical phenomena as well. Thus, he wrote, "The baby's body shows marks or defects at the sites of these [previous] wounds, but not the wounds themselves (except for occasional minor bleeding or oozing of fluid)."[19] Just as thoughts do not recur in exact detail, birthmarks and birth defects are not exact reproductions of bleeding wounds from previous injuries but are more like "mental scars" resulting from wounds affecting the previous body.

Reincarnation and past lives have received immense attention in the past few years—rightly, Stevenson believed. As he put it, "It has been wisely said that the question of a life after death is the most important one that a scientist—or anyone—can ask."

For those who prefer evidence to anecdote, Stevenson's work is a refreshing discovery. It is the result of an inspired researcher going methodically about his work, with a great deal of reserve and understatement. Do not think for a moment that Professor Stevenson's books are an exercise in science bashing. He was a physician who deeply respected the traditions of science and adored scientific methodology, which he used in his research.

As a physician practicing internal medicine, I often cared for patients who faced the impending or recent death of a beloved child. I often recommended they read Stevenson's book *Children Who Remember Previous Lives*. This was inevitably consoling because the book provided reasons for believing in the continuation of existence following death—not only for their child but for themselves as well, which held the prospect of being united with their child again.

The Research Continues

Dr. Stevenson's work has had a profound impact on many philosophers and scientists who are concerned with the origin, nature, and destiny of human consciousness. His work is carried on at the University of Virginia by two capable colleagues, Dr. Bruce Greyson and Dr. Jim B. Tucker. Both Greyson and Tucker worked closely with Dr. Stevenson prior to his death in 2007.

Dr. Greyson is the Carlson professor of psychiatry and neurobehavioral sciences and director of the Division of Perceptual Studies at the University of Virginia Health System. He is the co-author of the important book *Irreducible Mind*,[20] which I mention often in these pages. He is one of the most productive researchers in the field of near-death studies and is the co-editor of the *Handbook of Near-Death Experiences*.

Dr. Tucker is medical director of the Child and Family Psychiatry Clinic at the University of Virginia and associate professor of psychiatry and neurobehavioral sciences. His main research interests are children who seem to remember previous lives, and prenatal and birth memories. Tucker's book *Life Before Life: Children's Memories of Previous Lives* is an admirable survey of children's memories of previous lives, and it is a fine analysis of Dr. Stevenson's work.

Room to Maneuver

It is often assumed that belief in reincarnation is universal among Asians, but there are interesting exceptions. I have often encountered Buddhists who vigorously deny that any entity continues from one life to the next. Dr. Tucker has had similar experiences. In his book *Life After Life*, he explained that Theravada Buddhists, in their doctrine of *annata,* or "no soul," emphasize that there is no "self" and thus no entity that *could* continue from one life to the next. At the death of one personality, a new one comes into being, much as the flame of a dying candle can serve to light the flame of another. "Continuity between personalities [is said to occur]," Tucker wrote, "because the karmic forces that the previous person sets in motion lead to the subsequent rebirth, but no identity exists." Disqualifying himself as a Buddhist scholar, Tucker nonetheless said, "I have trouble embracing or even fully understanding this concept, but I can at least note that despite this doctrine, most practicing Buddhists do, in fact, believe that an actual entity gets reborn."

"As Dr. Stevenson notes," wrote Tucker, "our cases certainly suggest that some vehicle has carried the enduring memories with it to the next life. Something more seems to have survived than just the memories and emotions."

As in all major religions, there are many schools of Buddhism, and there are conflicting interpretations of what the Buddha really believed about whether some aspect of consciousness survives physical death. Like Dr. Tucker, I'm no scholar of Buddhism, and I stand bewildered before the thicket of disagreement among Buddhists on this question. Perhaps the diverging opinions are to be expected, for the Buddha's words were not written down until around four centuries after his death. Before that time, his teachings were passed down orally. Who knows how much interpretation was inserted? The disagreements on the soul issue are not trivial. As a single example, Nan Huai-Chin, a major figure in the revival of Chinese Buddhism, said, "But when this [doctrine of no self] flowed into the world of learning, especially when it was disseminated in the West, some people thought that the Buddhist idea of no self was nihilism and that it denied the soul, and they maintained that Buddhism is atheistic. This is really a joke."[21]

If the Buddha were to reappear today, what would he say about the scientific evidence favoring the One Mind? Would he agree or deny that it points toward a soullike aspect of consciousness? He might take the refreshing approach of His Holiness the Dalai Lama. In 1983, the Dalai Lama visited CERN, the European particle-physics laboratory, where he engaged a group of physicists in dialogue. When the physicists asked him how Buddhism would respond if it were clear that its tenets conflicted with the findings of modern science, the Dalai Lama responded through a translator, "We would have to study our scriptures very carefully, and, usually, there is some room for maneuver."[22] What a marvelous response! Would that all religions were as flexible.

The temporal nonlocality of consciousness, for which there is immense evidence, suggests that some aspect of the mind cannot die, even if it tried. The One Mind, Professor Ian Stevenson's psychophore, and researcher Lewis Thomas's biospherical nervous system are hypotheses that attempt to come to terms with these stubborn facts. Perhaps it is time for all religions, not just Buddhism, to "maneuver" in their direction.

CHAPTER 12

COMMUNICATION WITH THE DECEASED

C an the One Mind be an avenue through which a deceased individual can influence a living person? Reports have surfaced in all
cultures of persons who suddenly and inexplicably lose their normal
personality and skills and take on an entirely new mental makeup,
including a different personality and a new set of memories and abilities. The term usually used to describe this phenomenon is *possession,*
which implies that the changes are caused by the occupation of the
individual's body by someone who has already died, perhaps against
the recipient's will. Psychiatrists don't buy this explanation. They consider these bizarre instances as some type of mental disease, such as
dissociation or schizophrenia.

And Then There Were Two

In his intriguing book *Paranormal Experience and the Survival of
Death,* philosopher Carl Becker of Kyoto University reviews several
cases suggestive of possession that came under the scrutiny of Harvard psychologist William James.

One case involved Mary Reynolds, who was born in England in
1785 and moved with her family to Meadville, Pennsylvania. At 19,
she became blind and deaf for five or six weeks. Then one day she
awoke with no memory of her family or surroundings, and with no

knowledge of the things she had learned. Her family retrained her as if she were a baby, even though she had the body of an adult. As her reeducation proceeded, she took on a personality and character that were completely different from her previous self. She would alternate between the two personalities until around 15 years later, when at the age of 36 the second personality took over completely. She remained in the second state until her death at 61 years of age.[1]

One of the most dramatic cases of this sort is that of Iris Farczády, a well-educated Hungarian girl who was brilliant in mathematics and who had dabbled in séances. At age 15 she underwent a drastic personality change. She claimed to be Lucía Altarez de Salvio, a 41-year-old Spanish working woman who Iris claimed had died earlier that year in Madrid, leaving behind a widower and 14 children. Lucía was the antithesis of Iris—a working-class, poverty-stricken slum dweller who scrubbed floors, cleaned, washed, cooked, sang popular songs, danced Flamenco, married as a teenager, and hated the upper classes. After being transformed into Lucía, Iris ever afterward spoke fluent Spanish and no longer understood her native Hungarian. Iris had apparently never learned Spanish nor had the opportunity to acquire it, having never associated with any Spanish-speaking people.

In 1998 Iris/Lucía was interviewed by an investigative team of parapsychologists—Mary Rose Barrington, Peter Mulacz, and Titus Rivas.[2] Lucía, then aged 86, told them that Iris was a different person who ceased to exist in 1933. It remains a mystery, say the researchers in their exhaustive report, why Iris should have willed or submitted to her "replacement" by Lucía.

Iris came from a respectable, educated, cultured family. Because she had dabbled in séances as a girl, the investigators considered whether she had voluntarily opened herself up to invasion by a different personality, perhaps inventing it herself or by actually being taken over by the spirit of a deceased individual. Neither possibility made much sense. As the investigators explained, "We have to ask why a clever and successful schoolgirl should want, even subconsciously, to be transformed into an uneducated, middle-aged Spanish cleaning woman." Iris had had a very comfortable lifestyle and apparently took pleasure in intellectual pursuits, including literature and mathematics.

She had never undertaken rough domestic chores such as dishwashing and housecleaning, but this is what the transformed Iris inflicted on herself—the transition from "a studious, imaginative, moody, nervy intellectual into an uneducated, unthinking, crude, practical and cheerful domestic toiler . . ."

One of the most inexplicable elements of the case is Iris's acquisition of Spanish. In their analysis, the investigative team draws a distinction between knowledge and skills. They used the example of playing the piano. It is not sufficient to know the keys of the keyboard and to associate them with different tones on a sheet of music. Playing the piano requires much more, they say—training different muscle groups in order to hit several keys simultaneously, developing a sense of where those keys are on the keyboard while looking at a sheet of music, and so on. Learning a foreign language is similar. Simply knowing a vocabulary is insufficient; one needs a knowledge of grammar, idioms, phrases, and pronunciation. On top of that there are regional variants, such as the Madrileño dialect in Lucía's case.

An earlier investigator in the 1940s had suggested that Iris had learned Spanish through ESP (telepathy),[3] which the above team considered a "breathtaking" idea. Barrington, Mulacz, and Rivas rejected the possibility that telepathic communication between Iris and Lucía might explain the abilities that Iris came to possess. "[Even if] a large number of words of a foreign language could perhaps be attributed to ESP . . . the mastering of a language to the degree Lucía achieved most certainly could not," they wrote. "At least there is no precedent in the history of parapsychology of acquiring skills such as correct pronunciation of a language or a dialect by means of ESP. Mastering the choreography of Flamenco and other Spanish (or Gypsy) dances [which Lucía demonstrated] falls clearly into the same category of 'skills.'" The investigators also dismissed mental disturbances such as schizophrenia as an explanation. Although possession remains a possible explanation, Barrington, Mulacz, and Rivas were hesitant to invoke it, saying, "As the very existence of an entity able to 'possess' or 'overshadow' a human being is not proven it cannot be accepted as a 'causa vera' [true cause]. This would entail explaining one unexplainable by another unexplainable." In the end the investigations are inconclusive.

A possibility not considered by the investigators is the One Mind—Pearce's "cosmic soup," or the single mind posited by Nobel physicist Erwin Schrödinger. For reasons that remain unclear, Iris might have dipped into this informational dimension, ladled out what appealed to her and suited her needs, and returned as Lucía. This process would appear to outside observers as a dead ringer for possession.

Mediums

Mediums are persons who claim to be in contact with the spirits of the dead. They have been studied intensively since the earliest days of psychical research, beginning in the latter part of the 19th century. They have captured the interest of some of the leading figures in psychology, including William James and C. G. Jung. The history of this field is fascinating, exemplified in Pulitzer Prize–winning journalist Deborah Blum's engrossing book *Ghost Hunters: William James and the Search for Scientific Proof of Life after Death.*

Mediumship is one of the most contentious and controversial areas of consciousness research. I have no desire to enter the fray, nor am I endorsing mediums or mediumship. No doubt many or perhaps most instances of mediums' ostensible contact with the dead can be explained by mundane factors—fishing for information; reading the expression, voice, appearance, and body language of the so-called sitter; wishful thinking; or fraud, such as relying on a network of informants.[4] But as University of Virginia psychologist Edward F. Kelly and his colleagues say, when all such cases have been dismissed there remains a substantial number of really puzzling and carefully investigated cases that deserve attention, such as those that have attracted critical investigators such as William James.[5] Moreover, novel and ingenious methods of evaluating mediums are today being employed with intriguing results, as in the experimental work of researchers Julie Beischel and colleagues at the Windbridge Institute,[6] and Gary E. Schwartz, of the Human Energy Systems Laboratory in the Department of Psychology at the University of Arizona.[7]

Not Too Worried

Most individuals who consult mediums desire communication from their deceased loved one suggesting that he or she survives on the other side with personality intact. Is it important that our earth personality goes with us in the afterlife? I've never thought so. I don't want to lug around this personality eternally. I'm hoping for an upgrade.

Consciousness researcher Charles T. Tart agrees. He says, "Who am I? If I am someone who potentially has access to all the information in the universe, what makes me want to completely identify with the narrow version of myself that says I am nothing but my physical brain to begin with?"[8]

Mediums Not So Weird After All

The word *medium* is often associated with eccentrics, séances, and the occult, but many quite ordinary people appear to be mediums as well, without realizing it. Nurse-educator Barbara Stevens Barnum, Ph.D., R.N., former editor of *Nursing & Health Care,* has researched nurses' experiences of what she calls "expanded consciousness"—events that can't be explained rationally and that appear to transcend the physical senses. In a survey of 121 nurse leaders, all of whom held doctorates or master's degrees, she found that 41 percent of them described such experiences. They sometimes involved communication with the deceased.

One of these outstanding nurses described an event that took place a year after her husband died.[9] She remarried, and she and her new husband were cleaning the backyard of an old farmhouse they had rented. As she was picking up armloads of rotten, termite-infested lumber without gloves, she heard her deceased husband's voice say, in his Cajun accent, "Don't—step back—there's a rattler under there." She picked up the next layer of rotten boards with a pitchfork, saw the rattlesnake, and killed it. "Thank you," she said to her deceased husband. Two days later she revisited the site and saw him standing there. "No one can ever convince me this experience did not happen," she said. "I'm sane, mature, adult, productive, creative, active and *normal.* I only wish I knew how to be more receptive and to have more control over my 'extra' sense."

Scary? In Barnum's survey, "Not one account mentioned fear or dread; on the contrary, many described the comfort of the contact [with the deceased individual]."[10]

Experiences such as these are universal. When bereavement researcher W. D. Rees interviewed 227 widows and 66 widowers, he found that nearly half of them had "visitation experiences" from the deceased, almost 15 percent of which took the form of spoken messages. These experiences involved both sexes; cut across every culture; were common in small villages and large cities; and happened to agnostics, atheists, and believers alike.[11]

Reports of communication with the deceased, whether they come from mediums or other individuals, may be consoling to the living, but they are not the final verdict on survival. After all, skeptics will always contend they are products of disturbed minds. It is nonlocal awareness in general that is most important. Nonlocality involves infinitude in space and time. Infinitude in time is eternality. Therefore, nonlocal consciousness does not simply *imply* immortality, it *requires* it.

CHAPTER 13

EARLY ONENESS

Evidence suggests that oneness of mind between humans begins early in life in the mother-infant relationship. Developmental psychologist Joseph Chilton Pearce described a classical study of how bonded mothers in South America and Africa don't use diapers for their infants. They carry the infants in a sling yet are never soiled by them. They simply know when their baby is about to urinate or defecate.[1]

What Smoke Signals Really Meant

The possibility that minds could link together for practical purposes was taken for granted in premodern cultures. David Unaipon, a native Australian described in the Melbourne journal that reported his comments as those of "a Christianised and highly educated brainy Australian native," elaborated in 1914 how the use of smoke signals depended on this fact. Westerners who witnessed this custom assumed that some sort of code was involved in the signal. Not so, Unaipon explained; the function of the smoke signal was to get everyone's attention so that distant, mind-to-mind communications might then take place:

> He might want to give his brother, who might be twenty miles away, a message; so he would set to and make a smoke signal, and then sit down and concentrate his mind on his

brother. The column of smoke would be seen by all the blacks for miles around, and they would all concentrate their minds, and put their brains into a state of receptivity. Only his brother, however, would get in touch with him, and he . . . could then suggest to his [brother] the message which he wished to convey.[2]

Anthropologist Ronald Rose, who investigated the aborigines 40 years later, was also assured that smoke-signal messages were not in the smoke itself. "When we see smoke we think, and often we find clearness," a native told him. When the faraway person sees the smoke, "he gets to thinking. And I am thinking too, so that he thinks my thoughts."[3]

The fusion of minds and the sharing of thoughts among natives baffled Westerners whenever they came in contact with it, which was often. In his 1927 book, *The Sixth Sense,* author Joseph Sinel described how his son, who lived among the tribesmen of the southern Sudan, had found that "telepathy is constant." When he got lost on one occasion, tribesmen simply came out and collected him, aware of his plight. On another occasion, when he had picked up an arrow tip and brought it back with him, two natives, already aware of his discovery, met him and asked if they could examine it.[4]

Psychologist Joseph Chilton Pearce described a study of the original Anglo-Saxon settlers in the southern mountains of Appalachia, who were isolated for generations and who used "telepathy," as the researchers called it, as an everyday means of communication, without any self-consciousness of the novelty involved. "Virtually all these 'telepathic' communications involved the general well-being and emotional bonding within the family unit," Pearce wrote, "the mother calling the family in for dinner, sensing family members in distress, or whatever."[5]

British biologist Rupert Sheldrake suggests that throughout most of human history this sort of sensing ability was the norm. He asks, "Why have we lost so much of the sensitivity that our ancestors had? There are many stories from travelers in Africa, who say that it's taken for granted in many parts of Africa that members of a tribe will know when somebody's coming, when somebody's needed somewhere else, and they'll just go and they'll find someone who needs them 50 miles away. They respond to this all the time. Before the invention of telephones, this was what people did, and there are reports from the American Indians, Australian Aborigines, travelers' reports. Typically, anthropologists didn't study it, because they were convinced it was impossible. They went there with a rationalist frame of mind and didn't document the things in traditional cultures that are the most interesting features about them. . . . Even in our society [this capacity] has not been completely wiped out."[6]

More Than One Way to See

One individual who has studied distant knowing in premodern cultures is Douchan Gersi. An adventurer, explorer, and filmmaker, Gersi has spent most of his life in some of the most isolated regions on earth documenting cultures he calls "people of tradition." In his captivating book *Faces in the Smoke,* he described how nonlocal, One-Mind knowing is employed in a natural, seamless way in everyday life in these cultures.

One day while driving across desert wasteland in the Sahara, Gersi encountered a single Tuareg nomad sitting by his camel. Judging from the tracks, Gersi deduced that he had been occupying the same spot for several days. The location seemed to be in the middle of nowhere with no distinguishing features, just featureless sand, stone, and rocky hills. Intrigued, Gersi stopped and shared tea with the man.

The nomad explained that he was waiting for a friend. Seven months earlier, while in a town called Gao in Mali, 600 miles away, he had made a pact with his friend to meet at this particular place at this specific time. Each of them was on a journey and would be converging on this spot from different directions.

Looking around, Gersi was dubious that anyone could pick this place out of the surrounding immensity. The possibility that two people could converge here, from opposite directions, defied his imagination. "Can't miss the place," the nomad said, while giving names to everything that surrounded them. The only problem was that the nomad's water was about to run out; if his friend did not arrive in the next three days, he would have to move on.

The next morning the Tuareg told Gersi that things were on schedule. He had communicated with his friend during the night and he would arrive in two days. "Did you dream about him?" Gersi asked.

"No, I didn't dream about him. He just told me where he was," the nomad said. He explained that his friend had informed him that he had had to make a detour to fill his water bags.

"But how did he tell you?" Gersi asked.

"He told me that in my mind," said the nomad. "And in the same way I answered him that I will be waiting for him."

Still skeptical, Gersi waited to see the outcome. Two days later, right on schedule, the Tuareg's friend arrived.[7]

On another occasion, Gersi and his colleagues were facing a treacherous, 800-mile drive across the Sahara from Djanet, an Algerian city near the Libyan border, to Timbuktu in Mali. The route involved large expanses of sand dunes and dangerous quicksand, mountains, rocky volcanic areas, and deep valleys. The available maps were not specific, and it would have been foolish to attempt the journey without a guide.

Gersi met the head of the military outpost in Djanet, who recommended a man named Iken as the best guide for the trip. Gersi should not be concerned, the commandant said, that Iken was *blind.*

Iken, in his 50s, had spent his childhood and adolescence with his father, who led caravans throughout the Sahara. He then became a caravanner himself, and was eventually hired as a guide by the French Foreign Legion. Around age 30 he contracted trachoma, an eye infection, which eventually led to blindness.

"Have you made this trip before?" Gersi asked him.

"Not exactly . . . but I see very well what you want to do," Iken replied. He explained that it was necessary for him to sit on the spare tire that was strapped to the hood of the Land Rover. "I need to breathe the smell of the desert," he said, ". . . and hear the different noises the tires make on the ground; that tells me a lot about the terrain." He could do neither of these things from inside the car, he said. He added, "Don't talk while driving, but look carefully at the

landscape all around you. . . . That, too, helps me see where I am."
It was as if blind Iken could absorb information not just from the surrounding landscape but also from others. If they knew what things
looked like, so did he. It was as if his mind overlapped with the minds
of others. Iken's guidance was all the more remarkable considering
that Gersi's party often drove at night without headlights.

Iken turned out to be one big human sense organ that functioned
on every level except the visual. He would often stop the vehicle,
kneel, caress the sand, and contemplate its texture. He would breathe
deeply and smell the desert for long periods. Once, when water
ran short, he stroked the branches of a large dried bush, smelled all
around, and indicated new directions. Several hours later the group
found water.

With Iken's help Gersi's group made it to Timbuktu without
incident.[8]

Deprived of physical vision, Iken brought other ways of knowing
into play—including the knowing of others, made possible by the
linking, the coming together, of individual minds.

CHAPTER 14

SAVANTS

A body of evidence suggesting the existence of the One Mind comes from savants. *Savant* is derived from a French word meaning "learned one." Savants often possess knowledge they could not possibly have acquired on the basis of their experience or learning, and that they could not have formulated on their own. Although savants are often mentally or socially impaired, they frequently possess astonishing creative and intuitive powers of obscure origin in areas such as mathematics, art, or music.[1]

Illiterate, Untrainable, Uneducable—and Brilliant

Psychologist Joseph Chilton Pearce, who probes savant syndrome in his book *Evolution's End: Claiming the Potential of Our Intelligence,* stated, "Savants are untrained and untrainable, illiterate and uneducable . . . few can read or write . . . Yet each has apparently unlimited access to a particular field of knowledge that we know they cannot have acquired . . . Ask . . . [mathematical] savants how they get their answer and they will smile, pleased that we are impressed but unable to grasp the implications of such a question. . . . The answers come through them but they are not aware of how—they don't know how they know . . . The ones sight-reading music can't read anything else, yet display this flawless sensory-motor response to musical symbols . . . ." And here is the crux of the mystery: "The issue with these savants is that in most cases, so far as can be observed, *the savant has not acquired, could not have acquired, and is quite incapable of acquiring, the information that he so liberally dispenses* [emphasis added]."[2]

The "savant syndrome" was popularized in the 1988 movie *Rain Man*. Kim Peek, the developmentally disabled man who was the inspiration for the film, knew more than 7,600 books by heart, as well as every area code, highway, zip code, and television station in the U. S.[3]

Leslie Lemke, a blind savant, is developmentally disabled and suffers from cerebral palsy. He was born with glaucoma, and doctors were forced to remove his eyes. His birth mother gave him up for adoption, and May Lemke, a nurse, adopted him when he was six months old. He was 12 before he learned to stand and 15 before he learned to walk. When he was 16, May found him playing Tchaikovsky's Piano Concerto No. 1 in the middle of the night. He had recently heard the piece performed on television. Although he never studied piano, he was soon playing all styles of music, from ragtime to classical. He composed music and was able to play thousands of pieces flawlessly, even when he had heard them only once. Lemke became a sensation and toured in the United States, Scandinavia, and Japan.[4]

The abilities of savants are often thought to be curiosities with little practical value, but this is not always true. During World War II, the British government employed two mathematical savants to serve as human computers who were, so far as is known, infallible.[5]

Psychologist David Feinstein[6] reports that at least 100 savants with prodigious mental abilities have been identified in the past century. Darold A. Treffert, a psychiatrist who specializes in savant syndrome, described in his book *Extraordinary People*[7] a savant whose conversational vocabulary was limited to some 58 words but who could accurately give the population of every city and town in the United States with more than 5,000 people; the names, number of rooms, and locations of 2,000 leading hotels in America; the distance from any city or town to the largest city in its state; statistics concerning 3,000 mountains and rivers; and the dates and essential facts of more than 2,000 leading inventions and discoveries.[8]

One mathematical savant was shown a checkerboard with one grain of rice on the first of its 64 squares. He was then asked how many grains of rice there would be on the final square if the grains of rice were doubled on each square. Forty-five seconds later he gave the correct answer, which exceeds the total number of atoms in the sun.[9]

George and Charles are identical twins who are known as "calendrical savants." They are incapable of taking care of themselves and have been institutionalized since age seven. If you ask them on which date Easter will fall 10,000 years into the future, they answer immediately—not just with the date for Easter but also with other calendrical data such as the time of the tides. If you ask them for the date of an event prior to 1752, when Europe shifted from the Julian to the Gregorian calendar systems, their answers accommodate to the switch. They can tell you the day of the week of any date you choose, ranging 40,000 years into the past or future. Give them your birth date and they can tell you the Thursdays on which it might fall. In addition to their calendrical skills, they enjoy swapping 20-digit prime numbers, thereby showing a parallel ability that is uncommon in savants. In spite of these prodigious abilities, they cannot add the simplest numbers. If you ask them how they knew to switch from one calendrical system to the other in 1752, they will be confused by such an abstract question; indeed, they don't know what "calendrical system" means.[10]

Many clinicians have reported savants capable of extrasensory perception, or ESP, also called psi. In one case, George, an autistic savant who could not write his name or a sentence, would know when his parents unexpectedly decided to pick him up at school (he usually rode the bus). He would tell his teacher his parents were coming, and he would be at the door when they arrived. Other parents described their autistic-savant children as capable of hearing conversations that were out of range of hearing, and the ability to pick up thoughts not spoken. In one case, the father of one savant told how his watch crystal fell out in the bathroom and was immediately replaced, an occurrence known only to him. A short time later his savant daughter related the incident to him in accurate detail.

In another case, a savant girl was able to accurately predict a week before Christmas what her gift packages would contain, although she had no way of knowing and had been given no clues what her gifts might be. Another savant girl could predict when the telephone would ring and who would be calling. These and several dozen similar cases were reported by Dr. Bernard Rimland in a study of 5,400 autistic children. Rimland believed he was witnessing genuine psi abilities in many of these children, commenting, "Statistical probability of coincidental knowledge nil."[11]

How Do They Do It?

The usual explanations of savant syndrome rely on not-yet-understood genetic propensities and obscure brain processes. Psychiatrist Treffert, who has studied more savants than probably anyone, proposes "ancestral memory" as a key. He states, "Prodigious savants particularly 'know' things, or 'remember' things, they never learned. To explain that reality—and it is a reality—it seems to me one has to invoke a third type of memory—ancestral or genetic memory—that exists alongside the cognitive or semantic and the habit or procedural memory. . . . To me such ancestral memory is simply, and only, the *genetic transfer of knowledge.*"[12]

Treffert acknowledges the concept of the collective unconscious that pscyhologist Carl Jung used to account for "inherited traits, intuitions and collective wisdom of the past," and the notion of "racial memory" invoked by neurosurgeon Wilder Penfield. But for Treffert, all these proposals come down to genes. He states unequivocally, "Whether called ancestral or racial memory, intuitions or even collective unconscious, the concept of the genetic transmission of knowledge of a complex type is necessary to explain how the prodigious savant particularly *does* remember things he or she never learned. . . . The prodigious savant, it seems, comes with a great deal of software 'factory installed' which already contains a considerable amount of actual data or knowledge. It would appear that access to that 'factory installed' software may account for the innate, instinctive, exceptional skills, ability and 'knowledge' which is evident in the savant's vast and instant mastery of some particular area of functioning. . . . It is through that same transfer and mechanism that all of us 'know,' or 'remember,' to greater or lesser extent, things we never learned."[13]

All of which seems to be a violation of the basic tenet of evolutionary biology, which says that those abilities that contribute to individual survival and procreation are the ones that are genetically transmitted to succeeding generations. What is the survival value of knowing, as do some savants, nearly unlimited information that is utterly trivial? Why would this information have been factory installed in the savant's genes? How could it be "ancestral memory," as Treffert suggests, when information such as the above hotel facts did not exist when the savant's ancestors were alive?

Factory-installed knowledge and ancestor-derived information have little explanatory value. These proposals seem to be a desperate attempt to keep the brain and genes in charge of the savants' skills. If ever there were a promissory note in science with little redemption value, these attempts may be it, because no one has a clue how genes, which code for proteins, could account for these abilities, or how unlearned facts could be stored in ancestors' genes before the facts even existed.

The low intelligence of savants may be an advantage by limiting their attention to a narrow band and screening out extraneous stimuli. Fewer distractions might increase the "signal to noise" ratio from the timeless information source and heighten the reception of what comes through for the savant.

In our golden age of brain scanning, neuroscientists are exploring patterns of brain activity that correlate with the abilities of savants.[14] Geneticists may also identify patterns in the DNA of savants that correlate with their abilities. But in either case this will not prove that brain mechanisms or genes account for or cause these feats, any more than a television set produces the picture that appears on its screen. Rather, brains and genes may be a relay station for information originating outside themselves, just as a television's picture originates elsewhere. As the venerable tenet within science again has it, "Correlation is not causation."

Those who study savant syndrome sometimes admit they are baffled. They recognize they are confronting a conundrum that cannot be solved by continuing to focus on the usual suspects of genes and brains. Writing in *Scientific American* in their article "Inside the Mind of a Savant," Treffert and Daniel D. Christensen state, "Until we understand his [*Rain Man* Kim Peek's] abilities, we cannot pretend to understand human cognition."[15] Treffert also concedes, "There have been about as many theories that have attempted to answer this question as there have been investigators."[16] Although hypotheses continue to surface like spring weeds, no single model has emerged that can explain all savants. In the 1970s, researcher Jane Duckett of the University of Texas at Austin called for "extensive theory revision" in the quest to understand savants' abilities.[17] Her recommendation still applies.

It is tempting to view savants as entities unto themselves, cut off from those around them. In many instances, this is far from true. As Treffert notes, "One of the greatest lessons is that they have been shaped by far more than neural circuitry. The savants thrive because of the reinforcement provided by the unconditional love, belief and determination of those who care for them."[18] Perhaps the classic example is pianist Leslie Lemke, who probably owes his life to the love and caring of his adoptive mother and nurse who kept him alive through a decade of almost total dependency.

But the "social surround" may not be limited to the see-touch-feel world we are familiar with. It may also involve that great meeting place of consciousness, the One Mind. This may be the "extensive theory revision" that is required if we have any hope of penetrating the tantalizing mystery of savants. The One Mind that savants perhaps enter would be available to anyone. It would be a kind of watering hole for consciousness, where the thirst for information, creative solutions, and wisdom can be quenched. This Source would be a meeting place for all minds that have ever existed. It is Jung's collective unconscious, Emerson's Over-soul, and various other terms that have arisen throughout history for a spatio-temporally infinite dimension of mind.

CHAPTER 15

TWINS

Body and spirit are twins: God only knows which is which.

—ALGERNON CHARLES SWINBURNE[1]

I've been interested in identical twins since I was old enough to realize I am one. Being a twin is the major reason I was drawn to the concept of the One Mind. My twin brother and I have felt a deep connection all our life. Moreover, I am married to a twin. Barbara, my wife, has also shared One-Mind experiences with her fraternal-twin brother. Out of respect for privacy, I won't describe these experiences but will focus on twin research that has become public knowledge.

I was naturally fascinated when I first heard about the famous identical "Jim twins"—Jim Springer and Jim Lewis—who were united at age 39 after being separated in infancy and adopted into separate working-class homes in Ohio.[2]

Their reunion in February 1979 was a deeply emotional event for both of them. "I'm me and he's him, but at the same time he's me and I'm him. Do you understand?" said Jim Springer about his brother. Not only had each been named James by their adoptive families, but each had been married twice—the first time to wives named Linda, the second time to wives named Betty. Jim Lewis had had three sons, one of whom was named James Alan; his brother, Jim Springer, had three daughters and a son, James Allan. Both twins had previously owned a dog named Toy. Both preferred Miller Lite beer, chain-smoked Salem cigarettes, drove Chevrolets, enjoyed carpentry and had similar basement workshops in which they made similar things, disliked baseball, and relished stock-car racing. Both chewed their fingernails down to a nub. Each had been a lackluster student in high school; for both, their favorite subject was mathematics and their least favorite, spelling. They smoked and drank the same amount and got headaches at the same time of day. They had similar speech and thought patterns, similar gaits, and a preference for spicy foods. They shared peculiar behaviors, such as a preference for flushing the toilet before using it.[3] Both had served as sheriff's deputies in their respective communities. Each twin was demonstrative and affectionate, leaving love notes for his wife scattered around the house. They had voted identically in the past three presidential elections. Both men worried little about the past or future, dwelling mainly in the present. Each twin had vacationed in Florida at the same three-block-long beach.

Their medical histories were similar. Both had identical vision, blood pressure, pulse rates, and sleep patterns. Each twin suffered from hemorrhoids, had put on an extra ten pounds at the same time in life, and was afflicted with "mixed headache syndrome," a combination of tension and migraine headaches. The onset of headache in each was age 18, and in both twins the headaches occurred in the late afternoon. They even used similar phrases to describe them. Both had had what they felt were heart attacks in the past, although heart disease could not be demonstrated in either of them. Each had had a vasectomy. Their brain wave tests, recorded in response to various stimuli, were like carbon copies.[4] Jim Lewis lived in Elida, Ohio, in a modest frame house. His was the only house on the block with a white bench around a tree in the yard. Jim Springer lived in Dayton, some 80 miles south of Elida. His was also the only house on the block with a tree with a white bench around it.

When the story of the Jim twins was written up by a local reporter, it was picked up by the Associated Press. Psychologist Thomas J. Bouchard, Jr., of the University of Minnesota, read about it in the

Minneapolis Tribune and immediately realized that this was a rare opportunity to study identical twins reared apart. "It was just sheer scientific curiosity," Bouchard recalls. "I thought we were going to do a single study of a set of twins reared apart. We might have a little monograph."[5]

Bouchard was interested in the "nature versus nurture" controversy—the debate over the relative impact of genetic influences versus environmental factors in shaping one's overall makeup. Identical twins have the same genetic pattern. If they differ behaviorally, psychologically, or physically in significant ways, this strongly suggests that their different environments and upbringing are dominant over genetic influences. On the other hand, if they remain identical after being separated at birth into different environments, this suggests that genetic factors overshadow environmental influences.

Bouchard wasted no time. Within an hour of reading the story he had secured a preliminary grant from the university to fund an investigation of the Jim twins, including dozens of personality, aptitude, medical, and psychiatric evaluations. In one test measuring personality variables such as tolerance, conformity, self-control, sociability, and flexibility, the two Jims' scores were so close it was as if the same person had taken the test twice. Bouchard said, "In intelligence, in mental abilities, in their likes and dislikes, and their interests, they were remarkably similar . . . The pattern carried through in the little things that go together to form a personality . . . the way you sit or gesture, the pace of your voice, your body language. They were like bookends."[6]

At the time Bouchard began to study the Jim twins, only 19 cases of reunited twins had been reported in the United States and most had been reared by families who were biologically related. This made Springer and Lewis all the more unique and attractive to Bouchard, whose career had been dedicated to teasing apart the factors governing the human personality. The day the tests were to begin, Bouchard took the Jims to breakfast to brief them on the particulars of the study. It was the first time he had ever worked with identical twins, and he was shaken up. He found himself obsessing over little things about them—the way each one had bitten his nails, for example. Each of the Jims had a peculiar whorl in his eyebrow, and Bouchard started absently counting the number of hairs in their brows. "You're staring at us," one told him. Bouchard apologized. He had been staggered by the similarities of their gestures, their voices, and the morphology of their bodies. These two men had lived entirely separate lives, yet if Bouchard closed his eyes, he couldn't tell which Jim was talking.[7]

As news leaked out, the Jim twins became famous. They appeared on Johnny Carson's TV show, chatted with TV personality Mike Douglas, met fellow Ohioan Jonathan Winters, and appeared in articles in *Newsweek, People,* and other magazines.

As *Washington Post* journalist Arthur Allen wrote, "When journalists first began interviewing Bouchard's twins-raised-apart, they focused on the spectacularly similar pairs, like the Springer-Lewis twins. But those twins turned out to be outliers in the Minnesota study. Most of the other twins weren't nearly as alike. . . . Genes make proteins that contribute to chemical pathways that play a role in complex neurological and existential events. . . . Genes don't really make . . . violent kids or depressed adults, and no reputable scientist would claim that they do." Neither do they make twins-reared-apart flush the toilet before using it. So what's the explanation? In conventional science, there isn't one. Such anomalies are considered "noise in the system" or "outliers," terms that amount to a scientist's shrug.[8]

Writing in *Smithsonian,* journalist Donald Dale Jackson seemed to sense something of a sacred dimension in these phenomena:

> The final truth of the Jims' reunion [is] not the genetic similarities or the environmental differences but the joyous consummation of a bond restored, of love regained—the triumph of family. Both Jims recognized that truth intuitively and reacted to it identically—with gratitude. The scientists can't prove it, but maybe their souls are identical too.[9]

As a result of his investigation of the Jims, other sets of identical twins, also separated at birth, began to contact Dr. Bouchard. Within a year he had evaluated 15 pairs and had leads on 35 more. The project led to his founding of the Minnesota Center for Twin and Adoption Research in, appropriately enough, the Twin Cities. To date, more than 100 pairs of reared-apart twins have come through the program to spend a week in Elliott Hall in Bouchard's laboratories.

Two of Bouchard's most remarkable subjects were the middle-aged British twins Bridget Harrison and Dorothy Love, who were separated in infancy in World War II and raised apart in very different socioeconomic settings. When they got off the plane in Minneapolis, they were each wearing seven rings, two bracelets on one wrist, and a watch and a bracelet on the other wrist. Bridget had named her son Richard Andrew, and Dorothy had named hers Andrew Richard. The strange "naming phenomenon" went further. Bridget had named her daughter Catherine Louise; Dorothy named her daughter Karen Louise. Bouchard was struck by this, since the possibility of coincidence is lessened by the fact that choosing a name is a joint decision of husband and wife.

Another set of Bouchard's twins, Daphne Goodship and Barbara Herbert, also separated in World War II, were adopted separately as infants and reared apart. Like the two Jims, they were reunited after 39 years. When they met at King's Cross Station, London, in May 1979, each was wearing a brown velvet jacket and beige dress. They both had crooked little fingers that had prevented them from learning to type or play the piano. Both had the eccentricity of pushing up their noses, which they called "squidging." Both at age 15 had fallen down stairs and sustained weak ankles as a result. At age 16 each met at a dance the man she was going to marry, and each suffered a miscarriage with her first child, then had two boys followed by a girl. They both laughed more than anybody else they knew and are fondly remembered by the researchers as the Giggle Twins. Both were "great gigglers," always setting each other off. Yet when asked if there had ever been any gigglers in their adoptive families, both replied no.[10]

Another highly publicized set of twins was Oskar Stöhr and Jack Yufe, who had the most dramatically different backgrounds of any twins studied. They were born in Trinidad in 1933 to a Jewish father and a German mother and were separated shortly after birth. Oskar's mother returned with him to Germany, where he was raised as a Catholic and a Nazi youth by his grandmother. Jack was raised by his father in the Caribbean as a Jew, and spent part of his time as a youth on an Israeli kibbutz. When they reported to Bouchard, they led markedly different lives. Oskar was married, an industrial supervisor in Germany, a dedicated union man, and a skier. Jack ran a retail clothing store in San Diego, was separated, and was a workaholic. But similarities were evident from the moment they arrived at the airport in the Twin Cities. Both were wearing blue, two-pocket shirts with epaulets and wire-rimmed glasses, and had neatly clipped mustaches. Their idiosyncrasies meshed: they liked spicy foods and sweet liqueurs, were absentminded, and had a habit of falling asleep while watching television. Oddly, they shared the peculiar habit of sneezing loudly in public to get a reaction, a trait that baffled the scientists. They both flushed the toilet before using it, stored rubber bands on their wrists, read magazines back to front, and dipped buttered toast in their coffee. Said Bouchard, "With some of these things you can only shrug and say, 'It's in someone else's hands.'"[11]

Nature, Nurture, and the One Mind

Are these twin phenomena the results of "nature" or "nurture"—genetic or environmental factors? Bouchard's team leans predominantly toward a genetic explanation, since the environmental influences were so radically dissimilar in so many of their cases. But by focusing on only two possibilities to explain the strikingly similar thoughts and behaviors of identical twins reared apart, researchers may be omitting another key possibility. If consciousness is somehow unbounded and unitary, these similarities would not be surprising, because separated twins—or anyone else—could share thoughts across the separations of space and time. They could participate in each other's emotions and beliefs, which over time might distill into similar or identical behaviors. Nonlocal mind could act in concert with genetic factors, intensifying the tendency toward sameness. In that case, we might ask these questions: Why aren't we more alike than we are? In view of our sharing of consciousness, what keeps us from being clones of each other in word, thought, and deed? What makes possible our rich diversity? If the One Mind is real—if our minds are essentially unbounded and flow into each other—how do we become individuals?

Nonlocal mind, acting in concert with other factors such as genes and environment, gives us a more powerful explanatory model for the bizarre sameness seen in reared-apart identical twins. Currently, some of their behaviors are so outrageously similar that the most hard-core materialists have trouble explaining them; for example, wearing seven rings, sneezing in public, building white benches around a tree in the front yard, marrying serial mates with the same names, or naming children identically or similarly. The temptation is always to ascribe what can't be easily explained genetically or behaviorally to chance, that cherished, final dumping ground for the unexplained. A nonlocal, shared One Mind makes chance a less attractive explanation.

Bouchard and other twin researchers have found evidence that some identical twins reared apart are *more* identical than twins raised together. This may sound surprising until we consider what it is like to be a twin. Identical twins brought up together frequently have great difficulty establishing their individual identities. They are often encouraged to resemble each other as much as possible, such as being dressed alike. As a result they may go to great lengths to "be different" in order to assert their individuality. If identical twins are reared apart, they do not experience themselves as mirror images needing to struggle to establish their own identity. Thus their separation may paradoxically allow them to be more alike than if they were reared together.

Many people have responded to the twin data almost depressively, as if it is a curse. It isn't hard to see why. The research suggests that we can experience different environments, be raised by different parents, grow up in different countries, have different friends, and marry different people—and still emerge from these unique experiences to find ourselves a virtual clone of someone who has the same genes, someone we've never seen nor met. Our DNA seems to make a mockery of free will and volition. As Lawrence Wright stated in his summary of this field, "When we read about twins who were separated at birth and are reunited in middle age only to discover that in many respects they have become the same person, it suggests to us that life is somehow a charade: that we only *seem* to react consciously to events; that the life experiences we think have shaped us are little more than ornaments or curiosities we have picked up along the way; and that the injunctions of our parents and the traumas of our youth which we believed to be the lodestones of our character may have had little more effect on us than a book we have read or a show we have seen on television—that, in effect, we could have lived another person's life and still be who we are."[12]

Rather than evidence of a genetic curse, the twin studies may be precisely the opposite. The highly correlated behaviors of identical, separated twins may be lessons in freedom. Reared-apart twins may be coming together nonlocally in a particular dimension of consciousness, making unconscious choices to fit together, be alike, and share. They may illustrate the triumph of minds that, through their connectedness in the One Mind, are free to choose sameness and to delight in similarity. Their correlated thoughts and behaviors are perhaps not a reason to lament our enslavement to our genes but to celebrate our freedom from them.

The recurring tendency in materialistic science to deny free will is not limited to reared-apart identical twins, of course; it is widely applied to humans in general. This effort carries a hint of hypocrisy and illogic. As psychologist Lawrence LeShan wrote in his groundbreaking book *Landscapes of the Mind,* "Imagine someone who says, 'I have no free will. Everything I do or say is determined by mechanical forces. I am a robot.' We would send him to a psychiatrist. But if a person with a Ph.D. stands up in a lecture hall and says, 'All humans are mechanically determined and have no free will,' we would call him a behaviorist or a psychoanalyst or a philosophical determinist and applaud his brilliant thinking and make him chairman of his department."[13]

Philosophers may interpret the sameness of reared-apart identical twins as a curse, but the twins don't see it that way. For them, it's a cause for joy. Consider, for example, the comments of Jim Lewis. "My mother told me I had a twin when I was about six," he said. "I got a little more curious about it as I got older. . . . I always kinda felt like I wanted to have somebody close to me. I felt alone, I guess. . . . Once about five years ago, I took off . . . to see if I could find him. I didn't really know what I was looking for, just hoping to run into him,

I guess." After they were united, Jim Springer said, "God, we're just enjoying each other. Nobody can imagine what it feels like." Jim Lewis made a scroll and gave it to his brother. It read, "February 9, 1979 was the most important day of my life. On that day we started a lifetime relationship together and we will never be apart again."[14]

When the aforementioned identical twins Barbara Herbert and Daphne Goodship were reunited at age 40, they found they had both met their future husbands at a town hall dance at age 16. They both had fallen down stairs the same year, damaging their ankles, as mentioned, creating permanent difficulty walking down stairs without clutching the banister. In a comparison of their handwriting, when asked by the Minnesota researchers to choose any sentence, they both chose "The cat sat on the mat," and both misspelled "cat" as "cas." Both knitted cardigans in the same pattern and color. After being reunited, they both wrote to the same women's magazine on the same day to ask the same question, neither telling the other they'd done so. They both won ten pounds on the National Lottery in the same week. When Daphne won a bottle of Avon perfume in a raffle, Barbara won a prize in a drawing sponsored by her local Avon lady.[15] According to British twins researcher Guy Lyon Playfair, author of the insightful book *Twin Telepathy,* "What is being reflected in my findings is very clear: some twin coincidences are indeed due to genetic underpinning and some are not, and it is usually easy to tell which is which."[16]

It is not surprising, he wrote, that Jonathan and Jason Floyd, 17-year-old identical twins, required appendectomies within two days of each other, although 300 miles apart, since they were "genetic blueprints" of each other and had experienced correlated medical events all their lives. But there is also strangeness afoot. Playfair asked, "How can genetics explain why John and Michael Atkins both fell and broke legs at exactly the same time while skiing on different glaciers in the Alps, well out of sight of each other?"[17] Is there a gene for falling down while skiing? One is free, of course, to attribute all such happenings to genes, coincidence, or tiny Alpine gremlins tripping up skiers, but at some point, for most people, intellectual discomfort about genes and coincidence (and gremlins) sets in as the tally of uncanny happenings mounts.

The Casablanca Effect

Playfair considered examples such as these as evidence of the *Casablanca effect.* He derived this term from Humphrey Bogart's famous line in the movie *Casablanca,* when his ex-lover, Ingrid Bergman, appears: "Of all the gin joints in all the towns in all the world, she walks into mine."

Some coincidences seem *so* coincidental they beg for another explanation.

This suspicion surfaces even for skeptics such as Peter Watson, who wrote, "Are all the coincidences that are being collected at Minnesota a sort of camouflage, a signal for something else that is going on at a deeper level?"[18] Playfair gave a yes answer to Watson's query, and so do I. Playfair: "Something . . . continues to be demonstrated and reported regularly, with identical twins providing more than their fair share of such reports, despite the fact that there are still those who refuse to admit its existence, or even the possibility of its existence."

I suggest that this "something" is an expression of the One Mind.

CHAPTER 16

TELESOMATIC EVENTS

In the 1960s, the American neuropsychiatrist Berthold E. Schwarz coined the term *telesomatic* from words meaning "distant body."[1] Schwarz documented events in which individuals experience similar sensations or actual physical changes, even though they may be separated by great distances. Hundreds of telesomatic events have been reported over the decades. They suggest that the persons involved are somehow linked through consciousness, as if two bodies were sharing a single mind.

As if One Body

A classic example was reported by the English social critic John Ruskin, involving Arthur Severn, the famous landscape painter. Severn awoke early one morning and went to the nearby lake for a sail. His wife, Joan, who was Ruskin's cousin, remained in bed. She was suddenly awakened by the feeling of a severe, painful blow to the mouth, of no apparent cause. Shortly thereafter her husband Arthur returned, holding a cloth to his bleeding mouth. He reported that the wind had freshened abruptly and caused the boom to hit him in the mouth, almost knocking him from the boat at the estimated time his wife felt the blow.[2]

A similar instance was reported in 2002 by mathematician-statistician Douglas Stokes. When he was teaching a course on parapsychology at the University of Michigan, one of his students reported that his father was knocked off a bench one day by an "invisible blow to the jaw." Five minutes later his dad received a call from a local gymnasium where his wife was exercising, informing him that she had broken her jaw on a piece of fitness equipment.

Another example that also involved the Severn clan was more unfortunate. One day, while Joan Severn was sitting quietly with her mother and aunt, the mother suddenly screamed, collapsed back onto the sofa, covered her ears with both hands, and exclaimed, "Oh, there's water rushing fast into my ears, and I'm sure either my brother, or son James, must be drowning, or both of them." Then Joan looked out the window and saw people hurrying toward the nearby swimming place. Shortly thereafter her uncle came to the house, looking pale and distressed, and reported that James had indeed drowned.[3]

Empathic Resonance

David Lorimer, a shrewd analyst of consciousness and a leader of the Scientific and Medical Network, an international organization based in the U.K., has collected many telesomatic cases in his very wise book *Whole in One*. Lorimer is struck by the fact that these events occur mainly between people who are emotionally close. He makes a strong case for what he calls "empathic resonance," which he believes links individuals across space and time.

The late psychiatrist Ian Stevenson (1918–2007) of the University of Virginia investigated scores of comparable instances in which distant individuals experienced similar physical symptoms. Most involved parents and children, spouses, siblings, twins, lovers, and very close friends.[4] Again, the common thread seemed to be the emotional closeness and empathy experienced by the separated persons.

In a typical example reported by Stevenson, a mother was writing a letter to her daughter, who had recently gone away to college. For no obvious reason her right hand began to burn so severely she had to put down her pen. She received a phone call less than an hour later informing her that her daughter's right hand had been severely burned by acid in a laboratory accident at the same time that she, the mother, had felt the burning pain.[5]

In a case reported by researcher Louisa E. Rhine, a woman suddenly doubled over, clutching her chest in severe pain, saying, "Something has happened to Nell; she has been hurt." Two hours later the sheriff arrived to inform her that Nell, her daughter, had been involved in an auto accident, and that a piece of the steering wheel had penetrated her chest."[6]

The Twin Thing Goes Further

As we learned in the previous chapter, Guy Lyon Playfair is one of the best-known consciousness researchers in Great Britain and is the author of the revealing book *Twin Telepathy*. He collected a variety of documented telesomatic cases involving twins and nontwin siblings.

One case involved the identical twins Ross and Norris McWhirter, who were well known in Britain as co-editors of the *Guinness Book of Records*. On November 27, 1975, Ross was fatally shot in the head and chest by two gunmen on the doorstep of his north London home. According to an individual who was with his twin brother, Norris reacted in a dramatic way at the time of the shooting, almost as if he too had been shot "by an invisible bullet."[7]

Cases such as these are invariably considered by skeptics as coincidence, but other instances are harder to squeeze into this category. An example reported by Guy Lyon Playfair concerns two four-year-old identical twins, Silvia and Marta Landa, who lived in the village of Murillo de Río Leza in northern Spain.[8] In 1976, the Landa twins became celebrities after being featured in their local newspaper because of a bizarre event. Marta had burned her hand on a hot clothes iron. As a large red blister was forming, an identical one was forming on the hand of Silvia, who was away visiting her grandparents at the time. Silvia was taken to the doctor, unaware of what had happened to her sister. When the two little girls were united, their parents saw that the blisters were the same size and on the same part of the hand.

It wasn't the first time this sort of thing had happened to these girls. If one twin had an accident, the other twin seemed to know about it, even though they were nowhere near each other. Once, when they arrived home in their car, Marta hopped out and ran inside the house, where she suddenly complained that she could not move her foot. Meanwhile, Silvia had got tangled up with the seat belt and her foot was stuck in it. On another occasion when one of them had misbehaved and was given a smack, the other one, out of sight, immediately burst into tears.

Members of the Madrid office of the Spanish Parapsychological Society got wind of the burned-hand incident and decided the case was worth investigating. Their team of nine psychologists, psychiatrists, and physicians descended on the Landas' house, with the full cooperation and approval of the twins' parents. The researchers got to work with a series of tests disguised as fun games for the twins, so the little girls had no idea they were involved in an experiment.

While Marta stayed on the ground floor with her mother and some of the researchers, Silvia went with her father and the rest of the team to the second floor. Everything that happened on both floors was filmed and tape-recorded. One of the psychologists played a game with Marta, using a glove puppet. Silvia was given an identical puppet, but no game was played. Downstairs, Marta grabbed the puppet and threw it at the investigator. Upstairs, at the same time, Silvia was doing the same.

One of the team's physicians next decided to do a simple checkup exam and shone a bright light into Marta's left eye. Upstairs, Silvia began to blink rapidly as if trying to avoid a bright light. Then the doctor performed a knee-jerk reflex test by tapping Marta's left knee tendon three times. At the same time, Silvia began to jerk her leg so dramatically that her father, unaware the test was going on downstairs on Marta, had to hold it still. Then Marta was given some very aromatic perfume to smell. As she did so, Silvia shook her head and put her hand over her nose. Next, still in different rooms, the twins were given seven colored discs and were asked to arrange them in any order they liked. They arranged them in exactly the same order.

There were other tests as well. Not all were as dramatic as the knee reflex exam, but the team rated all but one of them as "highly positive" or "positive."

The Landa tests confirmed what most researchers have found—that children are more prone than adults to this sort of thing and that results are more likely to be positive when experiments are done not in sterile, impersonal labs, but in the natural habitat of the subjects and in a relaxed, supportive environment. This latter lesson has often been flagrantly ignored in consciousness research by experimenters who should know better. Researchers have had to learn repeatedly about the importance of "ecological validity"—the principle that what is being tested should be allowed to unfold as it does in real life.

A Survival Advantage

Telesomatic events are often viewed as little more than coincidences or weird curiosities, like the simultaneously burned hands of the Landa twins. But there are many instances in which telesomatic happenings are of life-and-death significance. These cases are important because they show that the telesomatic link has survival value, which is probably why it appears to be inherent in humans.

One such case reported to Guy Playfair involved identical twin boys, Ricky and Damien, only three days old. Anna, their mother, would feed them during the night in her bed, propping herself up with pillows. On this particular occasion she had one twin, Ricky, in front of her, while the other, Damien, lay on a pillow to the left. As she was changing Ricky's diaper, he suddenly began screaming. This was surprising; even though only three days old. "He was a really good baby," Anna said, as was his brother. She could not figure out what was wrong, since he had been cleaned and fed. Then, still screaming, Ricky's body began to shake, as if he were having a convulsion. Anna reports that the thought suddenly popped into her head that "twins relay messages to each other." She looked down to check on Damien and, to her horror, saw that he wasn't there—he was face down in the pillows behind her. She immediately grabbed him and saw that he was blue in the face with his mouth clamped shut. Damien was suffocating to death. She and her older daughter began artificial respiration and called an ambulance. The terrifying event had a happy ending. Anna concluded, "Without a doubt, Ricky saved his brother's life. Had it not been for him screaming and shaking, I never would have looked for Damien until I had finished with Ricky, and by then it would have been too late."[9]

Adult identical twins have similar experiences. An example involved Gloria Morgan Vanderbilt (1904–65) and her identical twin sister, Lady Thelma Morgan Furness (1904–70). In *Double Exposure: A Twin Autobiography*, they relate that when Lady Furness was expecting her baby in Europe, Gloria was in New York City. Gloria was planning to travel to Europe to be with her sister in May when the baby was due. Gloria relates that in late March, when she was preparing to go out to lunch, she developed such severe abdominal pains that she had to cancel her engagements and go to bed. She said, "I remember saying . . . that if I didn't know such a thing was out of the question, I would think I was having a baby." Gloria managed to sleep for a while, and on awakening she felt normal—and saw on the bedside table a cable from Lord Furness announcing the premature birth of Thelma's son.[10]

Sometimes the pain that is shared is emotional and not physical, as in another case reported to Playfair. It involved a young American academic who was an undergraduate at Stony Brook University in New York at the time. She awoke from a deep sleep at 6 A.M. New York time and cried out, knowing without doubt that her twin sister in Arizona was in trouble. She told her roommate what had happened, and called her mother as well. Her mother informed her that at 3 A.M. Arizona time a car bomb had exploded just outside her twin sister's apartment, shattering a window. Fortunately, her twin sister and her husband were unharmed. The time of the bomb blast in Arizona coincided with her terrified awakening in New York.

Although telesomatic exchanges are by no means limited to twins, they are undeniably frequent among them. As Playfair states, in twins we see "the telepathic signal at full volume, as it were, at which not only information is transmitted at a distance but so are emotions, physical sensations and even symptoms such as burns and bruises."[11] Even so, he has found that only around 30 percent of identical twins have these experiences, but in those who do, the phenomena can be mind-boggling.[12] Emotional closeness is an essential factor in the twin connection. Also, having an extroverted, outgoing personality has been shown to facilitate the link. And, as we see in the above examples, "what [twins] communicate best is bad news—depression, illness, accidents or of course death."

Intuitive Obstetrics

Connections that go beyond twins can be seen in physicians who emotionally and physically sense when their patients need their attention, as if the two individuals are sharing the same body-mind. A remarkable case is that of Larry Kincheloe, M.D., an obstetrician-gynecologist in Oklahoma City.[13] After completing his training in obstetrics and gynecology, Kincheloe joined a very traditional medical group and practiced for about four years without any unusual events. Then one Saturday afternoon he received a call from the hospital that a patient of his was in early labor. He gave routine orders, and since this was her first baby he assumed that delivery still would be some hours away. While sweeping leaves at home, he experienced an overwhelming feeling that he had to go to the hospital. He immediately called labor and delivery and was told by the nurse that everything was going fine; his patient was only five centimeters dilated and delivery was not expected for several more hours.

Even with this reassurance, the feeling got stronger and Kincheloe began to feel pain in the center of his chest. He described it as similar to the feeling people have when they are 16 years old and lose their first love—an achingly sad, melancholy sense. The more he tried to ignore the sensation the stronger it grew, until it reached the point where he felt he was drowning. By this time he was desperate to get to the hospital. He jumped into his car and sped away. As he neared the hospital he began to feel better, and when he walked onto the labor unit he felt an overwhelming sense of relief.

When he reached the nurses' desk, his patient's nurse was just walking out of the patient's labor room. When she asked why he was there, Kincheloe honestly admitted that he did not know, only that he felt he was needed and that his place was here. She gave him a strange look and told him that she had just checked the patient and that she was only seven centimeters dilated. At that moment a cry came from the labor room. Anyone who has ever worked in labor and delivery knows that there is a certain tone in a woman's cry when the baby's head is on the perineum, nearing delivery. He rushed to the patient's room just in time to help her deliver a healthy infant. Afterward, when the nurse asked how he had known to come to the hospital after being told that delivery was hours away, he had no answer.

After that day, Kincheloe started paying attention to these feelings. He's learned to trust them. Having experienced these intuitive feelings hundreds of times, he routinely acts on them. Usually by the time he gets a call from labor and delivery, he is already getting dressed or in his car on the way to the hospital. He often answers the phone by saying, "I know. I am on my way," knowing that it is labor and delivery calling him to come in. This is now such a common occurrence among the labor and delivery staff that they tell the new nurses, "If you want Dr. Kincheloe, just think it and he will show up."

Recently he had the old feeing, called in, and talked to a new nurse who was taking care of a patient of his who was in active labor. He asked her how things were going and she reported that the patient was resting comfortably with an epidural and that she had a reassuring fetal heart rate pattern. He again asked her if she was sure that nothing was happening that required his attention. Exasperated, she said, "I told you I just checked her and everything is fine." In the background Kincheloe heard another nurse say, "Ask him if he is having chest pains." Confused, the new nurse asked him. He replied yes. He heard the new nurse relay his response to the older nurse, who said, "If Dr. Kincheloe's having chest pains you had better go check the patient again."

"Just a minute," the new nurse said to Kincheloe, and she put down the phone and went to check the patient. Then he heard the sound of quick footsteps returning. She rapidly related that the baby was nearing delivery, and that he needed to hurry.

Dr. Kincheloe's experiences show how physical sensations can function as an early-warning system alerting us that something important is about to happen. Dr. Kincheloe may seem unique, but it's more likely that a lot of physicians and other health-care workers share his views and simply aren't talking.

Physicians, Scientists, and Professors: What They Believe

In his fascinating book, *The Witch in the Waiting Room,* Robert S. Bobrow, M.D., clinical associate professor in the Department of Family

Medicine at Stony Brook University, described how he discovered that many of his patients, nurses, and colleagues privately believe in powers of the mind that are not officially recognized in medicine. They keep their beliefs to themselves because of the stigma these views would evoke if they were made public.

Bobrow cited a 1980 survey published in the *American Journal of Psychiatry* that asked psychiatry professors, residents-in-training, other medical faculty, and medical-school deans the question "Should psychic studies be included in psychiatric education?" More than half said yes. The authors of the survey concluded, "Our results indicate a high incidence of conviction among deans of medical schools and psychiatric educators that many psychic phenomena may be a reality, psychic powers are present in most or all of us, nonmedical factors play an important part in the healing process, and, above all, studies of psychic phenomena should be included in psychiatric education . . ."[14]

Many skeptics have done their best to deny and obfuscate these trends. One often hears from skeptics that only a tiny percentage of practicing physicians and medical educators believe in the beyond-the-body, One-Mind happenings that we are examining in this book. These skeptics imply that physicians who believe these things are out of step with the scientific tradition and are trying to take medicine back to the Dark Ages. But as the above survey shows, belief in these matters is held not by a few renegades but is extensive in both clinical and academic medicine.

Another national survey in 2004 examined the beliefs of 1,100 U. S. physicians in various specialties. The surveyors found that 74 percent believe that so-called miracles occurred in the past, and 73 percent believe they can occur today. (I suspect that for most physicians *miracle* does not mean a violation, suspension, or breach of natural law, but an event that is not well understood. Most physicians would likely agree with St. Augustine that so-called miracles do not contradict nature, but they contradict what we know about nature. This is my view as well.) Fifty-nine percent of the physicians said they pray for their patients as individuals, and 51 percent said they pray for them as a group.[15] In a review of these trends, author Stephan A. Schwartz concluded, "There is a growing understanding that ineffable considerations, most subsumed under the concept of nonlocal mind, hold considerable sway in the thinking of both the general population and the medical community."[16]

Scientists in general hold similar beliefs. A 1973 survey of readers of the British journal *New Scientist* asked them to state their feelings about extrasensory perception, or ESP. (*New Scientist* defines its readers as being mainstream working scientists, or as science oriented.) Of the 1,500 respondents, 67 percent considered ESP to be an established fact or at least a strong probability. Eighty-eight percent considered psychic research to be a legitimate area for scientific inquiry.[17]

In another survey of more than 1,100 college professors in the United States, 55 percent of natural scientists, 66 percent of social scientists (psychologists excluded), and 77 percent of academics in the arts, humanities, and education reported believing that ESP is either an established fact or a likely possibility.[18]

Therefore the contention that belief in the beyond-the-body phenomena we are exploring is rare among veteran physicians, scientists, and academics may be dismissed as nonsense. This notion is perpetrated by skeptics who in general are woefully informed about the depth of research in this field and oppose it for ideological reasons.[19]

Telesomatic events are more than quirky, oddball happenings. They indicate communication channels between distant individuals, one of whom is often in need. They are reminders that beyond our apparent separateness there are nonphysical filaments that connect us in ways that are not limited by space, time, or material barriers. The fact that these linkages are catalyzed by emotional bonds suggests a more empathic, kinder side of existence than we have recently supposed.

CHAPTER 17

ABSOLUTELY CONVINCED

Contrary to the lamentations of skeptics, evidence favoring the One Mind is enormous and has been replicated by experimentalists in laboratories around the world.[1] As an example of a prominent scientist who has been intimately involved with these matters, I want to focus on the physicist Russell Targ.[2]

Targ's research pointing to an unbounded, nonlocal feature of consciousness is exemplary. Looking back on his career of four decades in consciousness research at Stanford Research Institute (SRI) and elsewhere, he does not equivocate. In a speech he delivered in Paris in 2010 entitled "Why I Am Absolutely Convinced of the Reality of Psychic Abilities, and Why You Should Be, Too," he said,

> The . . . data which track my career at SRI have convinced me, without a doubt, that our awareness is nonlocal, our consciousness is limitless, psi is real, and its accuracy and reliability are independent of distance and time. I believe that who we are is a reflection of our extraordinary nonlocal (and probably eternal) consciousness.[3]

Many events and experimental findings have led to Targ's view of consciousness. In 1974, he and his colleague at SRI, physicist Harold Puthoff, worked with Pat Price, a retired police commissioner of Burbank, California, in nine remote viewing experiments. In these tests,

Price was asked to describe the location of Puthoff, who had traveled to a remote site. From a pool of 60 possible locations, Price had seven first-place matches. The odds against a chance explanation of these results were 3 in 10,000. The Price and Hammid (see below) experiments were published in March 1976 in the *Proceedings of the IEEE* (Institute of Electrical and Electronics Engineers).

The CIA Comes Calling

In 1975, the CIA asked Targ and his team to find an inexperienced individual to participate in similar tests. Targ chose a good friend of his, photographer Hella Hammid. In nine double-blind trials of remote outdoor locations, she obtained five first-place matches and four second-place matches. The odds against chance were 1 in 500,000.

Why was the CIA interested? In 1972, Targ and Puthoff had founded the SRI remote viewing program, working with Pat Price and painter Ingo Swann. They successfully looked into and described a National Security Agency (NSA) secret cryptographic site in Virginia. Price named the site and read code words from the files, confirmed by both the NSA and CIA.

The CIA was interested in whether remote viewing could be used for spying. Their attention was riveted when Price described, and drew to scale, a Soviet Siberian weapons factory at Semipalitinsk, with a huge eight-wheeled gantry crane and a concealed 60-foot steel sphere under construction. Two years later these drawings were confirmed by satellite photography.

In 1974, Price identified and named the kidnapper of Patricia Hearst, from hundreds of photos in the mug book of the police department of Berkeley, California, two days after the kidnapping. Then he located and led police to the kidnap car 50 miles to the north.

Ingo Swann, in 1974, described a failed Chinese atomic bomb test for the CIA, using geographic coordinates. Swann drew the scene with colored pencils, including a line of trucks and a pyrotechnic display of the failed test. *All this was done three days prior to the actual test.*

In 1974, Targ and his SRI team received a NASA contract to develop a program to teach people ESP. Targ developed a four-choice ESP teaching machine that provided feedback and reinforcement to the user. The teaching machine was successful; people learned to recognize a "unique psychic feeling" that was accompanied by significant learning and success in the ESP task. This device, called ESP Trainer, is available as a free application for the iPhone.

The U. S. Army asked Targ and Puthoff to choose six Army Intelligence officers from a group of 30, who were then to be taught remote viewing as part of program they'd set up at Fort Meade, Maryland. They worked with the six officers in 36 trials. They obtained 18 first-place matches, in which four of the remote viewers achieved results with odds against chance of 3 in 1,000. The odds against chance for the overall group results were 3 in 10,000.

Working with psychologist Keith Harary, Targ organized an experiment to forecast silver commodity futures. They carried out nine trials in which they would predict the change in the silver market five days in advance. The predictions were successful nine out of nine trials, earning the team $120,000. An attempt to replicate their success the following year was not successful, possibly because, Targ says, they got greedy and tried to accelerate the trial rate, eliminating timely feedback to the viewer from the previous trial. Several attempts by other experimenters were successful, however.[4]

In 1996, working with Jane Katra, two mathematicians, and a so-called redundancy coding protocol, Targ and his team obtained 11 hits out of 12 trials for predicting silver futures.

In 1978, remote viewer Joe McMoneagle located a downed Soviet Tu-22 Backfire bomber with code books on board in an African jungle, when satellites were unable to do so. The success of this attempt was confirmed later by President Jimmy Carter.[5]

Two years later, McMoneagle described in detail the unique, secret construction of a 500-foot Soviet *Typhoon*-class submarine being built in a concrete-block building, a quarter-mile from the sea, six months before its launch.

The SRI remote-viewing program continued for 23 years, from 1972 to 1995, with $25 million funding from the CIA, DIA, NASA, Navy, Air Force, and Army Intelligence. As Targ stated, the scientific findings from this program were published in *Nature, Proceedings of the IEEE,* and journals sponsored by the American Institute of Physics, with replications conducted at Princeton, Edinburgh, and Utrecht universities.[6]

Summing up, Targ said, "I know, based on experimental data from psi research in my laboratory at SRI, that a viewer can focus attention at a specific location anywhere on the planet (or off of it) and often describe what is there. The SRI experiments showed that the viewer is not bound by present time. In contemporary physics, we call this ability to focus attention on distant points in space-time 'nonlocal awareness.' Data from the past twenty-five years have shown that a remote viewer can answer any question about events anywhere in the past, present, or future, and be correct more than two-thirds of the time. For an experienced viewer, the rate of correct answers can be much higher."[7]

How does it all work? How are people and things connected at a distance through space and time? Targ invokes models and metaphors we've already examined. One potential explanation, he suggests, is quantum entanglement.[8] Originally believed to exist only in the sub-atomic domain, entanglement is now known to also exist in living systems.[9] Another possibility involves physicist David Bohm's concept of the implicate order. The essential features of the implicate order are that the whole universe is in some way enfolded in everything, and that each thing is enfolded in the whole.[10] A related metaphor Targ finds useful is the hologram. "Like a hologram," wrote Targ, "each region of space-time contains information about every other point in space-time. This information is readily available to our awareness. In the holographic universe . . . there is a unity of consciousness—a 'greater collective mind'—with no boundaries of space or time."[11]

An Apple That Fell Close to the Tree

The Targ clan includes Elisabeth Targ (1961–2002), Russell's brilliant daughter, who was one of the most gifted consciousness researchers I have ever known. During the 1990s, our mutual interests brought us together at various conferences. Elisabeth was an academic superstar—not surprising, perhaps, considering her father and the fact that her mother's brother was Bobby Fischer, the famous world chess champion. From a young age Elisabeth collaborated with

Russell, both as a subject in his studies and as a co-experimenter. As a psychiatrist at California Pacific Medical Center in San Francisco, she conducted research in the role of spirituality, prayer, and intentionality in healing. She was a beautiful, compassionate, luminous individual who was adored by both her patients and colleagues. Elisabeth was also a healer, and her insights into the nature of the healing process were profound. Her career was cut short by her untimely death in 2002 at age 40.

Russell Targ's book *Limitless Mind*, written in the months following Elisabeth's death, is dedicated to her.

CHAPTER 18

DOWNED PLANES
AND SUNKEN SHIPS

R emote viewing is the purported ability of a person to acquire information about a target that is hidden from physical perception, usually at some distance. Physicists Russell Targ and Harold Puthoff introduced this term in 1974, based on experiments they conducted at SRI International, formerly known as Stanford Research Institute.[1]

Seeing Better than Spy Satellites

An example involving national security occurred during President Carter's administration, in which a Russian Tu-22 bomber crashed in a dense African jungle in Zaire. When spy satellites failed to locate the plane, the Air Force and CIA found it by adding remote viewing to their usual methods. Recounting the incident years later, Carter said, "She [the remote viewer] went into a trance, and while she was in a trance she gave some latitude and longitude figures. We focused our satellite cameras on that point and the plane was there." Carter's description, which he recalled years later, is a simplified account. Two remote viewers were actually involved, and several sessions were needed to match up their drawings with high-resolution photographic and map imagery. However, the end result was that they indeed located the downed Russian plane through remote-viewing input when conventional methods failed, and it was recovered for intelligence analysis.

When an actual photo of the crash site was made, it showed the tail of the aircraft jutting out of a brown, turbulent river. One of the remote viewer's sketches matched this photo in amazing detail.[2]

The One Mind renders the size of a group irrelevant. If one individual possesses information, in principle it is available to anyone, by virtue of the connectedness and integration of all minds as one. This does not mean the information in question will necessarily manifest in the minds of all 7 billion earthlings. Whether it does so depends on many factors, such as one's openness and the relevance of the information to an individual's needs, wishes, and intentions. Let's look further.

Operation Deep Quest

One of the most creative individuals I know is Stephan A. Schwartz, with whom I have the pleasure of working at *Explore: The Journal of Science and Healing,* where he is a columnist. Stephan is also a senior fellow at the Center for Brain, Mind, and Healing of the Samueli Institute, and a research associate of the Cognitive Sciences Laboratory of the Laboratories for Fundamental Research. He is the editor of the daily Web publication schwartzreport.net. Stephan is a real-life Indiana Jones. His research and adventures have taken him to the farthest corners of the planet. Schwartz's passion is exploring how consciousness operates in the world. He is perhaps best known for his role in developing remote viewing, which he has used for almost 20 years to locate and reconstruct archaeological sites around the world, many of which have eluded discovery for centuries. These include expeditions to Grand Bahama Bank to find the location of the brig *Leander*; to Jamaica with the Institute for Nautical Archaeology to survey St. Anne's Bay and locate the site of Columbus's sunken caravel from his fourth and last voyage; and to Alexandria, Egypt, which resulted in the first modern mapping of the Eastern Harbor of Alexandria and the discovery of numerous shipwrecks. The Egyptian venture also resulted in the discovery of Mark Antony's palace in Alexandria, the Ptolemaic Palace Complex of Cleopatra, and the remains of the Lighthouse of Pharos, one of the seven wonders of the ancient world.

Schwartz was fascinated by the early work in remote viewing. How could ordinary individuals know things remotely in space and time? How could they have premonitions of future events or describe remote sites they had never seen or heard of?

Most people who encounter this field for the first time imagine that some sort of signal must pass between the perceiver and the distant site, like the electromagnetic signals involved in radio and television transmissions. But when Schwartz reviewed the scientific experiments that were on the books, he found no evidence for the passage of any kind of electromagnetic signal. For one thing, distance was not a factor in these events; if an electromagnetic signal were involved, one would expect it to get weaker with increasing distance, meaning that the strength and accuracy of remote viewing should diminish with increasing distance between the remote viewer and the site or event he or she was attempting to access. The data showed that this was not the case: distance didn't matter. Moreover, remote viewing could not be blocked, even when the viewer was placed in mine shafts, caves, or Faraday cages, which are metal boxes that block most types of electromagnetic signals. All told, it appeared that nothing physical was transmitted or received in remote viewing.

There was one possible exception: extremely low-frequency, or ELF, electromagnetic waves. These are very long waveforms, on the order of miles, as opposed to the short, high-frequency waves seen in radio or television transmission. ELF waves have strong penetrating power and can pass through physical barriers. Deep sea water provides one of the few sure-fire shields against their passage.

Could the transmission of ELF waves explain remote viewing? One way of answering the question was to conduct a remote-viewing experiment with the viewer deep under the ocean's surface. If the experiment succeeded, this would be strong evidence that ELF waves were not involved in the process, since they would be blocked by seawater beyond a certain depth.

Schwartz had previously served at the highest echelons of the U. S. Navy, and he knew the movers and shakers in the naval hierarchy. In the summer of 1977, he gained access for three days to a small research submersible, the *Taurus,* which would be undergoing sea trials near Santa Catalina Island off the coast of Southern California.

By this time, Navy researchers had discovered the depth to which ELF waves penetrate seawater. So, if remote viewers in the sub could successfully describe persons, places, or events on the surface while below the penetrating level of ELF and higher-frequency electromagnetic waves, then the mechanism for remote viewing could not involve the transmission of electromagnetic signals. "And I thought," Schwartz says, "as long as I'm doing that, I'll also see if it is possible for remote viewers to locate a previously unknown wreck on the sea floor."[3]

The experiment became known as Deep Quest. Stanford Research Institute physicists Russell Targ and Hal Puthoff took part, as well as nuclear physicist Edwin May.

Schwartz gave nautical charts of the area to two remote viewers—New York City artist Ingo Swann and California photographer Hella Hammid. At the time, Swann and Hammid were regarded by many as the two most successful psychics in the United States. Schwartz asked them to mark the charts with the location of the unknown wreck and describe what would be found at the location. The two remote viewers sent back their charts marked with the locations of several sunken wrecks, many of which were verified as correct by the Bureau of Marine Sites of the U. S. Coast and Geodetic Survey. There was one site, however, marked by both Swann and Hammid, for which the Bureau had no record. Not only did both the remote viewers independently indicate this same site on their nautical charts, but they also described it in the same way—a sailing ship that had a small steam engine on the deck. They indicated that the ship's steam engine had caught fire around 90 years before, causing the ship to sink. The searchers would find the aft helm of the ship lying with the wheel down and the shaft coming out of it, they said, with a steam winch nearby. They drew pictures of these things. In addition, Hammid indicated that they would find a block of granite at the site, measuring about 5 feet by 6 feet by 7 feet.

Knowing that skeptics would try to debunk the experiment, Schwartz had invited senior scientist Anne Kahle, a renowned space expert and head of the Earth Applications Satellite Research Group of the Jet Propulsion Laboratory, to come along and witness everything, start to finish, and to hold and control all the records of the experiment. "I wanted to be certain," Schwartz said, "that we had a clear, unimpeachable chronology of when they [the remote viewers] made the predictions, what the predictions were, and what was discovered on the site." The goal was to close all the loopholes and rule out alternative explanations, so that if the experiment succeeded, the likeliest explanation would be the operation of a remote kind of knowing on the part of Swann and Hammid.

On the first day of the experiment, Schwartz assigned Swann and Hammid, the two remote viewers, to the submersible and asked them to describe where physicists Puthoff and Targ were hiding in the Palo Alto area, far up the California coast. One of the remote viewers indicated they were hiding in a huge tree and that they were climbing the tree. That's exactly what the physicists were doing at the time.

Then the submersible descended to a level below the ELF threshold for penetrating seawater. By this time, Puthoff and Targ had changed their location. One of the remote viewers identified the new location as "they're hiding in a shopping mall. There are big glass windows and there are people all around. There's red tile on the floor. There's this big turning wheel." The perception was again correct; all these features were in Puthoff and Targ's immediate surroundings. These hits seemed to rule out the possibility that any kind of electromagnetic signal was being exchanged between the surface targets and the remote viewers in the submarine.

The next day a surface ship dropped a radio homing device at the point where the remote viewers said the sunken ship would be, in order to guide the sub to the precise site. This was in an area where the submersible's crew had already been diving for weeks, well before Schwartz and his team arrived in the area. The crew was not enthusiastic, saying they'd already been all over the area and found nothing remotely like what Swann and Hammid were describing. Then the sub's radio device started pinging, and there it was, just as the remote viewers had described—the big block of stone, the steam winch, the aft helm with the wheel down and the shaft pointing up. "I think everybody," Schwartz said, "including me, and certainly the . . . submarine crew, and the guys at the Institute for Marine and Coastal Studies [of the University of Southern California], everyone was kind of stunned by this."

Schwartz, having compulsively filmed everything, made a movie of the event, called *Psychic Sea Hunt*.[4]

Could fraud have been involved? It isn't likely that Schwartz could have known where the wreck was located, when it was not even on the government's nautical charts. Could Schwartz and his team have "salted" the site, depositing the sunken ship parts and relics ahead of time, then saying "look here"? There is no evidence for this possibility and a lot of evidence against it. This would have been a huge undertaking that would have attracted a lot of attention. Moreover, when the submersible *Taurus* arrived at the site, the wreck was not discernible as such, being nothing more than a vague shadow on the ocean floor. Seaweed gradually grows over and around sunken objects on the ocean's floor. The fact that the seaweed lattice on the sunken ship's parts was intact was unimpeachable evidence that they had lain undisturbed for years and had neither been deposited there recently nor tampered with.

In his description of Operation Deep Quest in his book *Opening to the Infinite*,[5] Schwartz related how he was attacked at a dinner party by a skeptic following the discovery, who said, "How do you know they didn't find those things somewhere and just dump them overboard, then go back and mark your chart?" "It is the seaweed," Schwartz said, "that [brought] him to a sputtering silence."

Several other Deep Quest experts defended the discovery against skeptical charges. Don Walsh, then dean of the Institute for Marine and Coastal Studies of the University of California, who had made the deepest dive in a submersible, said in a TV documentary, "We know submersibles. We know deep ocean engineering. They [Schwartz and the remote viewing team] would have had to beat us across the board. I'm just saying that this didn't happen by chance."[6]

Neither could Schwartz's team have obtained the location in advance, for the plain fact that it was not known. Thomas Cooke, marine sites expert for the Bureau of Land Management, the government agency that keeps track of marine wrecks, said, "Based on intensive study of the sites in Southern California waters, I must conclude that the area selected by Schwartz's psychics was previously unknown and could not have been found by going through old papers, books at the library, or that sort of thing. . . . There are 1653 known wrecks along the Southern California Coast; [the one they found is not] one of them."[7]

Could the discovery have been a lucky hit, just "one of those things" that sometimes happens against great odds? "The target area equaled a rectangle 80 x 108 meters," said Schwartz. "It was located in a search area that was 3900 square kilometers. That meant if the search area was overlain with a grid made up of rectangles the same size as the target area, there would be 451,389 equal-sized rectangles in the grid. . . . What is the chance of locating the one correct grid box out of 451,389 similar boxes? It turns out to be very improbable to do this by chance."[8]

Schwartz and his team had apparently closed all the loopholes, just as they had set out to do. To this day, however, dissenters still insist that chicanery is the best explanation for this astonishing experiment. Schwartz no longer wastes time with them. He believes that if they are not convinced by Deep Quest that distant knowing is real, it is unlikely that they would be convinced by any evidence.

Anyone wishing to explore Deep Quest further can do so with the wealth of information available on Schwartz's website: http://www .stephanaschwartz.com.

Deep Quest was one of 12 archeological projects that relied successfully on remote viewers to locate lost or hidden sites. In his book *The Secret Vaults of Time,*[9] Schwartz discussed how archeologists for 100 years have used psychic methods to aid their discoveries. In his book *The Alexandria Project,* he discussed one of his projects in detail, his exploration of Alexandria harbor in Egypt.

"What we've learned," Schwartz wrote, "is that it's as easy to see something far . . . as something . . . near. Distance doesn't make any difference. It is as easy to see something that happens tomorrow as it is to see something that happens today."

Deep Quest involved two minds—Hammid's and Swann's—which, ostensibly working independently, came up with the location of the needle in the haystack at precisely the same place. Were they in fact working separately, or were they a duo in the One Mind? It's difficult to say. In any case, their success illustrates the hallmark of nonlocal knowing: distance and time are irrelevant.

CHAPTER 19

THE MISSING HARP
AND THE LIBRARY ANGEL

Elizabeth Lloyd Mayer was one of the most courageous psycho-analysts in confronting uncanny experiences I have ever known.[1] Many therapists consider such reports pathology; she considered them to be part of human experience and tried to understand them. An internationally acclaimed clinician-scholar who taught at the University of California at Berkeley, "Lisby," as she was known to her friends, was the author of scores of professional articles and books, including the posthumous *Extraordinary Knowing: Science, Skepticism, and the Inexplicable Powers of the Human Mind.*

Shortly before her untimely death in 2005, she invited me to her home in Oakland, California, to discuss some of the "inexplicable powers" she was exploring. Our paths had crossed earlier at Princeton University, at conferences conducted by the Princeton Engineering Anomalies Research (PEAR) project. Our interests in remote healing overlapped, and she wanted to discuss the research that had been done in this area. This was not a trivial pursuit; she was a member of the research faculty of the Institute for Health and Healing at California Pacific Medical Center in San Francisco. Word had leaked about the book she was writing; it was receiving notice long before it came off the press—an author's dream. Eyes were on her; her view of consciousness, expressed in her "coincidence theory," was named by *The New York Times Magazine* as one of the "most exciting" new ideas of 2003.

Lisby was also a talented musician with a lifelong interest in traditional folk and classical music. The first time I met her, she explained how her interest in "extraordinary knowing" had been triggered indirectly by music. A rare family possession—an antique harp—was stolen following a Christmas concert at a theater, where her 11-year-old daughter, Meg, was playing it. Lisby tried to recover it by going through the police, instrument dealers around the country, the American Harp Society newsletters, even a CBS TV news story. Nothing worked.

Eventually a close friend told her, "If you really want that harp back, you should be willing to try anything. Try calling a dowser." The only thing Mayer knew about dowsers was that they attempt to locate underground water with forked sticks. But really good dowsers, her friend said, can find not just water but also lost objects.

Mayer took her friend's dare and called Harold McCoy,[2] the president of the American Society of Dowsers, in Fayetteville, Arkansas, nearly 1,600 miles away. Could he help locate the lost harp? It may have been the most important call she ever made.

"Give me a second," McCoy said. "I'll tell you if it's still in Oakland." After pausing, he continued, "Well, it's still there. Send me a street map of Oakland and I'll locate that harp for you." Skeptical, but having nothing to lose, she overnighted a city map to McCoy. He called back two days later. "Well, I got that harp located," he said. "It's in the second house on the right on D------- Street, just off L--------- Avenue."

Mayer had never heard of either street, but she drove there, wrote down the address, then phoned the police and gave them the tip. They declined to get involved, however, saying that information from a dowser did not justify a search warrant. They were closing the case. They were sure that this valuable, highly marketable musical instrument was sold by now and was gone forever. The implicit message to Mayer was "Get over it."

The police underestimated Lisby. She didn't back off. She posted flyers about a lost harp in a two-block area around the house and waited. Three days later, a man called to say he'd seen a flyer, and that his next-door neighbor had recently obtained a harp like the one that was missing and had shown it to him. He offered to get the harp and return it. Two weeks later, after a complex web of phone calls, the harp was delivered to Mayer at 10 P.M. in the rear parking lot of an all-night Safeway.

As she pulled into her driveway a half hour later with the harp in the back of her station wagon, Mayer, an expert on the workings of the psyche, thought to herself, *This changes everything.*[3]

Harold McCoy, the dowser who located Mayer's precious harp, died in July 2010. He was a humble but savvy man who radiated confidence and intelligence—not surprising, because he was a retired military intelligence officer with 24 years of service to his country. McCoy founded the Ozark Research Institute in 1992, shortly after locating Mayer's harp. The ORI is dedicated to conducting research into the "power of thought." This involves, among other things, remote healing, which has long been of interest to me.[4]

These mutual concerns resulted in an invitation to speak at ORI in 2002 and to meet McCoy, who, in addition to being a dowser, was also a healer. I was impressed with his modesty and no-nonsense, down-to-earth approach. McCoy regarded his abilities as nothing special. He believed they are widespread and can be cultivated through proper training.

The episode of the missing harp is usually interpreted as an example of clairvoyance or "clear knowing"—the acquisition of information from the world unexplainable by sensory means. I suggest a One-Mind interpretation. The information about its location was a part of the universal or One Mind, of which all individual minds partake. Harold McCoy knew how to dip into this pool of information, bypassing the constraints that customarily limit our lives.

The Library Angel

The role of *need* in influencing the information that flows to us from the One Mind is suggested by the *library angel,* a term playfully coined by novelist Arthur Koestler. After reading through a score of reports in which a book, magazine, article, or quotation suddenly presents itself at a moment of need, Koestler said that "one is tempted to think of library angels in charge of providing cross-references."[5]

An example was reported to Koestler in 1972 by Dame Rebecca West, who was researching a specific episode that took place during the Nuremberg war crimes trials:

> I looked up the trials in the library and was horrified to find they are published in a form almost useless to the researcher. They are abstracts, and are catalogued under arbitrary headings. After hours of search I went along the line of shelves to an assistant librarian and said: "I can't find it, there's no clue, it may be in any of these volumes." I put my hand on one volume and took it out and carelessly looked at it, and it was not only the right volume, but I had opened it at the right page.[6]

Another researcher reports his experience in the British Library while researching clowns and tricksters. He came upon a book about synchronicity, opened it at random, and read about the above account involving Dame Rebecca West. Describing what happened next, he said:

> I put the book down and gazed over the reading desk at the person sitting in front of me. He was one of those characters that seem to dwell permanently in libraries, a large dusty sedentary bespectacled man, reading *A Train of Powder* by Rebecca West. The very book that collects her Nuremburg trials writings. Of all the hundreds upon thousands of volumes in the British library, of all the hundreds of seats in this reading room, how could it be that I happened to have sat in front of this person, with this particular book in his hands.[7]

British author Colin Wilson reports that when he was writing his book *The Occult,* he was searching for a piece of information when a book actually fell off the shelf and fell open to the right page.[8]

In his book *Notes From a Small Island,*[9] author Bill Bryson told of his encounter with the library angel. After pitching a story to a travel magazine on the topic of extraordinary coincidences, he realized that although he had plenty of information about scientific studies of probability and coincidence, he didn't have nearly enough examples of remarkable coincidences themselves. After writing a letter to the magazine saying he wouldn't be able to deliver on his commitment, Bryson left the letter on top of his typewriter to post the next day and drove to his job at *The Times of London*. On the door of an elevator, he saw a notice from the literary editor about the annual sale of review copies of books sent to *The Times*. Bryson described what happened when he went to the sale: "The place was full of mingling people. I stepped into the melee and what should be the very first book my eyes fell on but a paperback about coincidences. How's that for a remarkable true coincidence? But here's the uncanny thing. I opened it up and found that the very first coincidence it discussed concerned a man named Bryson."

Geoff Olson, the Vancouver-based writer and graphic artist, wrote, "The library angel and related phenomenon suggest something like a Google-search aspect to existence."[10] Unlike a Google search, however, this one appears to operate in reverse. The One Mind seems to be searching *us*, downloading information according to our needs, sometimes bursting into awareness as the library angel.

I have a Word of the Day screensaver, in which successive groups of words crawl across the computer screen and stop, at which point one word is selected and the definition is displayed. While searching for information about Koestler's idea of the library angel in his book *Janus*, I glanced up at my computer screen to see that the word "Janus" had been selected.

Coincidence? Perhaps. But science fiction writer Emma Bull may be closer to the truth: "Coincidence is the word we use when we can't see the levers and pulleys."[11] Or the One Mind.

I find Koestler's "library angel" a comforting metaphor. The idea that angels are attracted to books and libraries seems right. If we pay attention, perhaps we'll also detect evidence for a "computer angel" or a "digital angel," as the information once stored only on printed pages in libraries is becoming increasingly available online.

I regard these "angels" as emissaries of the One Mind, ambassadors who come calling when we least expect them, reminders of our connectedness within a unitary, universal web of intelligence.

CHAPTER 20

HEALING AND THE ONE MIND

D r. Jeanne Achterberg was a psychophysiologist and a pioneer of the integrative health-care movement. One of the earliest researchers in the use of imagery and visualization in healing, she was an authority in the psychological and spiritual dimensions of cancer. Her interest in healing led to a research opportunity in Hawaii, at the North Hawaii Community Hospital in Waimea on the Big Island. She was invited to direct a research effort funded by Earl Bakken, who invented the implantable cardiac pacemaker and founded Medtronic, the world's largest manufacturer of medical devices. Dr. Bakken has long had an interest in healing, specifically the techniques of Native Hawaiian healers. Like traditional healers in every culture, their methods often involved remote healing intentions, or healing at a distance. Are these claims valid? Can they be proved? Achterberg was determined to find answers.

She did not launch her research project right away. Instead, she set about meeting native healers and explaining her interests. The healers took her into their confidence and shared their methods. After two years, Achterberg was ready to begin.

She and her colleagues recruited 11 healers. These healers were not casually interested in healing; they had each pursued their tradition for an average of 23 years. Each healer was asked to select a person with whom they had successfully worked in the past, with whom they felt an empathic, compassionate, bonded connection, to be the recipient of their healing efforts. The healers described their healing efforts in a variety of ways—as prayer, sending energy, good intentions, or simply thinking and wishing for the subjects the highest good. Achterberg called these efforts distant intentionality (DI).

During the research, each subject was isolated from the healer while an fMRI brain scan was done. The healers sent DI messages to the subjects at two-minute random intervals, so the subjects could not have anticipated when the DI was being sent. Significant differences between the experimental (send) and control (no-send) conditions were found in 10 of the 11 subjects. During the send periods, specific areas within the subjects' brains "lit up" on the fMRI scan, indicating increased metabolic activity. This did not occur during the no-send periods. The areas of the brain that were activated during the send periods included the anterior and middle cingulate areas, precuneus, and frontal areas. There was less than approximately 1 chance in 10,000 that these results could be explained by chance (in the language of science, $p = 0.000127$).[1]

This study suggests that compassionate healing intentions can exert measurable physical effects on the recipient at a distance and that an empathic connection between the healer and the recipient is a vital part of the process.

Achterberg's study should have been front-page news in every major newspaper in the Western world when published in 2005, but it was ignored. The primary reason is that it ran counter to the neuromythology of the day, which insists that minds are completely separate, individual, and confined to the brain. Yet Achterberg's was only one among many studies that have yielded similar findings over the past four decades.

Healing and the One Mind

Entry into the One Mind can also transform one into a healer.

Since 1983, the remarkable John Graham has led the Giraffe Heroes Project, a nonprofit organization that honors people who stick their necks out for the common good. His organization has helped thousands of people around the world reach their potential through living a life dedicated to charitable work.

A natural adventurer, John shipped out on a freighter when he was 16. He took part in the first direct ascent of Mt. McKinley's North Wall at 20, a climb so precarious it has never been repeated. At 22 he hitchhiked around the world as a stringer for the *Boston Globe*. He was arrested as a spy and might have been shot. He graduated from Harvard with a degree in geology and obtained a graduate degree from Stanford in engineering. He spent 15 years in the United States Foreign Service and was caught up in the revolution in Libya that brought a young army lieutenant named Mu'ammar Qadhaafi to power. As an intelligence expert, he spent nearly two years in Vietnam in the war's final phase. He was later involved in strategic nuclear planning at the highest echelons. He was part of America's mission at the United Nations that promoted human rights during the late 1970s. Along the way he survived numerous close calls, including near drowning, an avalanche, being shot at by snipers, and almost perishing in a burning, sinking passenger ship in the North Pacific.

The fact that he seemed indestructible made him wonder if he was being spared to make some significant contribution in life. But in spite of his beyond-belief adventures, his life seemed increasingly empty and meaningless. On a lark, in his 30s he joined a meditation group. This proved to be his most significant adventure in a life packed with adventures. During meditation he began having out-of-body experiences. He sensed he was floating, weightless, with his consciousness in a corner of the ceiling, looking down at his own body sitting in a chair. He found he could control the floating with his mind, up and down, left and right. He moved through the wall of the house into the night, and back inside again. In his book, *Sit Down Young Stranger: One Man's Search for Meaning*, he described his One-Mind experience:

> [I] experienced a totality in which all souls melded, each being part of the whole, not as a petal is part of a flower, but as a wave is part of the ocean. And that "ocean" was God, the ultimate context for our lives, and the intelligent, organizing force for everything. God was not the separate,

anthropomorphic Almighty of my Catholic youth, on whose whims I was punished or rewarded, condemned or absolved. I—and everyone else—was part of God, part of the totality. Our connectedness at this level was a core aspect of creation and—if we choose to acknowledge it—a strong basis for compassion and co-existence in our earthly lives.

These insights didn't come in through my brain, as if I'd read a brilliant new book. I directly experienced these understandings without filtering them through my mind. I saw what I saw, learned what I learned, by being in the middle of it.

These out-of-body trips . . . were the most extraordinary experiences in my life. They were . . . meeting God face-to-face.[2]

During one session Graham described what sounds like a near-death experience. As he began to float outside his body, a pair of bright lights appeared. Although dazzlingly bright, they did not cause him to squint. They came up to him, then went forward a short distance and stopped. He began to follow them, and they went steadily forward. They led him to what appeared to be a bright tunnel that soon opened up into "what was not so much a place, as an extraordinarily peaceful state of being." He was now surrounded by a diaphanous white light, "as if walking in a damp meadow, watching ground fog burn off in the morning sun." Graham felt the presence of other beings, floating as he was floating, communicating greetings to him without words. The overall feeling was one of peace and joy.

Graham wondered whether these experiences were real or not. He acknowledged they might be hallucinations, dreams, or madness, and that he might be insane. But after reading several books on the history of these experiences, he concluded, "If I was crazy, then it was a remarkable coincidence that so many other people had been crazy in just the same way over four thousand years."[3] Still, he wanted a sign that the experiences were valid and that he had not gone off the deep end.

Through his meditative experiences, he had increasingly come to believe that the reason he came into this life, and the reason he had not been killed during the many close calls of his wild adventures, was to serve and to heal. Thus the sign he sought came through healing—not of himself, but of another.

In the late summer of 1975, he and his wife were visiting a friend's farm outside Charlottesville, Virginia. Several kids were frolicking on a hay wagon pulled by an old farm tractor, while the adults drank lemonade and watched from the porch of the farmhouse. Suddenly a four-year-old boy, the son of another couple, started shrieking and running to the house. The other kids reported that he had just placed his hand on the tractor's hot exhaust pipe. His hand was seriously burned. The owner of the farm, a doctor, raced to get his first-aid kit. The boy's mother held him, but the frightened little boy continued screaming in pain. Graham described what happened next:

> What I remember next is a feeling of immense personal calm and confidence. I quietly asked the mother to give the boy to me. When she did, I put the boy's burned hand between my hands, closed my eyes, and imagined myself back in the place of light. The boy stopped screaming. When I took my hands away, his hand showed no signs of being burned.
>
> It was impossible for me to pretend it hadn't happened. The mother took her son back, looking in my eyes without speaking. The others stared.
>
> . . . That boy was the only person I ever healed with my hands. . . . Given the skepticism of my science-trained mind, I needed that physical proof and the universe—God—provided it. Since the incident at the farm, I've never doubted that what I learned and did through [meditation] was real.[4]

Graham's experiences, which he vividly described in his enchanting book, are a classic example of someone catapulted into a realization of the One Mind through the time-honored practice of stilling and deepening the mind through meditation, contemplation, prayer, and the like.

Graham found that dimension of consciousness where "all souls meld," that "ocean" that is "God," that collective composite where diversity is made whole through oneness.

Graham returned from his near-death experience with the power to heal. Joyce W. Hawkes is another example. A biophysicist and cell biologist by training, with a doctorate from Penn State University, Hawkes is a fellow in the American Association for the Advancement of Science and the author of three dozen scientific publications. Following a near-death experience, she discovered she had the power to heal. Hawkes maintains a private practice in the Seattle area[5] and is the author of *Cell-Level Healing: The Bridge from Soul to Cell.*

Jane Katra, who holds a doctorate in health education and who taught at the University of Oregon, is another post-NDE healer. During a trip to Southeast Asia in 1974, she was struck with a horrific headache and a near-death-like dream, during which she was told that she would become a healer. To her dismay, the prophecy proved true. Back home, the new Jane did not go over well with university colleagues. She honored her calling, however, and began to use her healing gift. Katra's story is told in the book *Miracles of Mind: Exploring Nonlocal Consciousness and Spiritual Healing,* co-authored with physicist and psi researcher Russell Targ.

Perhaps it is appropriate that healing abilities sometimes result from an encounter with the One Mind, the All. "Healing," after all, is derived from Latin words meaning "whole."

CHAPTER 21

THE DARK SIDE

One-Mind experiences are often described as an epiphany or ecstasy, but there is a dark side to the One Mind that would be irresponsible to ignore.

Ian Stevenson, the late psychiatrist and consciousness researcher of the University of Virginia, described a patient of his whose clinical course suggested that mental symptoms may have been linked to the malevolent thoughts and intentions of others. The man was a 45-year-old professor who had become so depressed he required hospitalization. A major reason for his depression was disagreements with colleagues in his department. Although he seemed to be improving, one day he became much worse and complained of deteriorating feelings. "It turned out later," Stevenson wrote, "that this worsening of his condition coincided temporally with meetings of his opponents in his department who were, in effect, plotting to oust him from his position."[1] Stevenson implied that his patient was picking up on the negative wishes and thoughts of others. Are malevolent linkages inherent in the One Mind?

As reported by twins researcher Guy Lyon Playfair, the distant sharing of thoughts and feelings occasionally takes on macabre dimensions, as with the lives of male twins born in the spring of 1962 to Rozalia Cosma in Brasov, Romania.[2] She named them Romulus and Remus, after the legendary infant twins who were left to die but were rescued and suckled by a she-wolf. Romulus became the founder and first king of Rome. As is often the case with twins, the Romanian twins experienced the sharing of sensations at a distance.[3] While growing up, when one had an accident, the other often felt the pain.

As adults, Remus settled in Cluj in central Romania, and Romulus made a home in the Black Sea port of Constanta, 500 miles away. They continued to share emotions and physical feelings. The correspondence could be uncanny. They became ill with jaundice at the same time. When Romulus broke his leg during an excursion into the Carpathian Mountains, Remus fell down some stairs in Cluj and broke his leg.

In the fall of 1987, Remus began courting Monika Szekely. A week later, Romulus started courting a girl also named Monika. The following spring Remus married his Monika, and in 1989 they moved to a new apartment. The marriage soon fell on hard times and they quarreled daily. At 10 P.M. on May 16, 1993, Remus came home drunk and his wife screamed to him that she planned on taking a lover. He shoved her against a wall, whereupon she grabbed a knife. Remus wrested it from her and stabbed her 12 times. At midnight he went to the police station and turned himself in. At 11 P.M. that same evening, Romulus had a talk with Monika, his girlfriend. Although their relationship up to this point had been smooth, Romulus was inexplicably seized with rage and strangled her.

He told police in Constanta, "I don't know why I committed this monstrous crime. When I began to strangle my girlfriend, I felt impelled by an invisible force. I couldn't, or perhaps didn't want to, resist it."

Investigators discovered that Remus had committed his crime only a few minutes before that of his twin.

Nuremberg

Coherent, synchronized thinking and shared emotions of the One-Mind type can be valuable and even indispensable, as with members of an orchestra, a sports team, or a military unit. Yet there are other situations in which they can be disastrous.

The Nuremberg Rallies, held annually from 1933 to 1938 following Adolph Hitler's rise to power in Germany, were designed to promote coherent thought and solidarity between the German people and the Nazi Party. Eventually more than half a million people from the Nazi Party, the German army, and the populace attended these gatherings. They employed unique sensory experiences, as was the case during the 1937 rally in which Albert Speer's Cathedral of Light, made of 152 searchlights, cast vertical beams into the sky to symbolize the walls of a great building.[4] Deputy Führer Rudolf Hess, in his opening speech at the 1934 rally, whipped the crowd into frenzy. It was a classic example of how destructive ideas can cohere and spread in a large group and eventually throughout an entire nation.

The Madness of Crowds

The danger of coherent, unified thought is the subject of one of the most remarkable books of the 19th century, *Extraordinary Popular Delusions and the Madness of Crowds,* by Scottish journalist Charles Mackay, published in 1841 and still in print. In a passage that may sound uncomfortably contemporary, Mackay wrote, "In reading the history of nations, we find that, like individuals, they have their whims and their peculiarities; their seasons of excitement and recklessness, when they care not what they do. We find that whole communities suddenly fix their minds upon one subject, and go mad in its pursuit; that millions of people become simultaneously impressed with one delusion, and run after it, till their attention is caught by some new folly more captivating than the first. We see one nation suddenly seized, from its highest to its lowest members, with a fierce desire of military glory; another as suddenly becoming crazed upon a religious scruple; and neither of them recovering its senses until it has shed rivers of blood and sowed a harvest of groans and tears, to be reaped by its posterity."[5] Mackay's book is a withering indictment of customs and ideas that in retrospect appear absurd or lunatic, but which were embraced by the wider culture. Some of his examples are the passion for dueling, mesmerism, the Crusades, get-rich-quick schemes, the obsession with religious relics, and witch mania.

This theme has recently been taken up by Pulitzer Prize–winning geographer Jared Diamond in his insightful book *Collapse: How Societies Choose to Fail or Succeed.* Diamond shows how entire societies throughout history have blinded themselves through pathologically coherent ways of thinking, willfully following their certainties to their own destruction.

Groupthink

Another pathological form of coherent, One-Mind thought is groupthink, a type of discourse practiced by a cohesive in-group whose members try to minimize conflict and reach consensus without critically evaluating ideas. Groupthink extinguishes individual creativity and minimizes responsibility for what is decided. As individual doubts and alternatives are set aside, hasty, irrational decisions are made for fear of upsetting the group's consensus and balance. Irving L. Janis, a research psychologist at Yale University, analyzed examples in which groupthink likely played a role in American foreign-policy disasters, such as the failure to anticipate the Japanese attack on Pearl Harbor in 1941; the Bay of Pigs fiasco in 1961, when President John F. Kennedy's administration tried to overthrow Fidel Castro's government in Cuba; and the escalation of the Vietnam War during President Lyndon B. Johnson's administration.[6]

Groupthink in government is still with us. It has become epidemic in the U. S. Senate. Like a diseased heart with an unvarying rhythm, the Senate has become nearly paralyzed by ideology and partisan rigidity, making compromise, which is an indispensable element of democratic governance, almost impossible. Will Rogers's sarcasm still applies: "We could certainly slow the aging process down if it had to work its way through Congress."[7]

PART THREE

ACCESSING THE ONE MIND

CHAPTER 22

THE COSMIC SOUP

Something there is that doesn't love a wall,
That wants it down.

—Robert Frost[1]

One-Mind experiences come to some individuals, especially children, almost effortlessly.

When developmental psychologist Joseph Chilton Pearce was in his early 30s, teaching humanities in a college, he was engrossed in theology and the psychology of Carl Jung. Pearce described himself as "obsessed" by the nature of the God-human relationship, and his reading on the subject was extensive. One morning as he was preparing for an early class, his five-year-old son came into his room, sat down on the edge of the bed, and launched into a 20-minute discourse of the nature of God and man. "He spoke in perfect, publishable sentences," Pearce wrote, "without pause or haste, and in a flat monotone. He used complex theological terminology and told me, it seemed, everything there was to know. As I listened, astonished, the hair rose on my neck; I felt goose bumps, and, finally, tears streamed down my face. I was in the midst of the uncanny, the inexplicable. My son's ride to kindergarten arrived, horn blowing, and he got up and left. I was unnerved and arrived late to my class. What I had heard was awesome but too vast and far beyond any concept I had had to that point. The gap was so great I could remember almost no details and little of the broad panorama he had presented. My son had no recollection of the event."[2]

Pearce's interpretation was that his son, a bright, normal child, had responded to a field of information that he could not have acquired. So where is the information coming from? Physicist Russell Targ has suggested we live in a kind of "soup" that is the source of all the information and knowledge we know about the world. Pearce calls this the "cosmic soup," a highly organized domain from which we selectively extract information.

People use different language for the soup, as we've noted. Whether called the cosmic soup, the One Mind, the Source, a field of consciousness, or the collective unconscious, the Source is intelligence itself. Although the ingredients of the cosmic soup are the same for everyone, says Pearce, our sampling of the soup is different. Each individual ladles out what she needs. This causes our "soup perceptions" to be selectively perceived, resulting in individuality, diversity, and uniqueness.[3]

Pearce's young son seemed to have entered the One Mind and dipped from the cosmic soup the information that fulfilled a need at the time. The information arrived spontaneously, unasked, as a grace. Many people have learned not to depend on spontaneity, however, but have relied on time-tested methods to enter the One Mind at will.

During meditation, reverie, or prayer, time is often perceived as an eternal present in which the divisions of past, present, and future meld into an all-encompassing now. In this state, it is not just the separations in time that disappear, but also separations between people and things. This state is a doorway to the One Mind. This experience is amazingly common. It often erupts spontaneously, as when we are transfixed by a plangent musical note, the smell of fresh-baked bread, or a coyote's midnight howl.

For millennia humans have experimented with ways of being in the present and uniting time's divisions. Practitioners of various spiritual traditions have always known this territory; so, too, have poets and artists. Many outstanding scientists have also entered this time-less dimension and have left accounts of their experience. An example is Nobel laureate in genetics Barbara McClintock, who said, "Basically, everything is one. There is no way in which you draw a line between things. What we [normally] do is make these subdivisions, but they're not real. I think maybe poets . . . have some understanding of this."[4]

Creativity

The ability to dip into the cosmic soup has profound implications for creativity. Creativity is usually considered to be a process of discovering, making, or inventing something that did not exist before. But when time's divisions are overcome, there is no "before"; everything that can be known in some sense already exists and needs only to be realized, not brought freshly into existence.

The One Mind, Pearce's cosmic soup, or the Source that is not carved into subdivisions by space and time contains all the ingredients anyone could ever need to formulate a new idea, compose a sonata, or paint or sculpt a work of art. Tapping into the Source is the goal of every creative individual. As John Briggs wrote in his admirable book about creativity, *Fire in the Crucible*, "For the creative genius, the ancient perception that it is possible to invoke an identity between the universal and particular, between the personal and the vast impersonal, the part and the whole, is pervasive. It burgeons at all levels of the creative process and dominates creative vision. [In their] many moods and meanings, [creative individuals are involved in] a search for wholeness and a personal/universal identity . . ."[5] They are seeking the One Mind.

Systems theorist Ervin Laszlo, who is also a classical pianist and author of 75 books and more than 400 articles, knows a thing or two about creativity. He says, "We raise the possibility that the minds of exceptionally creative people would be in spontaneous, direct, though not necessarily conscious, interaction with other minds within the creative process itself."[6] He says, "To call individuals such as . . . a Mozart, a Michelangelo, or a Shakespeare . . . 'gifted' and their achievements 'works of genius' is not to explain their abilities, but only to label them." He proposes that some acts of creativity, particularly when sudden and unexpected, "are not due to a spontaneous and largely unexplained stroke of genius, but to the elaboration of an idea or a pattern in two or more minds in interaction . . ."[7]

Those who treasure uniqueness, individuality, and ownership are not thrilled with this scenario. The problem is this: if all minds are in contact and share information, who gets credit? If ideas cannot be assigned to specific persons, what, then, of originality and individual achievement? Who gets honored? Should the Nobel and Pulitzer prizes be put on hold? Should those already awarded be returned?

Others aren't troubled by this connection with the whole. Novelist Joseph Conrad wrote about "the latent feeling of fellowship with all creation—and to the subtle but invincible conviction of solidarity that knits together the loneliness of innumerable hearts."[8] Painter Piet Mondrian spoke of the artist's communion with something greater than the individual self, noting, "Art has shown that universal expression can only be created by a real equation of the universal and the individual."[9] Artist Paul Klee saw that the whole speaks through the part. The artist's "position is humble," he said. "He is merely a channel."[10] Psychologist Erich Fromm sanctioned Klee's view. Fromm said that the creator " has to give up holding on to himself as a thing and begin to experience himself only in the process of creative response; paradoxically enough, if he can experience himself in the process, he loses himself. He transcends the boundaries of his own person, and at the very moment when he feels 'I am' he also feels 'I am you,' I am one with the whole world."[11]

The creative individual often feels united not only with others, but also with his medium. As virtuoso pianist Lorin Hollander described, "By the time I was three, I was spending every waking moment at the keyboard, standing, placing my hands on the keyboard and pushing notes. And I would choose very carefully what tones I would choose because I knew that when I would play a note I would become that note."[12] Hollander also described merging with the great composers. I once asked his opinion of the movie *Amadeus,* which depicts the life of Mozart. He replied, "That wasn't Mozart." How did he know, I asked. "Because when I play Mozart, I *become* Mozart," he responded.[13]

The urge to become absorbed into something greater—God, Goddess, Allah, Brahman, Universe, the One, or Something with a capital S—underlies the drive of many highly creative individuals. Yet the creative individual can never see the entire whole, because he or she is mortal. But this is not fatal to one's vision; any part of the whole will do, because the truth is everywhere: Blake's "World in a Grain of Sand." For the artist, the whole must be refined, condensed, concentrated, focused. As Leonardo da Vinci said, "This is the real miracle, that all shapes, all colors, all images of every part of the universe are concentrated in a single point."[14] It is in fact a good thing for the writer and artist to try to communicate only a part of the truth, for few can stand truth unvarnished. Thus the Sufi saying "No one hath seen God and lived," and Emily Dickinson's dictum, "Tell all the Truth but tell it slant . . ."[15] Or as one wag said, "Consciousness is nonlocal, but sshh! Don't tell anyone!"

What about logic? What is its role in tapping the rich resources of the One Mind?

In 1945 the mathematician Jacques Hadamard conducted a survey of the most eminent mathematicians in America in an attempt to find out about their working methods. In response to his questionnaire, Einstein replied, "The words or the language, as they are written or spoken, do not seem to play any role in my mechanism of thought. . . . Conventional words or other signs have to be sought for laboriously only in a secondary stage . . ."[16]

Einstein's case was not unusual. Eugene Wigner, who was awarded the Nobel Prize in Physics in 1963, agreed with Einstein's views, saying, "The discovery of the laws of nature requires first and foremost intuition, conceiving of a picture and a great many subconscious processes. The . . . confirmation of these laws is another matter . . . logic comes after intuition.[17] Hadamard concluded from his survey that virtually all the mathematicians born or resident in America avoided not only the use of "mental words" but even "the mental use of algebraic or other precise signs. . . . The mental pictures [they employ] are most frequently visual."[18]

Cartoonists often portray scientists with thought balloons of mathematical equations floating above their heads, but mathematics, like language, is often on the sidelines during their creative processes. One of the most remarkable examples is that of the English physicist Michael Faraday, whom Einstein placed on a par with Newton. Faraday's thinking was almost entirely visual and was strikingly devoid of mathematics. Indeed, he had neither a mathematical gift nor any formal training in mathematics, and he was ignorant of all but the simplest elements of arithmetic. Yet Faraday could "see" the stresses surrounding magnets and electric currents as curves in space, and he coined the phrase *lines of force* to describe them. In his mind they were as real as if constituted of solid matter. Faraday saw the entire universe made up of these lines of force, and he saw light as electromagnetic radiation. But he was not merely a dreamer; his visualizations led to practical results, including the invention of the dynamo and the electric motor.[19]

Novelist-philosopher Arthur Koestler performed a historical survey of a large number of creative geniuses in science. In his monumental work *The Act of Creation,* he came to the conclusion that "their virtual unanimous emphasis on spontaneous intuitions, unconscious guidance, and sudden leaps of imagination which they are at a loss to explain, suggests that the role of strictly rational thought-processes in scientific discovery has been vastly over-estimated . . ."[20]

Milton's *Paradise Lost* was dictated by a muse, he said, as an "unpremeditated song."[21] But, as mentioned, throughout history people have cultivated nonordinary states of awareness such as meditation to attract the muses and nudge the creative process along. As Ervin Laszlo notes, "In some (relatively rare) cases these 'inspired states' are artificially induced—by drugs, music, self-hypnosis, or other means."[22] A notable example is Samuel Taylor Coleridge, who is said to have composed his epic poem *Kubla Khan* in an opium-induced sleep. Often, however, when people use drugs to boost creativity, although they may *feel* they have connected with "all there is," there is little or nothing to show for it when the drug wears off. Most "art" produced under the influence of mind-altering chemicals winds up in the wastebasket—which, Einstein once said, is the scientist's most important tool.

Urgency and "Hours by the Window"

A sense of profound urgency may catapult one into a state of heightened creativity. As Samuel Johnson wrote, "Depend upon it, sir, when a man knows he is to be hanged in a fortnight, it concentrates his mind wonderfully."[23] The French mathematician Evariste Galois, for instance, at the age of 20, wrote down his brilliant contributions to higher algebra in the three days before a duel in which he correctly believed he would be killed.

Arthur Koestler described a similar experiential crisis. Imprisoned for several months in Seville in 1937 during the Spanish Civil War, Koestler was threatened with execution as a suspected spy, and he did not know if he would be alive from one day to the next. He had experiences in solitary confinement he believed were close to the feelings described by mystics, a sense of oneness with all things. He called these experiences the "hours by the window." He wrote,

> The "hours by the window" had filled me with a direct certainty that a higher order of reality existed, and that it alone invested existence with meaning . . . that time, space and causality, that the isolation, separateness and spatio-temporal limitations of the self were merely optical illusions. . . . It was a text written in invisible ink; and though one could not read it, the knowledge that it existed was sufficient to alter the texture of one's existence, and make one's actions conform to the text.[24]

Preparation: "God Will Not Drive Flies away from a Tailless Cow"

Although creative breakthroughs and sudden revelations suggest that our entry into the One Mind is completely spontaneous, it helps if we open the door. This is most often done through preparation—perfecting one's craft or technique. It is not just chance that favors the prepared mind; the One Mind also favors preparation.

This has been emphasized especially in the spiritual world. As Huston Smith, the historian of religions, says, from the Christian tradition, "Everything is a gift, but nothing is free."[25] Vivekananda, from the Hindu tradition in the 19th century, agreed: "The wind of God's grace is always blowing, but you must raise your sail."[26] The message from Islam is the same. As the 9th-century Sufi mystic Bayazid Bastami said paradoxically, "The knowledge of God cannot be attained by seeking, but only those who seek it find it."[27] Lame Deer, a Sioux medicine man, expressed the sentiment that nothing is free in the spiritual domain: "But as I see it now, as I feel it, I want my visions to come out of my own juices, by my own effort—the hard, ancient way. I mistrust visions come by in the easy way. . . . The real insight, the greatest ecstasy does not come from this."[28] In the same spirit, the Fulani, a tribe in West Africa, extend this insight into a general principle: "God will not drive flies away from a tailless cow."

CHAPTER 23

THE SELF

*Why are you unhappy? Because nearly everything that you say
and do is for your "self"—and there isn't one.*

—CHINESE PROVERB

Some individuals resist the concept of the One Mind out of a desire to retain and protect their individuality, their sense of self. Take away the self, they say, and they'll be nobody. But how vital is the self?

For decades, the idea of the self has been the victim of a demolition derby within science. A steady torrent of books from materialistic scientists has made war on the sense of self—one's basic, essential sense of being, the object of one's introspection, what makes me "me" and not someone else. These days, scientists seem to vie with one another as to who can do the most thorough job of trashing the whole idea.

Buddhism could have saved them the trouble. The Buddha taught 2,500 years ago that there is no substantial self to make war *on*. The self, he said, is an illusion, a confection of emotions, fears, desires, wants, and strivings—what he called attachments—that get in the way of personal growth and transformation. So the Buddha would agree that the scientists who are trying to dismiss the self are on the right track because the self is a nonentity.

We must not confuse "self" and "I." As psychologist Arthur J. Deikman of the University of California at San Francisco states, "The core of subjectivity—the 'I'—is identical to awareness. This 'I' should be differentiated from the various aspects of the physical person and its mental contents which form the 'self.' Most discussions of consciousness confuse the 'I' and the 'self.' . . . The identity of awareness and the 'I' means that we know awareness by being it . . ." [1]

Even Einstein, arguably the most famous scientist in history, affirmed the value of breaking the bondage of the personal ego. In language that sounds decidedly Eastern, he said, "The true value of a human being is determined primarily by the measure and the sense in which he has attained liberation from the self." [2] The current situation is ironic. Modern science, the declared enemy of a spiritual realm, is in this instance in the service of spirituality. The message of science—that the self is an illusion—is consistent with many great wisdom traditions and may be a step along one's spiritual path. In this way, science has become an unwitting ally of spirituality.

But science's effort to eradicate the self is hypocritical as well. Anyone who has spent much time in academic science quickly realizes that scientists can have some of the most hypertrophied egos and bloated senses of self on the planet. They appear eager to dismiss the self in others but not in themselves.

The War on the Self

Typical of scientists who have attempted to bag the self was Nobelist Francis Crick, co-discoverer of the structure of DNA. In his book *The Astonishing Hypothesis,* he wrote, "[A] person's mental activities are entirely due to the behavior of nerve cells, glial cells, and the atoms, ions, and molecules that make up and influence them.[3] . . . 'You', your joys and your sorrows, your memories and your ambitions, your sense of personal identity and free will, are in fact no more than the behavior of a vast assembly of nerve cells and their associated molecules. As Lewis Carroll's Alice might have phrased it, 'You're nothing but a pack of neurons.'"[4]

But things don't stop there. Many materialistic scientists want to destroy not just the self, but the concept of consciousness as well. And here the game gets really bizarre, for in eradicating consciousness, materialistic scientists and philosophers make war on their own minds. For instance, philosopher and cognitive scientist Daniel Dennett of Tufts University has said that we're all zombies; no one is conscious.[5] He includes himself in this generalization and seems rather proud of it. Patients have been declared mentally incompetent for lesser reasons.

How has science become hostile to the self? Some of the steps in this direction include the following.

In the 1960s, Nobel laureate and neurophysiologist Roger Sperry and Michael Gazzaniga severed the corpus callosum in several individuals with intractable epilepsy. They discovered that the left hemisphere of the brain could be aware of things the right hemisphere was unaware of, and vice versa. This suggested that the idea of a single, undivided sense of self is an illusion.

In the 1970s, neurophysiologist Benjamin Libet discovered that certain bodily movements were registered in the brain 350 milliseconds before an individual was consciously aware of deciding to move that particular body part. This challenged the assumption of free will. It is as if the brain is telling the conscious self what to do, not vice versa. Other researchers such as Todd E. Feinberg and Antonio Damasio continued to investigate how a sense of self is developed and sustained.

Philosopher Julian Baggini of University College London, in his book *The Ego Trick,* explained that there is nothing fundamentally new about these developments. Dismissal of an essential self has been going on since the early days of science. In 1664, the English anatomist Thomas Willis published *Cerebri Anatome,* a detailed attempt to bypass the need for a self by explaining how different parts of the brain produced the different "animal spirits" that were believed to power thought and action. The British empiricists John Locke and David Hume maintained that what makes you the same person over time is the continuity of your mental life, not some independent self. Since these views were introduced, the knowledge of the brain has become more fine-grained and clinically useful, of course, "but philosophically speaking [modern science] really only filled in the details and hammered the last nails into the coffins of antiquated views of soul and self," wrote Baggini. The consensus now is that there is no place in the brain where "it all comes together," no spot in the brain where the sense of self or the soul resides. Soul and self are simply illusory constructs. These senses merely pop up—the in-word is *emerge*—when various parts of the brain are smoothly working together.

"Pretty much the same view was held by the Buddha, who believed that there is no abiding self, just a series of connected conscious experiences," Baggini wrote. "Neuroscience confirms this and explains the mechanics of this centreless self . . ."[6]

Again, however, echoes of contradiction can be heard, as when scientists experience a sense of *self*-accomplishment and *self*-satisfaction in having banished the notion of self. Or when cognitive scientists such as Dennett use their own consciousness to disprove the existence of consciousness. Mark Vernon, the British author, journalist, and physicist, captured the absurdity of this position, saying, "So when you next read that consciousness is an epiphenomenon, or that humans are zombies, or that we are disposable phenotypes, have a laugh. That human individuals can even pass such judgment upon themselves is itself proof that we are far more."[7]

Spirituality and the Self

The fact that science has successfully demolished the self is no big deal. Spiritual traditions have been doing this for millennia, as mentioned. And not just Buddhism. The same message is implied in the New Testament, when John the Baptist says, referring to Christ, "He must increase, but I must decrease."[8]

The problem is that science doesn't know when to stop. Instead of a single murder—the self—science has attempted a double homicide, killing off consciousness as well. The Self becomes collateral damage.

Carl Jung believed there is no way to avoid what he called the "psychic" side of life. As he put it, "It is almost an absurd prejudice to suppose that existence can only be physical. As a matter of fact, the only form of existence of which we have immediate knowledge is psychic. We might as well say, on the contrary, that physical existence is a mere inference, since we know of matter only in so far as we perceive psychic images mediated by the senses."[9]

Science's great failure is that, having stripped life of self and soul, it has nothing to put in their place except the notion that humans should simply man up, live nobly, and go bravely into the night. Many people perceive this as inadequate advice. This is a reason why the evidence pointing to the One Mind is important. The inclusive One Mind, of which all individual minds partake, nourishes the human drive toward transcendence.

Abundant evidence shows that people derive more than emotional satisfaction from spiritual beliefs that include a sense of being connected with "something greater." As social epidemiologist Jeff Levin and many other researchers have shown, hundreds of studies indicate that, on average, individuals who follow some sort of spiritual path in their life live significantly longer than people who do not, and they have a lower incidence of major diseases such as heart disease and cancer.[10] These tangible benefits of a spiritual direction are seldom acknowledged in the recent efforts to portray spiritual beliefs as nothing more than harmful fantasies by authors such as Richard Dawkins (*The God Delusion*), the late Christopher Hitchens (*God Is Not Great: How Religion Poisons Everything* and *The Portable Atheist*), Daniel Dennett (*Breaking the Spell: Religion as a Natural Phenomenon*), and Sam Harris (*The End of Faith*).

Nothing, No-Thing, Nobody

In her award-winning book, *Epiphanies*, psychotherapist Ann Jauregui said, "Ever since Freud . . . we have focused like a laser on the uniqueness of the individual. In the realm of psychotherapy there has been an extraordinary emphasis on the value of developing a 'sense of self' or an 'autonomous ego'; 'separation-individuation' is considered essential to growing up. All of this language has to do with the Western notion of a boundaried individual human mind."[11]

Yet there are outstanding examples of individuals who appear to thumb their nose at the idea of an intact self. They regard it as an arbitrary convenience that sometimes gets in the way. When it does so, they temporarily discard it and become in a sense a nonself, a nobody.

A Feeling for the Organism

To [properly] look at an object is to inhabit it.

— MAURICE MERLEAU-PONTY[12]

An example is Nobel laureate and geneticist Barbara McClintock, who worked with genes, chromosomes, and corn plants. She once said that her success resulted from the fact that she had "a feeling for the organism."[13] That's putting it mildly. McClintock would psychologically enter into a problem so deeply that she became the problem. She felt as if she could crawl down the microscope and stand toe to toe with the genes, getting an up-close look at their behavior. She would cease to exist as a person; on emerging from contemplating the issue, she literally could not remember her name. "Things are much more marvelous than the scientific method allows us to conceive," she said.

McClintock had always been a bit weird. Precocious from childhood, she repeatedly broke the mold. She practiced Eastern meditation, explored extrasensory perception, and experimented with mental control of her own blood pressure and temperature. On one occasion Joshua Lederberg, the Nobel laureate and molecular biologist and geneticist, visited her lab. "By God," he exclaimed, "that woman is either crazy or a genius!"

In order to experience "a feeling for the organism," one has to dare to *be* the organism. This means going beyond the boundaries that separate us from one another and from other life forms. It means entering the One Mind.

The German polymath Johann Wolfgang von Goethe knew this. Goethe, the author of *Faust* and many other diverse works, was opposed to the scientific method of the day, which emphasized objectivity, neutrality, and remoteness. He believed the understanding of nature came through participation. To understand a plant, for example, one must enter into the life of the plant. He called his scientific approach "a delicate empiricism which in a most inward way makes itself identical with the object and thereby becomes the actual theory."[14]

Goethe's theme of participatory science was taken up 130 years later by Heinz Kohut, the eminent Austrian-born American psychoanalyst. Kohut believed that conventional scientific methodology was "experience-distant," removed from actual observation. He proposed an "experience-near" approach as an alternative, in which data could be acquired directly from empathy and introspection. Empathy was crucial, he maintained, to prevent scientific pursuits from "becoming increasingly isolated from human life."[15] Eliminating empathy from science, he believed, had resulted in a cold, disinterested, and rational approach that fostered the aims of brutal totalitarian regimes and had led to "some of the most inhuman goals the world has ever known."[16] Summing up, Kohut said that the new ideal in science "can be condensed into a single evocative phrase: we must strive not only for scientific empathy but also for an empathic science"[17]—in other words, a science of love, a love that is made possible only by removing the razor-wire boundaries we employ in establishing the thing-ness of the world.

For those who argue that this would lead to sloppy, woo-woo science, the evidence suggests the opposite, as McClintock's experience and achievements show. As John Briggs shows in his book *Fire in the Crucible,* one can make a long list of great names in science who attribute their magnificent insights to moments in which the sense of self was temporarily abandoned.[18] They forgot who they were and where they were. They went somewhere else—in reverie, dreams, absent-mindedness—and the key insight burst upon them unexpectedly as an epiphany, a revelation, a dissolving of the boundaries between this world and another.

When the Self Disappears: The Journey of Suzanne Segal

But it is not always that simple.

In the words of the Buddha, "Events happen, deeds are done, but there is no individual doer thereof." Although the goal of many spiritual traditions is to transcend the illusory "individual doer," the experience of selflessness is not always pleasant.

One day in 1982, Suzanne Segal, a 27-year-old American woman living in Paris, stepped onto a city bus, and suddenly, without warning, found herself egoless and without any sense of a personal self. As she described the experience, "I lifted my right foot to step up into the bus and collided head-on with an invisible force that entered my awareness like a silently exploding stick of dynamite, blowing the door of my usual consciousness open and off its hinges, splitting me in two. In the gaping space that appeared, what I had previously called 'me' was forcefully pushed out of its usual location inside me into a new location that was approximately a foot behind and to the left of my head. 'I' was now behind my body looking out at the world without using the body's eyes."[19]

When she opened her eyes the next morning, the selfless feeling was still there. Her mind "exploded in worry." Was this psychosis? Schizophrenia? Would it go away? She was terrified and confused, drowning in mental agony. She was no longer certain she was sane. She felt as if her own name did not refer to anyone.[20] She felt as if her ". . . body, mind, speech, thoughts, and emotions were all empty; they had no ownership, no person behind them."[21] For years she saw a series of therapists in an attempt to make sense of what had happened. Her official diagnosis was depersonalization disorder.

Segal was no neophyte. Several years before her "bus stop hit," she had been a sincere spiritual seeker involved in meditation and retreats but had ceased these practices. She eventually turned for help to spiritual teachers within California's Buddhist community. As her story became widely known, she received congratulatory letters from numerous spiritual teachers, both East and West. Their view was that she had spontaneously entered the egoless state that many spiritual seekers struggle to attain. One letter she received from a famous guru in India said, "This is a wonderful experience. It has to stay eternally with you. This is perfect freedom. You have become (moksha) of the realized sages."[22]

Following her break with a sense of self, Segal managed to remain highly functional. She obtained a Ph.D. in psychology. She became well read in the psychological categories of depersonalization, dere-alization, and dissociation. When her autobiography, *Collision with the Infinite,* was published in 1996, she began giving public presentations and leading weekly dialogue groups.

Twelve years after her initial break with the self, Segal entered another phase of her experience. This involved a sense of oneness with all else. She wrote, "In the midst of a particularly eventful week, I was driving north to meet some friends when I suddenly became aware that I was driving through myself. For years there had been no self at all, yet here on this road everything was myself, and I was driving through me to arrive where I already was. In essence, I was going nowhere because I was everywhere already. The infinite emptiness I knew myself to be was now apparent as the infinite substance of everything I saw."[23] Segal had entered a state of nonlocal awareness. It would last for two years.

The earlier symptoms and old fears returned, however, this time more intense than before, and they became psychologically dis-ruptive. By February 1997, at the age of 42, she was in mental and physical decline. She entered the hospital, and her physicians discov-ered a malignant brain tumor. She died two months later. It remains unknown how much her brain tumor contributed to her experiences or whether it played any role at all.

There is a saying in transpersonal psychology: "Before you tran-scend the person, you first have to be one. And before you transcend the ego, you first must have one." The message is that the early, basic stages of psychological maturation cannot be short-circuited or bypassed without risk. Doing otherwise is like attempting to run with-out first learning to walk. There are suggestions that this sort of thing may have plagued Segal. During her final months she uncovered memories of childhood abuse. Yet no one can claim to understand fully the psyche of this endearingly complex, magnificent woman.

Suzanne Segal was a courageous explorer of the inner life. She bared her soul so that others might learn from her experience. Her legacy continues to inspire thousands. Her journey is a sober reminder that "transcending the self" is sometimes not as blissful as often assumed, and that spiritual paths that advocate self-transcendence are not for sissies.[24]

By the way, I've never been comfortable with the suggestions that Segal's negative experience of being nobody was the result of traumas buried in her past. I may be wrong, but there's a whiff of desperation in this reasoning, as well as a hint of blaming the victim. It would be far more honest, I believe, simply to say that the abandonment of the self is no guarantee of emotional delight. It simply is what it is.

This perspective—accepting one's experience on its own terms— is captured in the Taoist allegory of the Vinegar Tasters, which is set during the 6th century B.C.E. Confucius, the Buddha, and Lao Tzu, the founder of Taoism, are standing around a vat of vinegar. They each dip a finger in the vinegar and bring it to their tongue. "It is sour!" says Confucius. "It is bitter!" says the Buddha. "It is real!" says Lao Tzu. The followers of Lao Tzu may have invented this scenario as a promotional gambit. In any case, Lao Tzu's response is usually taken to mean that the unpleasant experiences of life are not to be sanitized, disregarded, or intellectualized but considered as part of the natural flow of life.

The Ordinary *Is* Extraordinary

The intimate connections between individuals via the One Mind are often associated with extraordinary happenings such as distant knowing, knowledge of events before they happen, communication between individuals remotely, and so on. I've known many individuals who become enchanted with these happenings and strive to manifest them in their own life, as if they were of supreme importance.

Yet, it is the ordinary, the plain, and the simple that are emphasized in the great spiritual traditions. Spiritual pyrotechnics are commonly viewed as distractions. An example is St. Teresa of Ávila, who in a letter written in January 1577 said, "I've had raptures again. They're most embarrassing. Several times in public . . . during Matins, for instance. I'm so ashamed, I simply want to hide away somewhere!"[25]

A student of Zen Buddhism reported to his master that during meditation he had experienced visions of Light and True Buddhahood. The master soberly responded, "Keep meditating. It will go away."[26]

In a comparable story, one day it was announced by Zen Master Joshu that the young monk Kyogen had reached an enlightened state. Much impressed by this news, several of his peers went to speak with him. "We have heard that you are enlightened. Is this true?" his fellow students inquired. "It is," Kyogen answered. "Tell us," said a friend, "how do you feel?" "As miserable as ever," replied the enlightened Kyogen.[27]

Individuals on their spiritual path often come to the realization of the preciousness of the moment. Thus Adair Lara, the author, journalist, and teacher, observed, "And some, like me, are just beginning to guess at the powerful religion of ordinary life, a spirituality of freshly mopped floors and stacked dishes and clothes blowing on the line."[28]

Yet even the ordinary can be misleading. If the ordinary is enshrined as a be-all, it can be as tyrannical as the desire for the extraordinary. It is equipoise that counts, a willingness to accept, without judging, whatever comes because one senses an underlying "fittingness" of all things. This is represented in the Zen teaching that "the making of distinctions is the sickness of the mind." And in Jesus's paradoxical identity as both Alpha and Omega, the first and the last. As Meister Eckhart, that troublemaking preacher of 14th-century Germany, said, "Everything praises God. Darkness, privations, defects, evil too praise God and bless God."[29] Paul Tillich, one of the most respected Christian theologians of the 20th century, endorsed this paradox, saying, "In its original sense the Holy denotes equally the divine and the daemonic. . . . Self-affirmation of being without non-being would not even be self-affirmation but a fixed and immovable self-identity. Nothing would be manifest, nothing expressed, nothing revealed. . . . Without the negative God has to overcome in himself and in his creatures, his positive self-affirmation would be a dead letter. There would be no life . . ."[30] Florence Nightingale, the founder of modern secular nursing, was a deeply spiritual woman who understood these intricacies. She said, "Everyone tells us that the existence of evil is incomprehensible, whereas I believe it is much more difficult—it is impossible—to conceive the existence of God (or even of a good man)—without evil. Good and evil are relative terms, and neither is intelligible without the other."[31] Jung agreed. "A whole person," he said, "is one who has both walked with God and wrestled with the devil."[32]

This uncompromising ambiguity is demanding and is one reason the esoteric spiritual paths have never been as popular as the comforting black-and-white certainties of most religions. But for those who penetrate these teachings, there is no going back.

In the same way, it is never a question of the One Mind versus the individual mind, or the collective versus the personal. There is no "versus," but an "and." The opposites go together, defining, illuminating, and invigorating each other. As the great Zen teacher Alan Watts put it, "The great metaphysical principle is this: Every inside has an outside, and every outside has an inside. . . . The entire universe can be understood as pulse/interval, on/off, peak/valley."[33]

My favorite Zen aphorism says, "After ecstasy, the laundry." Just as the divine waltzes with the mundane, the One Mind dances with the individual mind. In a healthy life, one never triumphs over the other.

CHAPTER 24

IS THE ONE MIND GOD?

*What a piece of work is man, how noble in reason, how
infinite in faculties, in form and moving how express and admirable,
in action how like an angel, in apprehension how like a god.*

—WILLIAM SHAKESPEARE, *HAMLET*, ACT **2**, SCENE **2**

*That which shows God in me, fortifies me. That which shows
God out of me, makes me a wart and a wen.*[1]

—RALPH WALDO EMERSON

The idea of the One Mind, of which all individual minds are a part, leads naturally to this question: is the One Mind God?

If the One Mind is the source of all information that is known and knowable, then it is omniscient. Omniscience is a characteristic usually assigned to the Divine. And if the One Mind is nonlocal—not localized to specific points in space, such as brains or bodies, and not confined to specific points in time, such as the present—then it is omnipresent and eternal. Omnipresence and eternality are also characteristics usually attributed to God, the Absolute, the Divine, the All.

The nonlocal One Mind, then, involves the inevitable premise that we share features commonly reserved to God. Is this why Jesus said, "Is it not written in your law, I said, Ye are gods?"[2] and "The kingdom of God is within you"[3]? And why India's ancient Upanishads proclaim *tat tvam asi,* "thou art that?"

The idea of an indwelling divinity does not sit well in Western cultures. Our predominant religions assure us that we are born as unworthy sinners doomed to perdition unless we are redeemed through an act of salvation. To claim natural divinity rather than acknowledging our natural unworthiness is considered blasphemous. People who have laid claim to this realization have often paid with their lives. One example is Meister Eckhart in 14th-century Germany. Eckhart preached to his flock, "If it is true that God became man, it is also true that man became God. . . . Where I am there is God, and where God is there I am. . . . To see God evenly in everything is to be a man . . ."[4] This sort of talk aroused the Inquisition, which fell on Eckhart with a vengeance. This gentle, compassionate man was convicted of heresy and would probably have been burned at the stake had he not died before his trial was completed.

One of most full-throated expressions in modern times of the joining of the divine and the human in a single mind is that of Nobel physicist Erwin Schrödinger. For him, "Consciousness is a singular of which the plural is unknown; . . . there *is* only one thing and that, what seems to be a plurality, is merely a series of different aspects of this one thing, produced by a deception (the Indian MAYA); the same illusion is produced in a gallery of mirrors . . . "[5] For Schrödinger, this singular One Mind *is* God. He did not equivocate. In the One Mind, humans are not "like" God or "similar" to God. They *are* God. Schrödinger realized the theological controversy this evokes, saying:

> In Christian terminology to say: 'Hence I am God Almighty' sounds both blasphemous and lunatic. But please disregard these connotations for the moment. . . . In itself, the insight is not new. The earliest records to my knowledge date back some 2,500 years or more. From the early great Upanishads the recognition ATMAN = BRAHMAN (the personal

self equals the omnipresent, all-comprehending eternal self) was in Indian thought considered, far from being blasphemous, to represent the quintessence of deepest insight into the happenings of the world. The striving of all the scholars of Vedanta was, after having learnt to pronounce with their lips, really to assimilate in their minds this grandest of all thoughts.

Again, the mystics of many centuries, independently, yet in perfect harmony with each other . . . have described, each of them, the unique experience of his or her life in terms that can be condensed in the phrase: DEUS FACTUS SUM (I have become God).

To Western ideology, the thought has remained a stranger, in spite of Schopenhauer and others who stood for it and in spite of those true lovers who, as they look into each other's eyes, become aware that their thought and their joy are *numerically* one, not merely similar or identical . . .

A drop of water in the ocean is one with the entire ocean in terms of chemical composition but not in terms of volume and power. Just so, a human may be identical to the Absolute in some ways but not in others. How far does our oneness with the Divine via the One Mind go?

The melding of the human and the divine is the theme of "the perennial philosophy," popularized in Aldous Huxley's great book of the same name. (Huxley acknowledged that it was Leibniz who coined the phrase *philosophia perennis*.) The perennial philosophy, wrote Huxley, is

. . . the metaphysic that recognizes a divine Reality substantial to the world of things and lives and minds; the psychology that finds in the soul something similar to, or even identical with, divine Reality; the ethic that places man's final end in the knowledge of the immanent and transcendent Ground of all being.[6]

No one has teased apart the connection between mankind and the divine better than philosopher of religion Huston Smith in his books *Forgotten Truth: The Primordial Tradition* and *Beyond the*

Post-Modern Mind. In order to make sense of the God-human identity that Schrödinger and Huxley expressed so forcefully, Smith employs the concept of hierarchy, which is simply a way of ranking things according to some criterion. "Hierarchy is an ugly word," said novelist Arthur Koestler, who nonetheless believed in its importance. "Loaded with ecclesiastical and military associations, [it] conveys to some people a wrong impression of a rigid or authoritarian structure." Even so, hierarchies permeate the natural world, Koestler added, "whether we are considering inanimate systems, living organisms, social organizations, or patterns of behavior."[7] (To minimize the resistance evoked by the concept of a vertical, ladderlike, higher/lower hierarchy, an alternate way of illustrating these relationships is the "nested" hierarchy. A nested hierarchy is illustrated as an arrangement of concentric circles, with the "lowest" member in the innermost center, with the "higher" elements occupying successive circles toward the periphery. The visual switch from a vertical ladder to concentric circles more effectively conveys "relationship with" rather than "power over.")

Smith finds the concept of hierarchy invaluable in answering the question of the human-God relationship. It is largely a matter of *being.* He wrote, "Reality is tiered; being increases as the levels ascend. Ascent is used here figuratively, of course. No literal up, or spatial move whatever, is involved."[8] Smith knows he has entered delicate territory to even bring up the concept of being. "Though it was commonplace to the point of being universal in the past, [being] is . . . most difficult for modern consciousness to grasp. What can it mean to say that X has more being than Y; or in ordinary parlance, that it is more real? . . . To have more being, or be more real, is to possess more of the properties of being per se."[9] Six of these properties, says Smith, are (1) power, (2) duration, (3) locale, (4) unity, (5) importance, and (6) worth.[10]

Unity and oneness involve gradations in these properties of being. A drop of ocean water may be united and one with the entire ocean, but as mentioned, it differs from the ocean in terms of power, locale, and importance. Just so, an individual mind may be nonlocally united with the One Mind, but differ from it, particularly in terms of power. As the Hindu sage Shankara put it in the 8th century:

> Though difference be none, I am of Thee,
> Not Thou, O Lord, of me;
> For of the sea is verily the Wave,
> Not of the Wave the Sea.[11]

Harvard philosopher Arthur O. Lovejoy's acclaimed book *The Great Chain of Being* dealt gracefully with these distinctions. He showed that the continuity and unity within the world are a graded, hierarchical spectrum, what Aristotle called the *scala naturae*. Lovejoy wrote:

> The result was the conception of the plan and structure of the world which, through the Middle Ages and down to the late 18th century, many philosophers, most men of science, and, indeed, most educated men, were to accept without question—the conception of the universe as a "Great Chain of Being," composed of an immense, or . . . infinite . . . number of links ranging in hierarchical order from the meagerest kind of existents . . . through "every possible" grade up to the *ens perfectissimum* . . .[12]

Ignoring the gradations of being can lead to what has been called a "category mistake" or "a category error," in which things of one kind are presented as if they belong to another kind or, alternatively, when a property is ascribed to something that cannot possibly have that property.[13] Oft-used examples of a category mistake are equating the menu with the meal or the map with the territory. An example that masquerades as science is the equating of nonmaterial consciousness with the material brain. An additional instance, to repeat our previous example, is when we say that a single drop of ocean water *is the same thing* as the ocean, without offering any sort of qualification. A similar error occurs when we say that an individual's mind *is the same thing* as the Divine Mind, without attention to the gradations of being, such as those mentioned by Huston Smith.

Integral theorist and author Ken Wilber discusses a similar mistake he calls the *pre/trans fallacy,* or *ptf.* The fallacy occurs when, for example, we equate "higher" with "lower" levels of psychospiritual realization. Wilber believes Freud committed a pre/trans fallacy when he equated the mystical realization of oneness with the Divine with regression to infantile states of oceanic oneness. He suggests that Jung unwittingly made the same mistake, only in the other direction, by failing to distinguish primitive, primordial myth-forms with truly archetypal divine realization. This forced Jung and his followers, wrote Wilber, into "the extremely uncomfortable predicament of having to view the archetypes as both very primitive and very divine." Jungian therapists are compelled, said Wilber, "to alternately worship archetypes and tremble in their presence because their 'archetypes'—being in fact a ptf mixture of real archetype and very primitive myth-forms—wobble between transrational glory and prerational chaos." Although Wilber considers himself a Jungian in many ways, he believes that in this matter "Jung's theories are in dire need of revision."[14]

Wilber believes that divine archetypes constitute a transcendent pull from in front rather than a primitive push from behind. This is where, he wrote, modern psychiatry has lost its way. "I hardly need to mention," he says, "the . . . fallacy [that] orthodox analysts and psychologists usually [make; they] take any truly archetypal material and hold it up as perfect examples of infantile or regressive mythic (or magic) cognition."[15]

So, are the claims of having entered the One Mind, of having experienced a God-connection, to be trusted? How do we know all these claims are not one gigantic category mistake or pre/trans fallacy? Schizophrenia and lunacy are real. But so, too, many scholars say, is the mystical realization of divine union, of merger with the Absolute, of citizenship in the One Mind. Wilber, in his inimitable style, weighed in on these questions in his book *A Brief History of Everything*:

> Are the mystics and sages insane? . . . [They all tell the same] story of awakening one morning and discovering you are one with the All, in a timeless and eternal and infinite fashion.

. . . It's at least plausible. And tell me: is that story, sung by mystics and sages the world over, any crazier than the scientific materialism story, which is that the entire sequence is a tale told by an idiot, full of sound and fury, signifying absolutely nothing? . . . Just which of those two stories actually sounds totally insane?

. . . And I think [the sages] point to the same depth in you, and in me, and in all of us. I think they are plugged into the All. . . . Your identity is indeed the All, and you are no longer *part* of that stream, you *are* that stream, with the All unfolding not around you but in you.[16]

So, to the question of whether the One Mind is God, we can give the answer: "No, but . . ." There are profound differences between these two dimensions, the One Mind of humans and the Absolute, as Huston Smith pointed out. Thus the ancient principle that "The higher contains the lower, but the lower does not contain the higher." Ignoring these differences can lead to ego inflation and hubris. Still, the similarities are real and should not be minimized. We share qualities with the Divine, just as the single drop of ocean water is a scaled-down version of the ocean itself. Ignoring these similarities can reinforce the dismal view that we are wicked, iniquitous, errant creatures from birth. As in most things, balance is the key.

The experience of Schrödinger's *Deus factus sum*—"I have become God"—should come with a warning: *This claim can be dangerous for your health*. The reasons were stated by Schrödinger himself: it "sounds both blasphemous and lunatic."

Mansur al-Hallaj (c. 858–922) was a writer and teacher of Sufism, the esoteric, mystical tradition of Islam. Many Sufi masters believed that mystical insights were not to be shared with the masses, but al-Hallaj proclaimed them. That is where the controversy surrounding him began. He began to make enemies. To make matters worse, he would occasionally fall into trances, which he attributed to being in the presence of God. During one of them, he uttered, "I am the Truth," which was interpreted to mean he claimed to be God, since "the Truth" is one of the ninety-nine names of Allah in Islam. He also once stated, "There is nothing wrapped in my turban but God." He would also point to his cloak and say, "There is nothing in my cloak but God." It was clear that he believed in complete union with the Divine, that God dwelled within him, and that he and God were not similar but had become one and the same. He called God his Only Self. These utterances led to his imprisonment. Before his execution, he asked his fellow Muslims to kill him, saying that what is important for the ecstatic is for the One to reduce him to oneness. He must have known what would happen. After ten years of imprisonment, he was condemned to die. His public execution was an example of the ferocity that can be evoked by claims of God-identity. He was led to the gallows amid taunts about being God and was given 500 lashes. His flagellation was stopped prior to killing him, so he could appreciate what followed. Al-Hallaj was then cut up into pieces. His arms, legs, tongue, and finally his head were sliced off. Even when he was beheaded, he was said to be smiling. The following day his trunk was burned; the next day his ashes were cast to the wind. His head was hung on the prison wall, then was carried throughout the surrounding districts to dissuade troublemakers.[17]

Countless individuals have sensed the affinity of all humans with the One, but without going as far as al-Hallaj. For instance, Mother Teresa was once asked by a brash young reporter, "Are you a saint?" She poked him in the chest with a bony finger and said, "Yes, and so are you."

Meister Eckhart was less hesitant, stating, "The eye by which I see God is the same as the eye by which God sees me. My eye and God's eye are one and the same—one in seeing, one in knowing, and one in loving."[18]

Plotinus also didn't hold back. Almost two millennia ago, he wrote, "No doubt we should not speak of seeing, but instead of seen and seer, speak boldly of a simple unity. For in this seeing we neither distinguish nor are there two. The man . . . is merged with the Supreme . . . one with it."[19]

Al-Hallaj would have agreed.

CHAPTER 25

REMOVING THE STUFFING
FROM THE KEYHOLE

. . . Celestial light
Shine inward, and the mind through all her powers
Irradiate, there plant eyes, all mist from thence
Purge and disperse, that I may see and tell
Of things invisible to mortal sight.

—JOHN MILTON[1]

We are "Peeping Toms at the keyhole of eternity," said novelist Arthur Koestler. "But a least we can try to take the stuffing out of the keyhole, which blocks even our limited view."[2] Thus people throughout history have used an astonishing variety of methods to overcome the brain's filter and increase what Aldous Huxley reffered to as the "measly trickle."

James Merrill, Pulitzer winner and one of the greatest American poets of the 20th century, used a Ouija board for this purpose, assisted by his longtime friend David Jackson. "The board goes along at a smart clip, perhaps 600 words an hour," Merrill reported. By this means Merrill would communicate, he said, with dead friends and spirits "in another world." The messages would be transcribed letter by letter, and then Merrill would edit and rewrite the transcriptions. Asked if he could have written his great poems without the help of the board, he replied, "It would seem not." How did the process work? "The point . . . [is] to be always of two minds," Merrill explained. "You could think of the board as a delaying mechanism. It spaces out, into time and language, what might have come to a saint or a lunatic in one blinding ZAP. Considering the amount of detail and my own limitations, it must have been the most workable method. . . . [It has] made me think twice about the imagination. . . . Victor Hugo said of *his* voices that they were like his own mental powers multiplied by five."[3]

William Butler Yeats used an unusual method for increasing the measly trickle, resulting in some of the most inspired poetry and prose of the 20th century. In *A Vision,* he declared that his recent "poetry has gained in self-possession and power." Yeats stated that he owed this change in his work to "an incredible experience" that took place on October 4, 1917, when his wife, Georgie Hyde-Lees, surprised him by attempting automatic writing. As philosopher Michael Grosso described the scene, "Profound and exciting utterances came forth, and an unknown writer (or writers) said: 'We have come to give you metaphors for poetry.' Thus commenced an extraordinary partnership in creativity that Yeats pursued with his wife for three years. . . [the] script was the product of a joint effort, transcending them both, who were more like secretaries to the psychological entity whom they jointly produced." A total of some 50 copybooks of automatic script were produced, which Yeats mined in producing some of his most majestic works.[4]

An Outsider Artist

Some of the most dramatic examples of the use of altered states of awareness to bypass the brain's filter mechanism are seen in so-called "outsider art," which includes "the work of children, primitives, the incarcerated, the elderly, folk art, *art brut,* psychotic art, and generally all forms of art and image-making produced by the untaught, the culturally deprived, the isolated, and the marginalized."[5]

An outstanding example is Adolf Wölfli (1864–1930), who was an institutionalized paranoid schizophrenic for most of his life. Growing up in poverty, abused both physically and sexually as a child, and orphaned at age ten, Wölfli was given to violent acts and sexual aggression. He spent much of life in solitary confinement in the Waldau Clinic in Bern, Switzerland, a psychiatric hospital.

In 1899, while hospitalized, he spontaneously began to write and draw. Walter Morgenthaler, a doctor at the Waldau Clinic, recognized the uniqueness and quality of Wölfli's drawings and wrote a book about him in 1921, which first brought him to the attention of the art world.

Wölfli's output was huge. As Michael Grosso reported, "From 1908 to 1930 he worked on a massive narrative . . . a mixture of authentic personal history and cosmic fantasy, a carefully unified whole, woven together with prose poetry, illustrations, and musical compositions. This mentally incompetent madman left behind him 45 volumes, 16 notebooks, altogether 25,000 packed pages, along with hundreds of drawings that now hang next to the work of Paul Klee in Switzerland."[6] His accomplishment is even more astonishing, considering his access to only the barest essentials. He would often trade small works with visitors to obtain pencils, paper, and other materials. Morgenthaler wrote:

> Every Monday morning Wölfli is given a new pencil and two large sheets of unprinted newsprint. The pencil is used up in two days; then he has to make do with the stubs he has saved or with whatever he can beg off someone else. He often writes with pieces only five to seven millimetres long and even with the broken-off points of lead, which he handles deftly, holding them between his fingernails. He carefully collects packing paper and any other paper he can get from the guards and patients in his area; otherwise he would run out of paper before the next Sunday night. At Christmas the house gives him a box of coloured pencils, which lasts him two or three weeks at the most.

Woelfli incorporated an idiosyncratic musical notation into his art. This started as a purely decorative effort, but later evolved into real compositions that he would play on a trumpet he made out of paper.

His musical works evoked wide interest. Professional recordings have been produced commercially, and free downloads are available.[7]

The French Surrealist André Breton described Woelfli's work as "one of the three or four most important oeuvres of the twentieth century."[8]

Woelfli said he had no idea how he did it. Somehow, this amazing man, under the most meager conditions, managed to increase the brain's measly trickle to a raging torrent.

Daimons

Some individuals describe what in today's terminology might be called personal assistants or coaches that guide their decisions invisibly from behind the curtains of consciousness, helping them overcome the everyday strictures imposed by the brain filter.

Socrates was guided throughout his life by a daimon, an intelligent inner voice, in matters large and small. "What makes Socrates so extraordinary is that he seems to have perfectly fused his conscious critical intellect with his subliminal daimon," wrote Grosso. "In the vast majority of human beings, the two are almost always thoroughly disjointed and disconnected, often at great emotional and spiritual cost."[9]

The daimon, or inner guide, sometimes has a voice of its own, as in the case of Joan of Arc, the virgin teenager who led France in its struggle against England in the Hundred Years War. Joan was guided by subliminal messages and voices throughout her brief life. These were sometimes associated with lights and visions of the saints. The voices began to speak to her at age 13, telling her to pray and go to church. Eventually they nudged her to save France and provided her with advice on military strategy and tactics. She could summon the voices with prayer. They kept her company during the court proceedings when her accusers charged her with witchcraft. They even predicted the exact time of her death.

An intelligence that is more profound than the rational, individual self appears to await us if we learn to access it. Sometimes it seems to meet us halfway, in the form of guides, daimons, or voices. In other instances, as with Merrill and Yeats, the informants are more impersonal.

This fusion of the individual mind with a greater mind is often experienced as an inspiration that lifts the individual above the immediate concerns of ordinary existence. Integrity of purpose becomes more important than life itself. Thus Socrates asserted that death with martyrdom is not a bad thing. When Joan temporarily recanted her mission, her voices urged her to recant her recantation. Earthly affairs and life itself were important, but they were trumped by higher values, meaning, and purpose, as revealed by the greater intelligence.

I am not suggesting that everyone who hears voices and claims a direct line to higher wisdom has accessed a valid depot of information. Mental illness is real. I am suggesting, however, that claimants such as Merrill and Yeats should be listened to.

Where have the voices gone? Apparently they are still around, should we care to listen. In a survey in the 1980s of 375 college students focusing on auditory hallucinations, 71 percent reported that they had experienced vocal hallucinations in waking life. Thirty percent reported auditory hallucinations as they were drifting off to sleep, and 14 percent reported vocal hallucinations as they were waking up. Almost 40 percent had heard their name called while outdoors. Eleven percent heard their name being called from the back seat of their car, while a similar percentage said they had heard God speak "as a real voice."[10]

The fact that the term *hallucination* is used in questionnaires such as these indicates the engrained skepticism in our culture toward these matters. Creative individuals such as Merrill and Yeats, however, are not concerned with the way in which researchers describe the source of their inspiration. Call it Factor X, for all they care. Is their experience real or imaginary? Does it originate in their unconscious or from another dimension? They do not struggle with such questions. What matters is that the filter has become porous, the reducing valve has been opened wide, and the measly trickle has become a flood.

The One Mind is not an encrypted information bank that is accessible by only a few. Any password will do. An entry method such as voices or Ouija boards may seem jejune or even repellent to some individuals, who may prefer instead the experience of reverie, a sunset, a line from Emily Dickinson, a Rebecca Bluestone tapestry, or the final sizzling chord of The Beatles' "A Day in the Life."

The Curse of Concreteness

There are no formulas that guarantee entry into the domain of the One Mind. Even when props are used, as with Merrill and Yeats, access remains what it has always been—a matter of *being,* not *doing.* One sets an intention, then ushers the conscious mind out of the way. That is why the most spectacular manifestations of the One Mind—revelations, epiphanies, creativity—occur when the discursive, striving, rational mind has been bypassed through reverie, meditation, dreams, or some other nonactivity. Muscular, aggressive, ego-oriented approaches do not work. Selfish entry—trying to access the One Mind in order to *get* something—is akin to burglary. Alarms get triggered and the delivery system shuts down. One approaches the One Mind respectfully, acknowledging a source of wisdom and intelligence greater than one's own. One then waits patiently and is grateful for what is given.

The One Mind thrives on uncertainty, unpredictability, and freedom. It is open to life, possibility, and endless variety. The surest way to doom our fruitful interaction with the One Mind is to concretize the process of entry, giving it a specific, definite form.

This is the curse of our age. When something is shown to be effective, websites and bestsellers erupt overnight that reduce the phenomenon in question to seven easy steps or a one-week plan, often with a money-back guarantee and celebrity endorsements.

Concretization is an attempt to reduce uncertainty, which we abhor. But when we concretize something, we narrow it and close it off to life, and it ceases to unfold in ways that are life affirming. In our attention-deficit culture, we want a sure thing, and we want it now. We are suckers for approaches that squeeze the life from things. When they disappoint, as they invariably do, we move on to the Next Big Thing.

An example of concretization is yoga, which evolved in ancient India as a discipline for obtaining spiritual insight and tranquility. We have narrowed it to a form of exercise that has become wildly popular. An effort is now underway to make it an Olympic sport. In one proposal, each yogi would have three minutes to do seven poses, five of which would be mandatory. They would be graded by a panel of judges on strength, flexibility, timing, and breathing.[11] What would Patanjali think?

Another example of concretization is the attempt of some researchers to study the healing effects of prayer in highly artificial ways that bear little resemblance to how prayer is employed in real life. It is not surprising that these efforts are often unsuccessful.

Where the One Mind is concerned, concretization is a trap. When entryways to the One Mind are formalized, the door closes. But to those who understand the interplay of emptiness and fullness, and the action that is inherent in letting go, the door to the One Mind is always open.

CHAPTER 26

DREAM PATHWAYS

Do you imagine you dream for yourself alone?

—DORIS LESSING, *THE MAKING OF THE
REPRESENTATIVE FOR PLANET 8*[1]

D reams are a universal doorway to the One Mind. In dreaming, our sense that we are an individual self that is confined to the here and now is suspended and replaced by experiences that know no personal, spatial, or temporal bounds. In dreams we are not fettered by contradiction, paradox, or reason. For these reasons, creativity often flourishes during dreams.

The role of dreams in the history of science and medicine has been undervalued, largely because scientists prefer the image of the logical, rational, analytical thinker to that of the dreamer. In general, information acquired in dreams is not something scientists are eager to talk about publicly.

There are, however, delightful exceptions. I was recently invited to address a large group of internal medicine physicians at a conference designed to update them on recent advances in our field. My topic dealt with the nature of consciousness and how it often behaves in ways not recognized in medical textbooks, including precognitive dreams, which I had written about in my book *The Power of Premonitions.*[2] I knew the topic was controversial, and as I began speaking I half expected the audience to leave. Nobody did, however, and during the question-and-answer period some people began to describe their own experiences. One female internist stood and boldly said, "I get numbers in my dreams. I see the results of my patients' lab tests—before I even order the tests." Other physicians disclosed experiences they had never revealed to anyone, and after the lecture still others approached me privately to do the same. This and other events lead me to believe that dreams and "weird knowings," as one of my colleagues calls them, are much more common than we assume.

Exploratory Dives into the Unconscious

The dream experiences of physicians, inventors, mathematicians, and scientists reinforce the image of the One Mind as a repository of information and intelligence that can be put to practical use. This view was sanctioned by Arthur Koestler in his brilliant exploration of creativity, *The Act of Creation*. Koestler called dreams an "essential part of psychic metabolism. . . . Without this daily dip into the ancient sources of mental life, we would probably all become desiccated automata. And without the more spectacular exploratory dives of the creative individual, there would be no science and no art."[3]

A spectacular "exploratory dive" into the unconscious was taken one night by Elias Howe. For years Howe had struggled unsuccessfully to perfect his sewing machine, but he was plagued by problems with the needle. Then one night he dreamed he was captured by savages who dragged him before their king. The king issued an ultimatum: if within 24 hours Howe did not come up with a machine that could sew, he would die by the spear. As time ran out, the menacing savages approached Howe, their spears raised for the kill. Holding up his hands to ward off the inevitable, Howe noticed that each of the spear points had an eye-shaped hole near the tip. He awoke full of excitement, realizing that the hole in the sewing machine needle must go at the tip, not at the middle or the bottom where he had been trying to place it. He raced from bed to his workshop, filed a needle to the proper size, drilled a hole near its tip, and inserted it in the machine.[4] The rest, as they say, is history.

In his monumental book *Our Dreaming Mind,* Robert L. Van de Castle, former director of the University of Virginia Medical School's Sleep and Dream Laboratory, cited several instances in which the minds of scientists frolicked nonlocally during dreamtime, with stunning consequences.[5] He reported that early in the 20th century, researcher Edmond Maillet sent a questionnaire to a group of mathematicians who had worked in their profession for at least ten years. Four of his respondents described "mathematical dreams" in which a solution actually occurred during the dream; eight acknowledged finding the beginnings of a solution or useful idea while dreaming; and another fifteen described how on waking they had achieved complete or partial solutions to questions posed the previous night.[6]

Srinivasa Ramanujan, the 20th-century mathematician, is considered a giant in his field. Certainly Ramanujan enjoyed an advantage over his colleagues: his dreams included an otherworldly mentor. In a 1948 article in *Scientific American* entitled "Mathematics and the Imagination," he reported how the Hindu goddess Namakkal would appear in his dreams and reveal to him mathematical formulae that he would verify on waking, a pattern that continued all his life.

A world-changing dream occurred in 1869 to Dmitri Mendeleyev, a professor of chemistry at Saint Petersburg, after he went to bed frustrated by his attempts to categorize the chemical elements according to their atomic weights. "I saw in a dream," he reported, "a table where all the elements fell into place as required. Awakening, I immediately wrote it down on a piece of paper. Only in one place did a correction later seem necessary." The result was the periodic table of the elements. The dream also enabled Mendeleyev to predict the existence and properties of three new elements, which were discovered within the next 15 years.[7]

Perhaps the most famous example of a dreaming scientist is that of Friedrich A. von Kekule, a professor of chemistry at Ghent, Belgium. Kekule was attempting without success to determine the structure of the benzene molecule. He fell asleep while sitting in a chair and saw atoms flitting before him in various structures and patterns. Soon long rows of atoms formed and took on a twisting, snakelike pattern. All of a sudden one of the snakes seized its own tail in its mouth and started to whirl in a circle. "As if by a flash of lightning" Kekule awoke and began to work out the implications of the dream images. This led to the idea that benzene was a six-carbon *ring* structure, which revolutionized organic chemistry. In an address to a scientific meeting in 1890, he concluded his talk to his colleagues by honoring his process of discovery: "Let us learn to dream, gentlemen, and then we may perhaps find the truth."[8]

One of the legendary discoveries in modern medical research, insulin, is dream related. Frederick Banting, a Canadian physician, was conducting research on diabetes. Awakening from a dream one night, he wrote down the following words: "Tie up the duct of the pancreas of a dog. Wait for a few weeks until the glands shrivel up. Then cut it out, wash it out and filter the precipitation." This procedure led him to discover the hormone insulin, which proved lifesaving for millions of diabetics. It also led to Banting's being knighted—an interesting word, considering his nocturnal revelation.[9]

The list of scientific discoveries influenced by dreams is quite long—James Watt's discovery of how to make spherical pellets that could be used as shot; David Parkinson's discovery at Bell Laboratories of the all-electric gun director known as the M-9 device, the precursor of guidance systems used later in antiaircraft and antiballistic missiles; Ernst Chladni's invention of the euphonium, a new musical instrument—on and on.[10]

Dreaming remains one of the most common pathways of entering the One Mind. As the collective nature of consciousness becomes more fully appreciated within science, skeptical scientists will understand that to be called a dreamer is a high compliment indeed.

Dream Premonitions

When people dream of things they have never known, and of events before they happen, the role of dreaming as an entryway into a possible storehouse of information such as the timeless One Mind seems especially plausible. A historical example can be found in the journal of Stephen Grellet, a French Quaker missionary.[11] Three months before Napoleon's army invaded Russia, the wife of Count Toutschkoff, a Russian general, had a dream that was repeated a second and third time on the same night. In the dream, Countess Toutschkoff was in an inn she had never seen before, in a town she did not know, when her father came into the room, leading her young son by the hand. In a gloomy tone he told her, "Your happiness is at an end. He"—meaning her husband, General Toutschkoff—"has fallen. He has fallen at Borodino."

The countess awoke in great anguish, roused her husband, and asked him where Borodino was. He had never heard of it. They looked for Borodino on a map and could not find it. Before the French armies reached Moscow, General Toutschkoff was placed in charge of the Russian reserve army. One morning not long after, the Countess's father, holding her son by the hand, entered her room at an inn where she was staying, and in great distress cried out, "He has fallen. He has fallen," the countess realized she was in the very same room as in her dream; even the scene outside the windows was as she had dreamed it. Then she learned that the battle where her husband was killed had been fought near an obscure village called Borodino.

Collective Dreaming

Collective or mutual dreams are those in which two or more people report similar dreams on the same night. *Shared* dreams are those in which two or more people dream of each other in a common space and time, independently reporting similar surroundings, conversations, and interactions within the dream.[12]

Psi researcher Stanley Krippner, in a cross-cultural study of dreams, reported a unique example of mutual dreaming involving two Japanese women. The first woman dreamed: "I am in the lobby of a big hotel. There is a large pillar made of marble. My friend Aiko is there and I stab her with a knife. I don't know why I stab her. Nobody seems to notice what I have done." The second woman dreamed: "I am in a hotel lobby. There is a big pillar there and I am standing by it. My younger sister comes in. She walks right up to me and stabs me with a knife. My younger sister's name is Tomoko. I die from the stabbing."[13]

These nearly identical dreams might be due, of course, to chance, coincidence, or inaccurate reporting. But in instances such as this, where there are no obvious shared events, sensory cues, or experiences that would have prompted the two women to dream the same dream (except for the identity of the assailant), one searches for other explanations. I propose we may be seeing the One Mind in action. In other words, dreams may coincide not because two people are dreaming but because only one mind is at work.

Neuroanthropologist Charles D. Laughlin of Carleton University in Ottawa, Canada, is an expert in shared or mutual dreaming.[14] He reported that when anthropologist Marianne George was doing fieldwork among the Barok of New Guinea, she developed a close relationship with an important female leader who was her sponsor among the tribe. George began having dreams in which her host told her to do certain things. In the morning the host's sons dropped by to make sure George understood the old woman's instructions during the night, and repeated verbatim what the old woman told her in her dreams. The sons told George that it made no difference how far away they might be when their mother wished to communicate with them; the dream would come through anyway. The old woman died, but the shared dreams kept happening. As during her life, the woman's sons continued verifying the dream visitation and the message, in one case directing George to the exact location of an ancient longhouse she had been trying to find for purposes of carbon dating.[15]

Shared anxieties and dreams sometimes enter through the nocturnal cracks in modern cultures, in spite of our insistence that they can't happen. In 1882 the Reverend A. B. McDougall of Hemel Hempstead in Hertfordshire in southeast England stayed with friends in Manchester, 143 miles away. He awoke to find a rat in his bed and informed his host. The same morning a cousin of his, staying at McDougall's home in Hemel Hempstead, came down to breakfast and related a weird dream she had "in which a rat appeared to be eating the extremities of my unfortunate self." McDougall's mother received a letter from her son telling her what had happened in Manchester. She wrote back, informing him of the woman's dream, saying that they had always considered the dreaming woman a witch because "she always knew about everything almost before it took place."[16]

Collective, mutual dreams are a calling card of the One Mind. They are reminders that the boundaries separating single minds are not absolute. When connections with others are realized in dreams, some dreamers describe this as an epiphany, a dramatic realization that their consciousness is infinite, transcendent, unbounded, and one with the consciousness of others.

A Caution, or How to Get Arrested

While collective dreaming can be very exciting, it can also cause problems, as in the case of Steve Linscott, who was awakened by a dream in October 1980 in Chicago. He dreamed that a man with a blunt object in his hand approached a girl. Falling asleep again, he dreamed the man "was beating her on the head. . . . She was on her hands and knees . . . and didn't resist . . . blood flying everywhere." Later that day he noticed police cars near his house. A young woman had been brutally beaten to death in a nearby apartment building. Linscott related the dream to his wife and to people at work; all of them urged him to report his dream to the police. When he did so, he was charged with the murder of the young woman a few weeks later. The police said he knew too many accurate details of the murder for it to be coincidental. Linscott was convicted and sentenced to 40 years in prison. Only after his defense attorneys lodged several appeals was the case dropped by prosecutors.[17]

This case provides a telling insight into the incredulity of our culture toward nonlocal knowing—gaining information beyond the reach of the physical senses. Not only do we have difficulty acknowledging this ancient way of knowing, but we are actually willing to imprison people who engage in it. We are not so far removed as we might like to think from the witch-burning days and the Spanish Inquisition, in which people were enthusiastically murdered for publicly acknowledging their gift of "second sight."

Randomania, Statisticalitis, and Coincidentitis

None of the preceding examples are likely to be taken seriously by those who are convinced that the mind is limited to brains, bodies, and the here and now. It has been my experience that no dream, no matter how dramatic or unlikely it may be, can shake the faith of those who "know" in advance that such things are impossible. Any dream that corresponds to reality can be dismissed as coincidence. This devotion to coincidence and randomness has been called *randomania* by British consciousness researcher David Luke of the University of Greenwich in London.[18]

One of the wisest critiques of the way in which skeptics play fast and loose with coincidence is that of the renowned British novelist and playwright J. B. Priestley, in his masterful book, *Man & Time.* In discussing precognitive dreams, he wrote:

> There is a point past which coincidences turn into something else, compelling us to demand an explanation, just as there is a point past which scientific detachment can turn into bull-headed prejudice. . . . People who adopt [this] standpoint pretend to write about an impossibly pure scientific detachment. All they ask, they tell us, is that those of us who are foolish enough to believe in such experiences should subject them to "well-controlled studies" and laboratory tests and the like.
>
> But we may be dealing here with a range of experiences that simply cannot be controlled and tested, that withers away when it is brought into the field of scientific experiment and proof. . . . And it does not surprise me that experimental psychologists—some of them attempting to deal with the psyche as if it were a lump of sodium—do not have precognitive dreams: Their minds are made up against them.[19]

Priestley was fascinated by precognitive dreaming. In 1963 he made an appeal to the British public while being interviewed on the BBC for accounts of precognitive dreams. He was flooded with responses.

One woman wrote she had told three people with whom she was breakfasting that she had just dreamed that as they were finishing breakfast a farmer arrived with 33 eggs in a bucket. Later, as she was standing halfway up the stairs, three more eggs were handed to her. That was her dream. Shortly following her actual breakfast, a farmer arrived and handed her a bucket, which he said contained three dozen eggs. She transferred them to a basket and paid the man. A few minutes later, her husband informed her that he had counted the eggs and found that there were 33 of them, not three dozen. While the woman was counting them for herself, she was called from below by an individual who met her halfway up the stairs. The individual explained that three eggs had been mistakenly removed from the bucket, and she handed her three eggs to boost the count to the proper tally.

Priestley stated, "Thirty-three and then three eggs in the dream; 33 and then three eggs in the real event. You can call it coincidence just as you can call it *boojum* or anything else. . . . But if you stop clinging to coincidence and try explaining this trumpery affair, you might shatter one kind of world."[20] The replacement for that shattered world is one in which linear time is no longer a tyrant, and causes do not always precede events.

CHAPTER 27

LOVE IS THE LAST WORD

The ways are but two: love and the want of love.

—MENCIUS, 300 B.C.E.

Love is a gateway to the One Mind because love tempers the forces of isolation, separateness, and individuality. Individuality is a valuable complement to connectedness and unity, but in excess it can lead to an overblown sense of self and obstruct the felt realization that we are united with one another and all things. As D. H. Lawrence trenchantly put it, "Hate is not the opposite of love, the opposite of love is individuality."[1]

This is more than idle speculation. Overcoming separateness results in effects that can be measured in lab studies. In three decades of experimental research at the Princeton Engineering Anomalies Research (PEAR) lab, Robert G. Jahn, the former dean of engineering at Princeton, and his colleagues have demonstrated that emotionally bonded couples are uniquely gifted in their mental ability to impart order to strings of random ones and zeros produced by random event generators. Moreover, pairs of emotionally close individuals can mentally exchange information even when separated at continental or global distances. Summing up how it all happens, Jahn wrote, "[The] successful strategy . . . involves some blurring of identities between operator and machine, or between percipient and agent [receiver and sender]. And, of course, this is also the recipe for any form of love: the surrender of self-centered interests of the partners in favor of the pair."[2] Put simply, love can change the state of the physical world.

Overcoming Loneliness

Because love transcends individuality, as Lawrence saw, it can help overcome isolation and loneliness, which have been associated with a host of health problems.[3] On the surface, the high prevalence of loneliness doesn't make sense. In our electronically obsessed age, aren't we connected more intimately than ever before? Not necessarily. "In an overcrowded world," wrote physician Eva Bell, "where billions of people are in close connectivity with each other through print or electronic media, it seems paradoxical that loneliness has become a rapidly growing malady of the 21st century. High-rise building[s], claustrophobic box-like flats, stressful jobs and impersonal city life do not encourage friendliness."[4] Thoreau's definition still applies: "A city is a place where hundreds of lonely people live together."[5]

Although cell phones are seen as devices that connect people, they may have the unexpected consequence of decreasing the desire to socially connect with others, contributing to loneliness and isolation in the long run. In a study at the University of Maryland, researchers conducted a series of experiments on test groups of cell-phone users, described in their paper, "The Effects of Mobile Phone Use on Prosocial Behavior." Prosocial behavior was defined as action intended to benefit another person or society as a whole. The researchers discovered that after a short period of cell phone use, the subjects were less likely to volunteer for a community service activity when asked compared to a control group. The cell-phone users were also less persistent in solving word problems, even when they knew their answers would be matched by a monetary donation to charity. The reduced focus on others held true even when the cell-phone users were asked to draw a picture of their cell phones and think about using them. The reasons? The researchers say, "The cellphone directly evokes feelings of connectivity to others, thereby fulfilling the basic human need to belong." This results, they suggested, in reducing one's desire to actually connect socially with others or to engage in empathic and prosocial behavior.[6]

Loneliness also correlates with Internet use.[7] In one study, chatting online resulted in increased loneliness, not less.[8] This was especially obvious in the "I am lonely will anyone speak to me" website that became the top online hangout for lonely folk in 2004.[9] Because of its enormous popularity, the site was featured in *Wired,* the *Guardian,* and the *New Yorker.*[10]

Jacob Needleman, professor of philosophy at San Francisco State University, bumped into the problem of loneliness quite unexpectedly. He asked one of his classes what they considered to be the major problems in our society. He got the usual answers—the breakdown of the family, nuclear war, the environment, and so on. Then a student said "loneliness," and Needleman asked, "How may people here feel basically lonely?" Everyone raised their hands. "I was astonished," he said. Then he asked another, larger class, with a much broader spectrum of people, and all but two individuals raised their hands. Then a 35-year-old student from Nigeria said, "You know, when I first came from Nigeria to England, I didn't understand what people meant when they said they were lonely. It's only now, after I've been living in the United States for two years, that I know what it means to be lonely." He explained that in his culture loneliness simply did not exist. There was not even a word for it. Although there was plenty of pain, suffering, and grief, he said, there was no loneliness.

"So what is this loneliness we're experiencing?" Needleman asks. "People are cut off, not just from each other, but also from some harmonizing force in themselves. It's not just that 'I am lonely;' it's that the 'I' is lonely. We are lacking an essential harmonious relationship with some universal force."[11]

The "essential harmonious relationship" that is lacking is not one that will be achieved by Twitter, Facebook, or any other of the hundreds of available social networking websites.[12] A candidate for a universal connecting force that *is* up to the task is the One Mind. No membership fee, computer, or smart phone required. The One Mind is already installed as part of our original equipment.

The Return of Love

Philosopher Neal Grossman, a former professor at the University of Illinois at Chicago, has spent decades analyzing near-death experiences (NDEs). NDEs, as we have seen, suggest that an element of consciousness exists outside the brain and that it may persist following physical death. Those who recover from NDEs often report that they underwent an experience that transcends individual consciousness. This awareness is universally accompanied by a profound sense of love that remains following the NDE. Grossman wrote, "There is a message hidden in all this [NDE] research. . . . The message is universal love. Every near-death experiencer is convinced that the purpose of life is to grow in our ability to give and receive love."[13] NDEs are an entry point to the One Mind, whose calling card is love.

For some, injecting love into science—as Jahn, Grossman, and others attempt to do—is the final straw. It is the ultimate proof that we are out to drag science into the gutter of sentimentality, which will be its ruin. But there is another view—that love *redeems* life and, by extension, science as well. Aldous Huxley wrote:

> Of all the worn, smudged, dog's-eared words in our vocabulary, "love" is surely the grubbiest, smelliest, slimiest. Bawled from a million pulpits, lasciviously crooned through hundreds of millions of loud-speakers, it has become an outrage to good taste and decent feeling, an obscenity which one hesitates to pronounce. And yet it has to be pronounced, for, after all, Love is the last word.[14]

It is also the *first* word in medicine, my field. Consider the art of diagnosis, on which all else is based. *Diagnosis* comes from Greek words roughly meaning "a knowing that exists between two people." Diagnosis is not a one-person event, not something that is performed only by someone wearing a white coat and stethoscope. It works best when doctor and patient come together in what Whitman called a "similitude." Diagnosis involves the "blurring of identities" that Jahn sees in his successful laboratory experiments.

Throughout history, the primacy of love has been confirmed countless times by those who have experienced various versions of the One Mind—in altered states, mystical experience, reverie, epiphany, or highly creative moments. Psychologist Carl Rogers called these experiences a "delicate and sensitive tenderness towards others"—to which Huxley added, "And not only *your* tenderness, the cosmic tenderness, the fundamental all-rightness of the universe—in spite of death, in spite of suffering."[15]

From the standpoint of common sense, Huxley acknowledged, the assertion that the universe is fundamentally all right is "the raving of a lunatic." The assertion that God is love "flies in the face of all experience and is totally untrue. But common sense is not based on total awareness; it is a product of convention, of organized memories of other people's words, of personal experiences limited by passion and value judgments, of hallowed notions and naked self-interest."[16]

Attempts to purge life of love can lead to situations that would be comical were they not so serious. This is particularly obvious in health care. In a major hospital with which I was acquainted, a group of staff nurses interested in adding another dimension to their conventional skills journeyed out of town one weekend to take a course in Therapeutic Touch, a healing technique that involves loving, compassionate intentions. When the director of nursing got wind of this, she was furious. When the nurses reported for duty the following Monday, there was a large sign in the nursing department saying, THERE WILL BE NO HEALING IN THIS HOSPITAL!

In another instance, a nationally prominent nurse I know was invited to give a lecture at a major hospital. But when the hosts found out she planned to discuss various healing techniques, they canceled the invitation, saying, "We're not ready for your visit yet, but we plan to reinvite you when we get into healing." The disinvited nurse said wryly, "I wonder what they're into now?"

In another large hospital, nurses were prohibited from touching patients except for procedures such as taking their pulse and blood pressure. "Excessive touch," such as back rubs and foot rubs, were off limits. The purpose of this regulation was to bar nurses from practicing hands-on healing techniques, which are becoming increasingly popular in American nursing.

I am delighted to say that American nurses are out front in reintroducing healing into health care.[17] Were it not for their enduring courage and wisdom, health care in the United States would be even more dismal than it currently is.

Some of the founding fathers of modern medicine knew that love heals, whether it was called caring, empathy, compassion, or good bedside manner. Sir William Osler is widely considered the father of Western scientific medicine. After revolutionizing how medicine was taught and practiced in Canada and the United States, in 1905, at the peak of his fame, Osler was lured to England, where he was appointed to the Regius Chair of Medicine at Oxford.

One day he went to graduation ceremonies at Oxford wearing his academic robes. On the way, he stopped by the home of his friend and colleague Ernest Mallam, whose young son was seriously ill with whooping cough. The child would not respond to the ministrations of his parents or the nurses and appeared to be dying. Osler loved children greatly, and he had a special way with them. He would often play with them, and children would invariably admit him into their world. So when the familiar Osler appeared in his impressive ceremonial robes, the little boy was captivated. Never before had he seen such a spectacle! After briefly examining the child, Osler slowly peeled a peach, cut and sugared it, and fed it bit by bit to the enthralled patient. Although Osler felt recovery was unlikely, he returned for each of the next 40 days, each time dressed in his awe-inspiring robes, and personally fed the young child nourishment. Within just a few days the tide had turned and the little boy's recovery became obvious.[18]

I suspect Osler knew that loving, compassionate thoughts of a healer create measurable, physical changes in others, as Jeanne Achterberg's experiments and other healing studies show.[19] Individuals can respond physically to our thoughts, as the EEG and fMRI studies of distant brains reveal, even when the distant individual is unaware we are having them. The attempt to strip loving intentions from healing in an attempt to sanitize it and make it objective is based on a misunderstanding of what decent medical care is all about.

A Wonderful Cliché

To say "God is love" is a cliché, but a good one. Jung thought so. In his autobiography, *Memories, Dreams, Reflections,* he said, "Man can try to name love, showering upon it all the names at his command, and still he will involve himself in endless self-deceptions. If he possesses a grain of wisdom, he will lay down his arms and name the unknown by the more unknown . . . by the name of God."[20]

The entire universe may be suffused by love. It may even be possible to detect rudimentary expressions of love, a kind of proto-love, in the subatomic domain. As we move from there toward systems of increasing complexity, love becomes more recognizable, reaching its fullest expression in humans, with our participation in the One Mind. I've illustrated this Universal Spectrum of Love in the following figure:

The Universal Spectrum of Love

Biological Complexity →

Interacting Systems	Evidence of Interaction	Expression of Interaction
Humans and humans	Humans interact with each other nonlocally—at a distance, without benefit of sensory- or energy-based exchanges of information. Many controlled studies of distant healing intentions and hundreds of telesomatic events and remote viewing have been reported.	Love, empathy, compassion, caring, unity; collective consciousness; the Universal or One Mind; God, Goddess, Allah, Tao, the Absolute
Humans and animals	Scores of studies involving various types of distant healing intent have been done using higher animals as subjects. Lost pets return to owners across vast distances to places they have never been.	Love, empathy

Interacting Systems	Evidence of Interaction	Expression of Interaction
Humans and living organisms	Scores of controlled studies have dealt with the distant effects of prayer and other types of positive, distant healing intent, in which various "lower" organisms—bacteria, fungi, yeasts—are the subjects, as well as seeds, plants, and cells of various sorts.	Love, empathy
Humans and complex machines	Humans can mentally influence the behavior of sophisticated electronic biofeedback devices, affirmed by the collective record of over 40 years of biofeedback research in hundreds of laboratories. Humans can also mentally influence random event generators and other electronic devices at a distance, demonstrated at the Princeton Engineering Anomalies Research (PEAR) lab and other institutions.	"Becoming one" or "falling in love" with the machine; interconnectedness; unity
Humans and simple machines	Humans can interact with and influence the behavior of freely swinging pendulums, mechanical cascade devices, and other relatively simple apparatuses at a distance—affirmed by studies conducted at the Princeton Engineering Anomalies Research (PEAR) lab and elsewhere.	"Becoming one" or "falling in love" with the machine; interconnectedness; unity

Biological Complexity

Biological Complexity ↑

Interacting Systems	Evidence of Interaction	Expression of Interaction
Complex physical devices/systems	According to commonly accepted principles in physics, coupled harmonic oscillators, all common musical instruments, and radio and television circuitry interact and resonate with each other. In general, all manner of physical systems—whether mechanical, electromagnetic, fluid dynamical, quantum mechanical, or nuclear—display synergistically interactive vibrations with similar systems or with their environment.	Sympathetic or harmonic resonance
Subatomic particles	Subatomic particles such as electrons, once in contact, demonstrate simultaneous changes—no matter how far apart—to the same degree. Bell's Theorem, the Aspect experiment, and many others affirm these phenomena.	Nonlocally correlated behavior; rudimentary or proto-love?

"All manner of physical systems," wrote Robert G. Jahn, "whether mechanical, electromagnetic, fluid dynamical, quantum mechanical, or nuclear, display capacities for synergistically interactive vibrations with similar systems, or with their environment. Coupled harmonic oscillators, all common musical instruments, radio and television circuitry, atomic components of molecules, all involve this 'sympathetic' resonance, from which strikingly different properties emerge than those that characterize their isolated components."[21]

What does it mean to say that all manner of physical systems are in "sympathetic resonance" with each other or their environment? "Sympathy" comes from the Greek *sympatheia*, "feeling together"; "resonance" is derived from the Latin *resonantia*, "an echo." Is the universe one vast echo of feeling and sensitivity? Of love?

A universal spectrum of feeling, sensitivity, and love that culminates in the One Mind—Walt Whitman, America's bard, saw it, wrote it, lived it. And so I give Walt the last word on this topic:

A vast similitude interlocks all . . .
All souls, all living bodies though they be ever so different . . .
All identities that have existed or may exist on
this globe, or any other globe,
All lives, and deaths, all of the past, present, future,
This vast similitude spans them, and always has spann'd,
And shall forever span them and compactly hold
and enclose them.[22]

PART FOUR

THE WAY FORWARD

CHAPTER 28

EXPANDING SCIENCE

If the evidence I've presented so far is as abundant and compelling as I suggest, why do the controversies about consciousness persist? Why is there such resistance to the premise that individual minds can act beyond the body, violating the limitations of space and time, and to the possibility that they might come together in the Great Connect, the One Mind? Why don't all veteran scientists agree on these matters? The reasons are enormously complex and too varied to analyze here in detail. However, at the risk of seeming quarrelsome, I want to look at some of the most obvious reasons these disputes never end. It's important to examine them because they constitute logjams. If science is to expand, they must somehow be removed.[1]

Science has regularly skimmed off the top, so to speak, admitting data that the scientific community approves of and ignoring data it finds objectionable. Thomas Kuhn, the science historian and philosopher who introduced the term *paradigm shift,* described this pattern in his influential book *The Structure of Scientific Revolutions.*[2] What gets denied publication in professional journals sometimes has little or nothing to do with the veracity of the data itself. Decisions about the awarding of research grants and the publication of papers often appear to be made by what's been called the GOBSAT method— good old boys sat around a table.[3] Among the information that has been shoved to the side is a vast body of evidence dealing with how consciousness manifests nonlocally in the world, unconstrained by space, time, and the physical limitations of the brain and body.

These charges may seem overreaching and unfair to those who are unacquainted with the day-to-day ways in which science is actually done. The image preferred by scientists is that they are open-minded individuals who are willing to accept any proof as long as it *is* proof. But this is often not the case. Science is like sausage: while you may like it, you may not want to tour the factory and see how it is made.[4]

For a look at the arbitrary, capricious, and sometimes malicious ways in which scientists sometimes respond to new ideas, I recommend science writer Hal Hellman's entertaining account of "ten of the liveliest disputes ever" in each of his twin books *Great Feuds in Science* and *Great Feuds in Medicine*.[5] Titanic feuds among scientists and physicians are nothing new. Sometimes they are ferocious. When physician William Harvey produced detailed evidence for the circulation of the blood in 17th-century England, he was accused, says historian Roger French, of "attempting to overturn the rationality and providence not only of nature, but of God."[6] Almost as bad, Harvey had the audacity to contradict the greats. "As for Aristotle," huffed a contemporary physician, "he made observations of all things and no one should dare contest his conclusions."[7] Harvey carried a dagger with him at all times, perhaps because he feared retribution for his renegade ideas, which some considered not just scientific but also theological heresy. This would be like Jonas Salk packing a .45 after developing the polio vaccine.

A snapshot of the ridicule that then prevailed is the comment of the distinguished 18th-century German physician Leopold Auenbrugger, who remarked, "It has always been the fate of those who have illustrated or improved the arts and sciences by their discoveries to be beset by envy, malice, hatred, destruction and calumny."[8]

Auenbrugger knew what he was talking about. He invented the art of percussion in 1761, by which one can determine the density and size of the underlying tissues and organs in the body by lightly tapping over them. His technique was the X-ray and scan of his day, an era when "digital" still referred to fingers. He hit on the technique by testing the level of wine in casks in the cellar of his father's inn. Although today this finger-tapping skill is taught to all medical students and is a mainstay in physical diagnosis, originally no one cared. Auenbrugger's discovery was met with such complete indifference that it was stillborn. The technique had to be reintroduced in 1808, one year before his death, by Jean-Nicolas Corvisart, Napoleon's personal physician and the most famous doctor in France. Auenbrugger's contribution was important. It led to the development of the stethoscope in 1816 and the art of auscultation by the French physician René Laennec.[9] So the next time your doctor listens to your heart or chest, say thanks to the thankless Auenbrugger.

Auenbrugger got off easily compared to the Hungarian physician Ignaz Semmelweiss. When in 1848 he produced overwhelming evidence for the effectiveness of hand washing by obstetricians in reducing maternal mortality following childbirth, his colleagues could not believe it. At that time the germ theory of disease did not exist, and the idea that a doctor should wash his hands before delivering a baby was considered preposterous. Evidence didn't matter. Semmelweiss was disgraced and was hounded out of Vienna. He fled to Budapest, where he eventually committed suicide.

Similar events took place in America. When the well-known physician Oliver Wendell Holmes proposed hand washing and scrupulous cleanliness to his colleagues in Boston in 1843, he was violently opposed by several of the prominent obstetricians of his day.[10]

The image of the scientist as an open-minded seeker of truth has been dashed by some of the greatest figures in modern science. This was expressed pointedly—and arrogantly—by a true science insider, Nobel laureate James Watson, co-discoverer of the structure of DNA. Watson proclaimed, "One could not be a successful scientist without realizing that, in contrast to the popular conception supported by newspapers and mothers of scientists, a goodly number of scientists are not only narrow-minded and dull, but also just stupid."[11] Or as the distinguished psychologist Hans Eysenck observed, "Scientists, especially when they leave the particular field in which they have specialised, are just as ordinary, pig-headed and unreasonable as anybody else, and their unusually high intelligence only makes their prejudices all the more dangerous . . ."[12] I warned you I might be quarrelsome.

Prejudice against the consciousness research we've examined throughout this book is openly admitted. An example is Ray Hyman, a University of Oregon psychologist who regularly denounces nonlocal, beyond-the-body research findings. Hyman conceded, "The level of the debate [in this field] during the past 130 years has been an embarrassment for anyone who would like to believe that scholars and scientists adhere to standards of rationality and fair play."[13]

The attempts to ignore consciousness have not banished it. Rather, these attempts have paradoxically made consciousness the elephant in the living room of science.[14] Future consciousness researchers would do well to heed the words of astronomer Carl Sagan: "It is the responsibility of scientists never to suppress knowledge, no matter how awkward that knowledge is, no matter how it may bother those in power; we are not smart enough to decide which pieces of knowledge are permissible and which are not . . ."[15]

CHAPTER 29

TRANSCENDENCE

*And in that day men will be weary of life, and they will cease to
think the universe worthy of reverent wonder and of worship. . . .
They will no longer love this world around us . . . this glorious
structure. . . . As to the soul, and the belief that it is immortal
by nature, or may hope to attain immortality . . . all this they
will mock at, and will even persuade themselves it is false.*[1]

—HERMES TRISMEGISTUS, 2ND CENTURY B.C.E.

Anything we love can be saved.

—ALICE WALKER[2]

"**I** know a way out of hell."

This arresting statement is from a galvanizing scene in Richard Attenborough's 1982 biographical film of Mahatma Gandhi. The
setting is 1947 India. The country is involved in a ferocious Hindu
versus Muslim civil war after gaining independence from British colo-
nial rule, spearheaded by Gandhi's nonviolent resistance movement.
With blood running in the streets of Calcutta and the city aflame, a

crazed Hindu father has come to Gandhi's bedside. The Mahatma is weak from fasting, which is his way of trying to stop the nationwide bloodbath. He is nearing death. The man offers Gandhi food. "Here! Eat! Eat! I'm going to hell—but not with your death on my soul!" Gandhi calmly replies, "Only God decides who goes to hell." Then the guilt-stricken man confesses that he has killed a Muslim child. "I smashed his head against a wall!" Gandhi asks the man why he killed the child. "Because they killed our son . . . my boy! The Muslims killed my son!" For such a heinous act of revenge, however, there is no easy fix. Gandhi's way out of hell for the man is severe. "Find a child," he gently advises, "a child whose mother and father have been killed—a little boy—and raise him as your own. Only be sure that he is a Muslim. . . . And you must raise him as a Muslim." The Hindu is horrified; he has not counted on such an extreme payback for atonement. But he senses the truth in Gandhi's prescription and falls to his knees and sobs.

I have intended this book to be a way out of hell—the hell of this particular moment in history where we confront threats to our existence that our forebears never imagined, an earth that is being degraded by the sheer fact of our existence and shortsighted choices. It is a hell from which, beyond a certain point, experts say, there may be no escape—and, unlike the Calcutta scenario, perhaps no atonement.

The evidence for our global predicament is based on abundant science, not on some sidewalk lunatic wearing a sandwich board yelling, "The end is near!" Only through willful blindness can one *not* be aware of the challenges we face—global climate change, polluted air and water, exploding populations, habitat and species loss, water scarcity, desertification, murderous ideologies, resource depletion, grinding poverty, endless wars of choice, ethnic and religious hatreds, on and on, all abetted by the "I've got mine/every man for himself" philosophy that currently infects our society. I have chosen not to dwell on the specific threats themselves, however; many other writers have done so brilliantly. My approach, rather, has been roundabout and sideways—to "tell all the truth but tell it slant," as poet Emily Dickinson advised.

My message is that there is a way of recalibrating our collective response to *all* of these problems—a move that then permits a cascade of solutions to fall into place. This approach requires rebooting our ethical and moral stance toward the earth and toward one another. It is about changing channels, redialing our basic concepts of who we are and how we are related to one another and to the terrestrial crucible that sustains us. I believe that the concept of the unitary, collective One Mind, a level of intelligence of which the individual minds of all sentient creatures are a part, is a vision that is powerful enough to make a difference in how we approach all the challenges we face—not as a mere intellectual concept, but as something we feel in the deepest way possible. As Hesse said in the prologue to *Demian,* "I have been and still am a seeker, but I no longer seek in stars and books; I have begun to listen to the teachings my blood whispers to me."[3]

Responsibility to Something Higher

Vaclav Havel, the author, poet, and playwright who was the first president of the Czech Republic, saw a hell looming in our world and had the guts to say so on the international stage. As a solution, he endorsed a collective entry into a One-Mind type of awareness he called "responsibility to something higher." As he said in a speech delivered to a joint meeting of the United States Congress on February 21, 1990:

> Consciousness precedes Being, and not the other way around . . . for this reason, the salvation in this human world lies nowhere else than in the human heart. . . . Without a global revolution in the sphere of human consciousness, nothing will change for the better in the sphere of our being as humans, and the catastrophe toward which this world is headed—be it ecological, social, demographic or a general breakdown of civilization—will be unavoidable. If we are no longer threatened by world war or by the danger that the absurd mountains of accumulated nuclear weapons might blow up the world, this does not mean that we have definitely won.

We are still capable of understanding that the only genuine backbone of all our actions, if they are to be moral, is responsibility. Responsibility to something higher than my family, my country, my company, my success—responsibility to the order of being where all our actions are indelibly recorded and where and only where they will be properly judged.[4]

Transcendence

In a subsequent speech at Independence Hall in Philadelphia in 1994 titled "The Need for Transcendence," Havel spoke of a unified humanity held together by a state of consciousness he called *transcendence:*

> In today's multicultural world, the truly reliable path to coexistence, to peaceful coexistence and creative cooperation, must start from what is at the root of all cultures and what lies infinitely deeper in human hearts and minds than political opinion, convictions, antipathies, or sympathies—it must be rooted in self-transcendence: Transcendence as a hand reached out to those close to us, to foreigners, to the human community, to all living creatures, to nature, to the universe. Transcendence as a deeply and joyously experienced need to be in harmony even with what we ourselves are not, what we do not understand, what seems distant from us in time and space, but with which we are nevertheless mysteriously linked because, together with us, all this constitutes a single world. *Transcendence as the only real alternative to extinction* (emphasis added).[5]

In the preceding pages, we've explored many ways of experiencing a transformative engagement with a transcendent, unifying state of being I've called the One Mind.

These transcendent experiences often shake us up, turn us inside out, and momentarily "stun the mind into a blur," as Frederick Turner puts it.

Astronaut Edgar Mitchell, whom I have known and admired for years, is an iconic example of what can happen as a result of a collision with wholeness. As the lunar module pilot of Apollo 14, Mitchell was the sixth human to walk on the moon. On his return flight to Earth, he felt an extraordinary connection with the planet. "It was a beautiful, harmonious, peaceful looking planet, blue with white clouds, and one that gave you a deep sense . . . of home, of being, of identity. It is what I prefer to call instant global consciousness."[6] Speaking of other astronauts, he observed, "Each man comes back with a feeling that he is no longer an American citizen—he is a planetary citizen." Astronaut Russell Schweickart, the lunar module pilot of Apollo 9, said much the same thing: "You recognize that you are a piece of this total life. . . . And when you come back there is a difference in that world now. There is a difference in that relationship between you and that planet and you and all those other forms of life on that planet, because you've had that kind of experience."[7]

Of course, we don't have to go into outer space to experience these transcendent, transformative moments; we can journey into *inner* space. As we've seen, these experiences are always hammering on the door of awareness, just waiting for an opportunity to burst into the living room of our conscious life. They intrude in a dazzling variety of ways—in mundane situations such as sitting quietly, listening to music, viewing art, meditating, worshiping, praying, washing dishes, gardening, or doing nothing; or they may occur in dramatic, desperate moments such as near-death or life-threatening situations.

The Spiritual Side of One-Mind Experiences

But how can One-Mind experiences such as those we've examined in this book lead us out of the dark future that confronts us? How does the process work?

Most of these experiences are considered paranormal or parapsychological because they involve nonlocal ways of knowing that bypass the physical senses. These experiences reveal linkages and connections between distant individuals. But linkages between distant people are common—think cell phones and telephones—so there is nothing that is *necessarily* transformational about connectedness. Even One-Mind experiences can be ho-hum. As Hoyt L. Edge, professor of philosophy at Florida's Rollins College, wrote, "Parapsychological phenomena are no more spiritual than any other phenomena in themselves . . ." But that is not the whole story. "There is an implication of the paranormal that is profound: the data of parapsychology provide evidence for the view that there is a connectedness to all things, and that this related-ness is natural, not a result of human artifact (i.e. the telephone). . . . If psi indirectly suggests that all aspects of the cosmos are intimately interrelated and I am in a significant way part of this unity, then spiritual meaning can be developed out of this view."

Professor Edge sees immense significance in this larger view because it can transform our way of being in the world. "The point of spirituality is not to separate oneself from the natural world and from others; rather, it is to make one's own actions in the natural world and one's interactions with others sacred," he said. "Parapsychology gives evidence that supports a more relational and connected view of the world . . ." Professor Edge cited the feelings of one of his students in an experiment designed to produce mystical experiences. The student said, "I was at the source of awareness, enlightenment, and exis-tence, manifested in a form of energy linking all objects animate and inanimate. . . . I felt morally elevated to a state of pure and simple existence flowing like a continuous current through a waterfall, going deeper and deeper within all existence while feeling more and more at peace and content. . . . I was surrounded by meaning and freed from the despair of meaninglessness, guilt, and time."[8]

Consciousness researcher and experimental psychologist William Braud sees One-Mind-type experiences as a potential way out of hell. "We could, no doubt, treat one another with kindness, understand-ing, and compassion even if we were not profoundly and intimately interconnected in nontrivial ways," he wrote. "However, having direct knowledge and direct experience of our interconnections can greatly increase our love for one another and enhance our ethical behaviors toward one another."

Another way in which One-Mind-type experiences can aid in one's spiritual growth is to shock one into a realization that the con-stricting worldview of conventional science, which prohibits these phenomena, is inadequate. "Sometimes the only way that such a worldview can be undermined is by a powerfully impressive paranormal experience which the skeptic undergoes," wrote philosopher Donald Evans. "I have seen this happen in workshops designed to evoke various paranormal powers of intuition. The whole reality issue shifts. . . . Sometimes, of course, this happens spontaneously."

Evans sees two appropriate ways we can interpret these experiences. "On the one hand, I know that I am not separated from anyone or anything because of mystical experiences in which my own spirit is connected with everyone and everything through a *cosmic spirit* that is a pervasive *medium*. On the other hand, I know that I am not separated from anyone or anything because of mystical experiences in which my own conscious soul is united with the *conscious Source* of everyone and everything, which *simultaneously* lives in us and as us."[9]

Are there dangers? Of course. Any lofty human experience can be hijacked by narcissism and selfishness, and converted into an ego trip. For this reason, some spiritual traditions have devalued and even derided *siddhis,* or paranormal powers, which not infrequently crop up in one's process of personal transformation. But surely an absolute prohibition of these experiences is improper because they can be powerful indicators of the connectedness that underlies the world of which we are a part. These experiences, as Evans said, can provide "the necessary though elemental basis for what can follow: the arduous process of radical transformation or transfiguration in which we gradually uncover and surrender whatever prevents our being lived by God, resonating and channeling the divine love."[10] Through these One Mind experiences we can learn to become "transparent to transcendence," as Karlfried Graf Dürkheim, the German psychologist and Zen master, put it.[11] We become a transmitter of the circuits of consciousness, life, empathy, and love. With this realization we no longer *have* One-Mind-type experiences—we *live* the One Mind.

Russell Targ, whose experiments helped put remote viewing on the scientific map, wrote in his book *The Reality of ESP: A Physicist's Proof of Psychic Abilities,* "Western science had given us great accomplishments and shown us the far reaches of space. But it has shrunken our mental space down to the size of a coconut. I think it is past time start questioning this reality and to claim the unobstructed reality that is available to us."[12] Our future likely depends on our acknowledgement of this "unobstructed reality" that is defined by our nonlocal, intimate connections with one another and our world.

Targ believes spirituality and One-Mind-type experiences are intimately related, and as evidence he cited the description of telepathy and precognition in the powerful Buddhist text known as *The Flower Ornament Scripture,* which dates to 100 C.E.[13] "This Buddhist compendium," Targ wrote, "teaches that there is no paradox in precognition or in communicating with the dead because past, present, and future are all infinite in extent and *dependently co-arising.* Thus, the future can affect the past—and, since our awareness is timeless and nonlocal, it should not be surprising that we can and do experience manifestations of the deceased or communications from the future in precognitive dreams." All these forms of "super-knowledge," Targ said, "should be expected to appear in our lives as the natural outcome of nonlocal consciousness." And they can help us on our spiritual journey, if experienced through a discriminating, clear mind refined through spiritual disciplines such as meditation, contemplation, and the like.

Targ showed how these same examples of "super-knowledge" are found also in Hinduism, particularly in the writings of the sages Patanjali (2nd century B.C.E.) and Shankara (8th century C.E.). He concluded, "I hope that my Buddhist friends never tell me again that Buddhists aren't interested in psychic abilities."[14]

I hope my Christian friends, too, will cease suggesting to me that these nonlocal ways of knowing are theologically suspect. Christianity still suffers from a hangover from centuries past, when nonlocal phenomena such as telepathy, clairvoyance, and precognition were considered the devil's work and when individuals professing them were often executed in God's name. These suspicions no longer become our species. These abilities should in fact be encouraged, because our struggling species requires the full spectrum of consciousness if we are to survive.

The Eye of the Needle

The common pathway in all One-Mind moments is the experience of a hyperreal level of awareness, connection, intimacy, and communion with a greater whole, however conceived—the Absolute, God, Goddess, Allah, Universe, and so forth—all of which is marinated in an experience of intense love. There follows a profound shift in the existential premises on which one's life is based. One ceases to be "a thing or process, but an opening or clearing through which the Absolute can manifest."[15]

This is the eye of the needle through which, having passed, there is no going back. It is our best hope, but it is more than hope: it is a possibility within the reach of everyone and that many have experienced already.

If this great earth were to speak to us, it might summon us with the words of Rumi, the luminous Sufi poet of 13th-century Persia: "Come, come, whoever you are, wanderer, fire worshiper, lover of leaving. This is not a caravan of despair. It does not matter that you have broken your vow a thousand times, still come, and yet again come."[16]

And if summoned by the earth, how shall we answer? Each of us has broken our responsibilities to our earth and environment, therefore to ourselves and to one another, a thousand times. Yet it is within our power to redeem our shortcomings by reclaiming our nonlocal nature—the One Mind that unites us with all else, including our earth; the One Mind whose calling card is love, caring, affection. When we sense our place in this Great Connect, our response is to honor that with which we are linked, as if it were our lover. This connection is eternal; no assembly required. Rumi again: "Lovers don't finally meet somewhere. They're in each other all along."[17]

ENDNOTES

Acknowledgments

1. Krishna, *The Biological Basis of Religion and Genius:* 35–36.
2. Baldwin, *Edison:* 376.

Author's Note

1. Yu, *The Great Circle:* 160.
2. Rao, *Cognitive Anomalies, Consciousness, and Yoga:* 352.
3. Ibid., 335; Emerson. *Self-Reliance and Other Essays:* 53. Compare Professor Rao's language to that of Emerson: "The soul in man . . . is not a faculty, but a light . . . from within or from beyond, a light [that] shines through us upon things, and makes us aware that we are nothing, but the light is all." (Emerson. *Self-Reliance and Other Essays:* 53.)
4. Tzu, *Tao Te Ching.*
5. And as in the East, so in the West, as in Emerson: "It [the soul] is too subtle. It is undefinable, unmeasurable, but we know that it pervades and contains us." (Emerson, *Self-Reliance and Other Essays:* 53).
6. Heisenberg, *Physics and Beyond:* 137.
7. Planck, *Where is Science Going?:* 217.

Introduction

1. Schiller, "The Progress of Psychical Research."
2. For those who would like to consult a single additional source that examines in detail many of the phenomena I discuss, I recommend the scholarly *Irreducible Mind* by University of Virginia psychologist Edward F. Kelly and colleagues. This landmark book has rightfully been called "brilliant, heroic, . . . astonishing . . . [and] scientifically rigorous . . ." Comment of Richard Shweder on the back cover of: Kelly, et al. *Irreducible Mind.*
3. Dossey, *Recovering the Soul:* 1–11.
4. Thomas, *The Medusa and the Snail:* 174–75.
5. Raffensperger, "Moral Injuries and the Environment."
6. Karpf, "Climate Change."
7. Mead, Quotationspage.com.
8. Barasch, Green World Campaign.
9. Rifkin, *The Empathic Civilization:* 599–600.
10. Josephson, "Pathological Disbelief."
11. Sturrock. *A Tale of Two Sciences:* 95.
12. Milton, *Alternative Science*: 3; Lindsay. "Maskelyne and Meteors"; "History of Meteoritics"; Ensisheim meteorite, Encyclopedia of Science.
13. Einstein, *The New York Times;* Wikiquote.

14. Johnson, "The Culture of Einstein."
15. Emerson, *Essays: First Series:* 1.
16. Ibid., 96.
17. Lovejoy, *The Great Chain of Being.*
18. Akashic Records, Wikipedia; Laszlo, *Science and the Akashic Field.*
19. Luke 17:21, King James Version.
20. John 10:34, King James Version.
21. Trismegistus, *Hermetica:* 203.
22. Plato, *Collected Dialogues of Plato:* 520–25.
23. Pierce, *Irish Writing in the Twentieth Century:* 62.
24. Kerouac, *Scattered Poems:* 54.
25. There are three common forms of materialism. (1) Epiphenomenalism holds that consciousness somehow emerges from the brain, like steam from a kettle. Remove the kettle and there is no steam. (2) Identity theory alleges that consciousness and brain states are identical. (3) Eliminative materialism is the view that consciousness does not exist.
26. Hoffman, "Conscious Realism and the Mind-Body Problem."
27. Pinker, *How the Mind Works:* 146.
28. Huxley, *Tomorrow and Tomorrow and Tomorrow:* 32; Huxley's observation should not be interpreted as an endorsement of intellectual laziness or antiscience. He is honoring a kind of wisdom that does not conform to the language and equations of science—a wisdom that, as Emerson says, comes from "revelation . . . the disclosure of the soul." Emerson asserted that this kind of knowing is degraded when it is used to answer mundane questions. "We must check this low curiosity," he said. "We must pick no locks." (Emerson, *Self-Reliance and Other Essays:* 58.)
29. Thomas, *The Medusa and the Snail:* 73.
30. Ibid., 174–75.
31. Sheldrake, *Science Set Free.*
32. Nisker, *Inquiring Mind:* 1.

Chapter 1: Saving Others

1. Buckley, "Man is Rescued by Stranger on Subway Tracks."
2. Trump, "The Time 100."
3. Campbell and Toms, *An Open Life:* 53.
4. Ryder, *Animal Revolution:* 57.
5. Campbell, *The Inner Reaches of Outer Space:* 84.
6. Dossey, *Healing Beyond the Body:* 79–104.
7. Pearce, *Evolution's End:* 221.
8. Huxley, *The Perennial Philosophy:* 6.
9. Ibid., 9.

Chapter 2: The Patron Saint of the One Mind

1. Schrödinger, *What is Life?* and *Mind and Matter:* 145.
2. Moore, *Schrödinger: Life and Thought:* 107–10.
3. Ibid., 111.
4. Koestler, *The Roots of Coincidence:* 107–8.
5. Moore, *Schrödinger: Life and Thought:* 112.
6. Schopenhauer, *Sämtliche Werke:* 224–25; Koestler, *The Roots of Coincidence:* 107–8.
7. Moore, *Schrödinger: Life and Thought:* 113.
8. Schrödinger, *What is Life?* and *Mind and Matter:* 139.
9. Ibid., 133.
10. Ibid., 145.

11. Ibid., 165.
12. Schrödinger, *My View of the World:* 21–22.
13. Ibid., 22.
14. Moore, *Schrödinger: Life and Thought:* 348–49.
15. Ibid., 173.
16. Huxley, *The Perennial Philosophy.*
17. Underhill, *Mysticism:* 80.
18. Moore, *Schrödinger: Life and Thought:* 114.
19. Gandhi, *The Evolution of Consciousness:* 215–51.
20. Dossey, *Space, Time & Medicine.*
21. Dossey, *Recovering the Soul:* 1–11.

Chapter 3: One-Mind Experiences

1. Stein, *Everybody's Autobiography:* 289.
2. Van Oss, "Hunch Prompted Dutch Man to Cancel Flight on Air France 447."
3. Winkler, Personal communication to the author.
4. Beloff, *Parapsychology:* xiv.

Chapter 4: The One Mind Is Not an Infinite Blob

1. Pearce, *Evolution's End:* 30.
2. Ibid., 95.
3. Grann, *The Lost City of Z:* 122–23.
4. Walach and Schneider, *Generalized Entanglement From a Multidisciplinary Perspective.*
5. Nadeau and Kafatos, *The Non-Local Universe:* 65–82.
6. Herbert, *Quantum Reality:* 214.
7. Einstein, Podolsky, and Rosen, "Can Quantum-Mechanical Description of Physical Reality Be Considered Complete?"
8. Kafatos and Nadeau, *The Conscious Universe:* 71.
9. "How old is the universe?" Universe 101.
10. Vedral, "Living in a Quantum World"; Thaheld, "Biological Nonlocality and the Mind-Brain Interaction Problem"; Thaheld, "A Method to Explore the Possibility of Nonlocal Correlations Between Brain Electrical Activities of Two Spatially Separated Animal Subjects."
11. Bohm, *Wholeness and the Implicate Order:* 145.
12. Cook, *Hua-Yen Buddhism:* 2.
13. Bohm, *Wholeness and the Implicate Order:* 149.
14. Bohm and Krishnamurti, *The Limits of Thought.*
15. Lachman, Lachman, and Butterfield, *Cognitive Psychology and Information Processing:* 137.
16. Sheldrake, McKenna, and Abraham, *The Evolutionary Mind:* 109–21.
17. Turner, *Natural Religion:* 213.
18. Best, *Five Days That Shocked the World:* 79.
19. Gonin, "Extract from the Diary of Lieutenant Colonel Mervin Willett Gonin."
20. Bohm, *Wholeness and the Implicate Order.*
21. Eckhart, "Spiritual Practices: Silence."
22. Keating, "Spiritual Practices: Silence."
23. Vivekananda, "Spiritual Practices: Silence."
24. Alexander, *Proof of Heaven;* Alexander, "Neurosurgeon Eben Alexander's Near-Death Experience Defies Medical Model of Consciousness."
25. Eckhart, *Meister Eckhart:* 243.

Chapter 5: The Sense of Being Stared At

1. Longworth, *Churchill by Himself:* 322.

2. Sheldrake, *The Sense of Being Stared At;* Braud, Shafer, and Andrews, "Electrodermal Correlates of Remote Attention"; Cottrell, Winer, and Smith, "Beliefs of Children and Adults About Feeling Stares of Unseen Others."
3. Sheldrake, *The Sense of Being Stared At:* 5.
4. Ibid., xiii.
5. Matthew, "Sixth Sense Helps You Watch Your Back."
6. Sheldrake, *The Sense of Being Stared At.* London. Arrow; 2003: 139.
7. Ibid., 139–40.
8. Ibid., 157.
9. Cottrell, Winer, and Smith, "Beliefs of Children and Adults About Feeling Stares of Unseen Others."

Chapter 6: They Moved as One

1. Sandoz, *The Buffalo Hunters:* 3–5.
2. Ibid., 102.
3. Ibid., 103–4.
4. "Project Passenger Pigeon: Lessons from the Past for a Sustainable Future."
5. Winter, Starlings at Otmoor; For another breathtaking starling display, see: Clive, Murmuration.
6. Shadow, Dailygrail.com.
7. Ibid.
8. Miller, "The Genius of Swarms."
9. "Planes, Trains, and Ant Hills." ScienceDaily.com.
10. Miller, "The Genius of Swarms."
11. "Caribou." U. S. Fish and Wildlife Service.
12. Miller, "The Genius of Swarms."
13. Sheldrake, *The Sense of Being Stared At:* 113–21.
14. Potts, "The Chorus-Line Hypothesis of Manoeuvre in Avian Flocks."
15. Sheldrake, *The Sense of Being Stared At:* 115; Selous, *Thought Transference (or What?) in Birds:* 931; Long, *How Animals Talk.*
16. Sheldrake, *The Sense of Being Stared At:* 119.
17. Ibid., 83.

Chapter 7: The One Mind of Animals and Humans

1. Watson, "Natural Harmony."
2. Alexander, *Bobbie, A Great Collie:* 103–13.
3. Harness, "The Most Famous Mutts Ever"; Rin Tin Tin's story is told in Orlean. *Rin Tin Tin;* Stelljes, *Wonder Dog, the Story of Silverton Bobbie;* Schul, *The Psychic Power of Animals:* 52; Rhine and Feather, "The Study of Cases of 'Psi-Trailing' in Animals."
4. Scheib, "Timeline."
5. Trapman, *The Dog, Man's Best Friend.*
6. Rhine and Feather, "The Study of Cases of 'Psi-Trailing' in Animals."
7. "Of All the Pigeon Lofts in the World."
8. Rhine and Feather, "The Study of Cases of 'Psi-Trailing' in Animals."
9. Sheldrake, *Dogs That Know When Their Owners Are Coming Home;* Sheldrake, Commentary on a paper by Wiseman, Smith, and Milton on the "psychic pet" phenomenon.
10. Armstrong, "Souls in Process: A Theoretical Inquiry into Animal Psi." *Critical Reflections on the Paranormal:* 134.
11. Ibid., 135.
12. Ibid.
13. Sheldrake and Smart, "Psychic Pets."
14. Scheltema, *Something Unknown Is Doing We Don't Know What.*

15. Wiseman, Smith, and Milton, "Can Animals Detect When Their Owners Are Returning Home?"
16. Wilson, Quoted at GoodReads.com.
17. Schul, *The Psychic Power of Animals:* 142–43; Telepathy. *Gale Encyclopedia of Occultism and Parapsychology.*
18. Kane, "Do Dogs Mourn?"
19. Harrison, *Off to the Side:* 47–48.
20. Ibid., 48.
21. "NZ Dolphin Rescues Beached Whales." BBC News online.
22. Gessler, "Couple Alerted by Dolphins about Tired Dog Tells Story."
23. Cellzic, "Dolphins Save Surfer from Becoming Shark's Bait."
24. "Dolphins Save Lifeguards from Circling Great White Shark." www.joe-ks.com; Thomson, "Dolphins Saved Us From Shark, Lifeguards Say."
25. "Amazing Moment Mila the Beluga Whale Saved a Stricken Diver's Life by Pushing Her to the Surface."
26. "Heroic Horse Halted Cow's Attack." BBC News online.
27. "Gorilla Rescues Child." Year in Review: 1996; "Gorilla at an Illinois Zoo Rescues a 3-Year-Old Boy." *The New York Times* archives; "Gorilla's Maternal Instinct Saves Baby Boy Who Fell into Zoo Enclosure from Coming to Harm." *The Independent* online.
28. Buchmann, *Letters from the Hive:* 123.
29. Anonymous, "Telling the bees." Dailygrail.com.
30. Schul, *The Psychic Power of Animals:* 146; "Telling the Bees." SacredTexts.com.
31. Whittier, "Telling the Bees": 167.
32. Shadow, "Telling the Bees." Dailygrail.com.; J. K. Rowling may not have known about "telling the bees" and the reverence of ancient cultures toward them. One source says that Rowling knew that *Dumbledore* was an old English word for bumblebee and that, because her character Albus Dumbledore is very fond of music, she always imagined him as sort of humming to himself a lot. See: Rowling. "What Jo says about Albus Dumbledore."
33. Rogers. Quoted at GoodReads.com.
34. Twain. Quoted at GoodReads.com. Dogs.
35. De Gaulle. Quoted at GoodReads.com.
36. Schulz. Quoted at GoodReads.com.
37. Kundera. Quoted at GoodReads.com.
38. "Cat Heroes." Squidoo.com.
39. Dosa, "A Day in the Life of Oscar the Cat."
40. Twain. Quoted at GoodReads.com. Cats.
41. Da Vinci. Quoted at GoodReads.com.

Chapter 8: Atoms and Rats

1. Feynman, *Six Easy Pieces:* 20.
2. Radin, *Entangled Minds:* 19.
3. Vedral, "Living in a Quantum World."
4. Mermin, "Extreme Quantum Entanglement in a Superposition of Macroscopically Distinct States."
5. Kafatos and Nadeau, *The Conscious Universe:* 71.
6. Nadeau and Kafatos, *The Non-Local Universe:* 65–82; Kafatos and Nadeau. *The Conscious Universe.*
7. Kelly, et al., *Irreducible Mind;* Carter. *Parapsychology and the Skeptics;* Tart. *The End of Materialism.*
8. Vedral, "Living in a Quantum World."
9. Wilber, *Quantum Questions:* back cover quotation.
10. Socrates. QuotesEverlasting.com.

11. Dawkins, *The Selfish Gene.*
12. Ibid., 3.
13. Ibid.
14. Bartal, Decety, and Mason, "Empathy and Pro-Social Behavior in Rats."
15. Kane, "Study Shows Lab Rats Would Rather Free a Friend than Eat Chocolate."
16. Mitchum, "Rats Free Trapped Companions, Even When Given Choice of Chocolate Instead."

Chapter 9: Mind Beyond Brain

1. Brunton, *Network Newsletter:* 18.
2. Lashley, "In Search of the Engram": 478.
3. Lorber, "Is Your Brain Really Necessary?"
4. Brian, *Genius Talk:* 367.
5. Wigner, "Are We Machines?"
6. Maddox, "The Unexpected Science to Come."
7. Hippocrates, *Hippocrates:* 179.
8. Carter, *Science and the Near-Death Experience:* 14.
9. Bergson, *The Creative Mind.*
10. Carter, *Science and the Near-Death Experience:* 15.
11. Bergson, Presidential address.
12. James, *Human Immortality:* 15.
13. Ibid., 1113.
14. Huxley, *The Doors of Perception:* 22–24.
15. Fenwick and Fenwick, *The Truth in the Light:* 235–36.
16. Ibid., 260.
17. Ibid.

Chapter 10: Immortality and Near-Death Experiences

1. Ramachandran, "The Limbic Fire."
2. Dickinson, *The Complete Poems of Emily Dickinson:* 708.
3. Benedict, "Mellen-Thomas Benedict's Near-Death Experience."
4. Ibid.
5. Benedict, *Wisdom.*
6. Benedict, "Mellen-Thomas Benedict's Near-Death Experience."
7. Plato, "The Myth of Er."
8. Jung, *The Collected Works of C. G. Jung.* Princeton University Press; 1969: 43.
9. Jung, *The Symbolic Life.*
10. Jung, *Memories, Dreams, Reflections:* 325.
11. Taylor, *Orwell:* 239.
12. Bohm, *Omni.*
13. De Beauregard. Address to the Third Annual Meeting of the Society for Scientific Exploration.
14. Stevenson, *Where Reincarnation and Biology Intersect;* Tucker. *Life Before Life.*
15. Darling, *Soul Search:* 179.
16. Gefter, "Near-Death Neurologist."
17. Russell, *The Basic Writings of Bertrand Russell:* 370.
18. Thomas,"The Long Habit."
19. Alexander, *Proof of Heaven.*
20. Alexander, "Life Beyond Death."
21. Alexander, Interview with Alex Tsakiris.
22. Moody, *Life After Life.*
23. Gallup Poll. "New Poll Gauges Americans' General Knowledge Levels."
24. Flat Earth Society.

25. Gallup and Proctor. *Adventures in Immortality*; Perera, et al. "Prevalence of Near-Death Experiences in Australia": 109; Knoblauch, et al. "Different Kinds of Near-Death Experience": 15–29.
26. Van Lommel, et al., "Near-Death Experience in Survivors of Cardiac Arrest": Clinical death is "unconsciousness caused by the loss of heartbeat and respiration. Unless patients are resuscitated within five to ten minutes, they will die."; Van Lommel. *Consciousness Beyond Life:* 398.
27. Gallup and Proctor. *Adventures in Immortality:* 198–200.
28. "Key Facts about Near-Death Experiences." Prevalence of NDEs.
29. Clark, *Divine Moments:* 54.
30. Ibid., 51.
31. Moody, *Life After Life.*
32. Clark, *Divine Moments:* 34–40.
33. Emerson, *Essays: First Series:* 1.
34. Clark, *Divine Moments:* 45.
35. Ibid.,188.
36. Ibid., 212.
37. Ibid., 23–27.
38. Van Lommel, *Consciousness Beyond Life:* 8–9.
39. Van Lommel, *Consciousness Beyond Life:* 9; Van Lommel, et al., "Near-Death Experiences in Survivors of Cardiac Arrest"; Greyson, "Incidence and Correlates of Near-Death Experiences in a Cardiac Care Unit."
40. Hoffman, "Disclosure Needs and Motives after Near-Death Experiences."
41. Van Lommel, *Consciousness Beyond Life:* 10.
42. Clark, *Divine Moments:* 53.
43. Moody, *Paranormal:* 227–42.
44. Borysenko, "Shared Deathbed Visions."
45. Moody, *Paranormal:* 239–41.
46. Rominger, "An Empathic Near-Death Experience."
47. "Group Near-Death Experiences"; This account is also available in Gibson, *Fingerprints of God:* 128–30.
48. Moody, *Paranormal:* 227–42.
49. Clark, *Divine Moments:* 177.
50. Ibid., 103–4.
51. Ibid., 157–58.
52. Ibid., 137.
53. Ibid., 187.
54. Ibid., 193.
55. Ibid., 221.
56. Greyson, "Increase in Psychic Phenomena Following Near-Death Experiences"; Sutherland, "Psychic Phenomena Following Near-Death Experiences."
57. Clark, *Divine Moments:* 244–47.

Chapter 11: Reincarnation

1. Voltaire, "La Princesse de Babylone": 366.
2. Tucker, *Life Before Life:* 211.
3. Schopenhauer, *Parerga and Paralipomena:* 368.
4. Pew Forum, "Many Americans Mix Multiple Faiths."
5. Stevenson, *Where Reincarnation and Biology Intersect:* 9.
6. Ibid., 7.
7. Ibid., 12.
8. Stevenson, *Telepathic Impressions.*
9. Schmicker, *Best Evidence:* 223.
10. Stevenson, *Where Reincarnation and Biology Intersect:* 180–81.

11. Ibid., 3.
12. Ibid., 180.
13. Ibid., 181.
14. Ibid.
15. Thomas, *The Lives of a Cell:* 52.
16. Stevenson, *Where Reincarnation and Biology Intersect:* 181.
17. Ibid.
18. Ibid., 181–83.
19. Ibid., 182.
20. Kelly, et al., *Irreducible Mind.*
21. Nan Huaijin, *Basic Buddhism:* 46.
22. Bernstein, *Quantum Profiles:* 82.

Chapter 12: Communication with the Deceased

1. Mitchell, "The Case of Mary Reynolds"; Putnam, *A History of Multiple Personality Disorder:* 357.
2. Barrington, Mulacz, and Rivas, "The Case of Iris Farczády."
3. Warcollier, "Un Cas de Changement de Personnalité avec Xénoglossie": 121–29
4. Kelly, et al., *Irreducible Mind:* 282.
5. Ibid., 283.
6. Beischel and Rock, "Addressing the Survival vs. Psi Debate Through Process-Focused Mediumship Research." Rock, Beischel, and Cott, "Psi vs. Survival."
7. Beischel and Schwartz, "Anomalous Information Reception by Research Mediums Demonstrated Using a Novel Triple-Blind Protocol."
8. Tart, "Who or What Might Survive Death?" in *Body Mind Spirit:* 182.
9. Barnum, "Expanded Consciousness."
10. Ibid., 264.
11. Rees, "The Bereaved and Their Hallucinations."

Chapter 13: Early Oneness

1. Ainsworth, "Deprivation of Maternal Care"; Geber, "The Psycho-motor Development of African Children in the First Year and the Influence of Maternal Behavior."
2. Inglis, *Natural and Supernatural:* 34.
3. Rose, *Primitive Psychic Power:* 49–50.
4. Inglis, *Natural and Supernatural:* 33; Sinel, *The Sixth Sense.*
5. Pearce, *Evolution's End:* 149.
6. Sheldrake and Wolpert, Telepathy Debate.
7. Gersi, *Faces in the Smoke:* 84–86.
8. Ibid., 86–91.

Chapter 14: Savants

1. Dossey, *Healing Beyond the Body:* 265–68.
2. Pearce, *Evolution's End:* 3–5.
3. Treffert and Wallace, "Islands of Genius."
4. Ibid.
5. Pearce, *Evolution's End:* 4.
6. Feinstein, "At Play in the Fields of the Mind."
7. Treffert, *Extraordinary People.*
8. Ibid., 1–2.
9. Pearce, *Evolution's End:* 4.
10. Treffert, *Extraordinary People:* 59–68.
11. Rimland, "Savant Capabilities of Autistic Children, and Their Cognitive Implications."

12. Treffert, *Extraordinary People:* 396.
13. Ibid., 396–97.
14. Ibid., 196–97; Treffert and Wallace, "Islands of Genius."
15. Treffert and Christensen, "Inside the Mind of a Savant."
16. Treffert, *Extraordinary People:* 163.
17. Duckett, "Adaptive and Maladaptive Behavior of Idiot Savants"; Duckett. "Idiot Savants."
18. Treffert and Wallace, "Islands of Genius."

Chapter 15: Twins

1. Swinburne, "The Higher Pantheism in a Nutshell": 14.
2. Dossey, "Lessons from Twins."
3. Allen, "The Mysteries of Twins."
4. Jackson, "Reunion of Identical Twins, Raised Apart, Reveals Some Astonishing Similarities": 48–56.
5. Wright, "Double Mystery."
6. Holden, "Identical Twins Reared Apart": 1323–1328.
7. Jackson, "Reunion of Identical Twins, Raised Apart, Reveals Some Astonishing Similarities": 50.
8. Allen, "The Mysteries of Twins."
9. Jackson, "Reunion of Identical Twins, Raised Apart, Reveals Some Astonishing Similarities": 56.
10. Holden, "Identical Twins Reared Apart": 1324.
11. Jackson, "Reunion of Identical Twins, Raised Apart, Reveals Some Astonishing Similarities": 48–56.
12. Wright, "Double Mystery": 62.
13. LeShan, *Landscapes of the Mind:* 186–87.
14. Jackson, "Reunion of Identical Twins, Raised Apart, Reveals Some Astonishing Similarities": 55–56.
15. Playfair, *Twin Telepathy:* 69.
16. Ibid., 77.
17. Ibid.
18. Ibid., 81.

Chapter 16: Telesomatic Events

1. Schwarz, "Possible Telesomatic Reactions."
2. Gurney, Myers, and Podmore, *Phantasms of the Living:* 188–89.
3. Ibid., 132.
4. Stevenson, *Telepathic Impressions:* 5–6.
5. Rush, "New Directions in Parapsychological Research."
6. Rhine, "Psychological Processes in ESP Experiences."
7. Playfair, *Twin Telepathy:* 11–35.
8. Ibid., 52–55.
9. Ibid., 55–56.
10. Vanderbilt and Furness, *Double Exposure:* xi–xii.
11. Playfair, *Twin Telepathy:* 16.
12. Ibid., 51.
13. Kincheloe, "Intuitive Obstetrics."
14. Dean, Plyler, and Dean, "Should Psychic Studies Be Included in Psychiatric Education?"
15. *Survey of Physicians' Views on Miracles;* Schwartz, "An American Profile."
16. Schwartz, "An American Profile."
17. Evans, "Parapsychology—What the Questionnaire Revealed."
18. Bem and Honorton, "Does Psi Exist?"

19. Hansen, *The Trickster and the Paranormal:* 148–61; Hansen, "CSICOP and the Skeptics"; Carter, *Parapsychology and the Skeptics.*

Chapter 17: Absolutely Convinced

1. Radin, *The Conscious Universe;* Radin, *Entangled Minds.*
2. The following publications are relevant to Russell Targ's research: Targ, *Do You See What I See?;* Targ, *Limitless Mind;* Targ and Puthoff, *Mind-Reach;* Targ and Puthoff, "Scanning the Issue"; Targ and Puthoff, "Information Transmission under Conditions of Sensory Shielding"; Targ, "Remote Viewing at Stanford Research Institute in the 1970s."
3. Targ, "Why I Am Absolutely Convinced of the Reality of Psychic Abilities and Why You Should Be Too."
4. Dossey, "Making Money": 49–59.
5. Puthoff, "CIA-Initiated Remote Viewing Program at Stanford Research Institute."
6. Targ, "Why I Am Absolutely Convinced of the Reality of Psychic Abilities and Why You Should Be Too."
7. Targ, *Limitless Mind:* 7–8.
8. Ibid., 83.
9. Vedral, "Living in a Quantum World"; Dossey, "All Tangled Up."
10. Targ, *Limitless Mind:* 8; Bohm and Hiley, The Undivided Universe: 382–86.
11. Targ, *Limitless Mind:* 8.

Chapter 18: Downed Planes and Sunken Ships

1. Targ and Puthoff, *Mind Reach.*
2. Schnabel, *Remote Viewers:* 215 ff; Swanson, *The Synchronized Universe:* 33.
3. Schwartz, "Nonlocal Awareness and Visions of the Future."
4. *Psychic Sea Hunt.*
5. Schwartz, *Opening to the Infinite:* 180–201.
6. Ibid., 199.
7. Ibid., 197–98.
8. Ibid., 198–99.
9. Schwartz, *The Secret Vaults of Time.*

Chapter 19: The Missing Harp and the Library Angel

1. Gallagher, "Psychoanalyst and Clinical Professor Elizabeth 'Lisby' Mayer Dies Jan. 1 at Age 57."
2. McCoy, *Power of Focused Mind Healing.* 1–3.
3. Mayer, *Extraordinary Knowing:* 1–3.
4. Ozark Research Institute.
5. Miller, *Emerging Issues in the Electronic Environment:* 24.
6. Combs and Holland, *Synchronicity:* 21.
7. Jordan, "In the Footnotes of Library Angels."
8. Wilson, *The Occult:* xxxix.
9. Bryson, *Notes From a Small Island:* 181.
10. Olson, "Is the Universe Friendly?"
11. Bull, Thinkexist.com.

Chapter 20: Healing and the One Mind

1. Achterberg, et al., "Evidence for Correlations Between Distant Intentionality and Brain Function in Recipients."
2. Graham, *Sit Down Young Stranger:* 179–94.
3. Ibid., 186.
4. Ibid., 190.
5. Hawkes, Website.

Chapter 21: The Dark Side

1. Stevenson, *Telepathic Impressions:* 131–32.
2. Romania's murderous twins; Playfair, 79-80.
3. Dossey, "Lessons from Twins."
4. "Propaganda in Nazi Germany." History Learning Site.
5. Mackay, *Extraordinary Popular Delusions and the Madness of Crowds:* xix.
6. Janis, *Victims of Groupthink.*
7. Will Rogers. Quoted at Dartmouth.org.

Chapter 22: The Cosmic Soup

1. Frost, *The Poetry of Robert Frost:* 33.
2. Pearce, *Evolution's End:* 8–9.
3. Ibid., 10–11.
4. Keller, *A Feeling for the Organism:* 48.
5. Briggs, *Fire in the Crucible:* 68.
6. Laszlo, *The Interconnected Universe:* 129.
7. Ibid., 130; Dossey, *Healing Beyond the Body:* 268–69.
8. Conrad, *Typhoon and Other Tales:* 21.
9. Ross, *Art and Its Significance:* 555.
10. Herbert, *Modern Artists on Art:* 77.
11. Fromm, *Creativity and Its Cultivation:* 51.
12. Hollander, "Child's Play."
13. Hollander, Personal communication.
14. Valletin, *Leonardo da Vinci:* 151–52 and 111.
15. Dickinson, "There's a Certain Slant of Light": 248.
16. Hadamard, *The Psychology of Invention in the Mathematical Field:* 142–43; Koestler, *The Act of Creation:* 171.
17. Greene, "Toward a Unity of Knowledge."
18. Hadamard, *The Psychology of Invention in the Mathematical Field:* 85.
19. Koestler, *The Act of Creation:* 170.
20. Ibid., 208.
21. Laszlo, *The Interconnected Universe:* 131.
22. Ibid.
23. Boswell, *Life of Samuel Johnson.*
24. Koestler, *Janus:* 284–85.
25. Smith, *Forgotten Truth:* 113.
26. Ibid., 113–14.
27. Ibid., 114.
28. Erdoes, *Lame Deer—Seeker of Visions:* 217.

Chapter 23: The Self

1. Diekman, "'I' = Awareness."
2. Einstein, *Ideas and Opinions:* 12.
3. Crick, *The Astonishing Hypothesis:* 271.
4. Ibid., 3.
5. Dennett, *Consciousness Explained:* 406.
6. Baggini, "The Self: Why Science Is Not Enough." 34–35.
7. Vernon, Philosophy and Life blog.
8. John 3:30, King James Version.
9. Jung, *Psychology and Religion:* 12.
10. Levin, *God, Faith, and Health;* Hummer, Rogers, Nam, and Ellison, "Religious Involvement and U. S. Adult Mortality."
11. Jauregui, *Epiphanies:* 70.
12. Merleau-Ponty, "Primordial Wholeness."

13. Keller, *A Feeling for the Organism:* 101.
14. Goethe, *Maximen und Reflexionen:* 435.
15. Kohut, *The Search for the Self:* 82.
16. Ibid., 174.
17. Ibid., 609.
18. Briggs, *Fire in the Crucible:* 68.
19. Segal, Collision with the Infinite: 49.
20. Simeon and Abugel, *Feeling Unreal:* 143–45.
21. Ibid., 63.
22. Segal, *Collision with the Infinite:* 122.
23. Ibid., 49.
24. Forman, *Enlightenment Ain't What It's Cracked Up to Be.*
25. Lanier, "From Having a Mystical Experience to Becoming a Mystic."
26. Ibid.
27. Syfransky, *Sunbeams:* 45.
28. Lara, *The Sun.*
29. Eckhart, *The Sun.*
30. Tillich, *The Courage to Be:* 179–180.
31. Cook, *The Life of Florence Nightingale:* 481.
32. Attributed to Jung.
33. Alan Watts. Quoted at Secondattention.com.

Chapter 24: Is the One Mind God?

1. Emerson, *Self-Reliance and Other Essays:* 108.
2. John 10:34, King James Version.
3. Luke 17:21, King James Version.
4. Eckhart, *Meister Eckhart: A Modern Translation:* 233–50.
5. Wilber, *Quantum Questions:* 92.
6. Smith, *Beyond the Post-Modern Mind:* 36.
7. Koestler, *Janus:* 289–91.
8. Smith, *Beyond the Post-Modern Mind:* 37.
9. Ibid., 38–39.
10. Ibid., 40.
11. Falk, *The Science of the Soul:* 2.
12. Lovejoy, *The Great Chain of Being:* 59.
13. Blackburn, *The Oxford Dictionary of Philosophy:* 55–56.
14. Wilber, *Eye to Eye:* 219.
15. Ibid., 243.
16. Wilber, *A Brief History of Everything:* 42–43.
17. Mason, *Al-Hallaj:* 30–96.
18. Meister Eckhart. Quoted at Goodreads.com.
19. Brown, "The Man from Whom God Hid Nothing."

Chapter 25: Removing the Stuffing from the Keyhole

1. John Milton, *The Oxford Book of English Verse:* No. 322, lines 51–55.
2. Koestler, *Janus:* 282.
3. Merrill. Interview by Helen Vendler.
4. Grosso, "The Advantages of Being Multiplex": 225–246.
5. Hall and Metcalf, *The Artist Outsider.*
6. Grosso, "The Advantages of Being Multiplex": 225–246.
7. Wölfli. Recited and set to music.
8. Breton. Quoted at the Adolf Wölfli Foundation website.
9. Grosso, "The Advantages of Being Multiplex": 241.
10. Posey and Losch, "Auditory Hallucinations of Hearing Voices in 375 Subjects."

11. *The Week* Staff, "Should Yoga Be an Olympic Sport?"

Chapter 26: Dream Pathways

1. Lessing, *The Making of the Representative for Planet 8.*
2. Dossey, *The Power of Premonitions.*
3. Koestler, *The Act of Creation:* 181.
4. Chesterman, *An Index of Possibilities:* 187.
5. Van de Castle, *Our Dreaming Mind:* 34–39.
6. De Becker, *The Understanding of Dreams and Their Influence on the History of Man:* 85.
7. Kedrov, *Voprosy Psikologii.*
8. Van de Castle, *Our Dreaming Mind:* 35–36.
9. Ibid., 36.
10. Ibid., 34–39.
11. Grellet, Wikipedia; Seebohm, *Memoirs of the Life and Gospel Labors of Stephen Grellet:* 434; Maeterlink, *The Unknown Guest:* 98–99.
12. Krippner, Bogzaran, and Percia de Carvalho, *Extraordinary Dreams and How to Work with Them:* 6.
13. Krippner and Faith, "Exotic Dreams: A Cross-Cultural Survey."
14. Laughlin, "Transpersonal Anthropology"; Laughlin, "Transpersonal Anthropology, Then and Now."
15. George, "Dreams, Reality, and the Desire and Intent of Dreamers as Experienced by a Fieldworker."
16. Inglis, *Natural and Supernatural:* 333.
17. Wagner-Pacifici and Bershady, "Portents or Confessions."
18. Luke, "Experiential Reclamation and First Person Parapsychology."
19. Priestley, *Man & Time:* 190–91.
20. Ibid., 211–12.

Chapter 27: Love Is the Last Word

1. Bell, *D. H. Lawrence:* 51.
2. Jahn and Dunne, *Margins of Reality:* 343.
3. Marano, "The Dangers of Loneliness."
4. Bell, "Ways of Overcoming Loneliness."
5. Ibid.
6. Pocheptsova, Ferraro, and Abraham, "The Effect of Mobile Phone Use on Prosocial Behavior."
7. Hu, "Will Online Chat Help Alleviate Mood Loneliness?" 219–223.
8. Hu, "Social Use of the Internet and Loneliness."
9. "I Am Lonely Will Anyone Speak to Me."
10. Andrews, "Misery Loves (Cyber) Company"; Burkeman, "Anybody There?"; Ratliff. "Hello, Loneliness."
11. Needleman, "The Heart of Philosophy."
12. List of social networking websites. Wikipedia.
13. Carter, *Science and the Near-Death Experience:* xv–xvi.
14. Huxley, *Tomorrow and Tomorrow and Tomorrow:* 57.
15. Ibid., 56.
16. Ibid., 56–57.
17. Dossey and Keegan, *Holistic Nursing.*
18. Golden, "William Osler at 150."
19. Achterberg, et al., "Evidence for Correlations Between Distant Intentionality and Brain Function in Recipients."
20. Jung, *Memories, Dreams, Reflections:* 354.
21. Jahn, "Report on the Academy of Consciousness Studies."

22. Whitman, *The Complete Poems:* 288–89.

Chapter 28: Expanding Science

1. For those who want an in-depth analysis of the incessant disagreements about the nature of consciousness, I recommend philosopher Chris Carter's discussion of consciousness in his book *Science and the Near-Death Experience.*
2. Kuhn, *The Structure of Scientific Revolutions.*
3. Greenhalgh, *How to Read a Paper:* 6.
4. I am by no means denigrating the great achievements of science nor the many great journals that have played a role in these accomplishments. I have served as executive editor for medical journals for 15 years.
5. Hellman, *Great Feuds in Science;* Hellman, *Great Feuds in Medicine.*
6. French, *William Harvey's Natural Philosophy:* 233–34.
7. Chauvois, *William Harvey:* 222–23.
8. Hellman, *Great Feuds in Medicine* by *Publishers Weekly.*
9. Nuland, *Doctors:* 168.
10. Garrison, *An Introduction to the History of Medicine:* 435–37.
11. Watson, *The Double Helix:* 14.
12. Koestler, *The Roots of Coincidence:* 15.
13. Kurtz, *A Skeptic's Handbook of Parapsychology:* 89.
14. One of the most recent examples of these periodic spasms of intolerance against so-called paranormal science was recently played out in the *New York Times.* (Dossey, "Why Are Scientists Afraid of Daryl Bem?")
15. Splane, *Quantum Consciousness:* 80.

Chapter 29: Transcendence

1. Trismegistus, *Hermetica:* 344; Compare with Emerson: "The doctrine of the divine nature being forgotten, a sickness infects and dwarfs the constitution. Once man was all; now he is an appendage, a nuisance. . . . The doctrine of inspiration is lost. . . . The doctrine of the soul . . . exist[s] as ancient history merely . . . [and]when suggested, seem[s] ridiculous. Life is comic or pitiful, as soon as the high ends of being fade out of sight, and man becomes near-sighted, and can only attend to what addresses the senses." (Emerson, *Self-Reliance and Other Essays:* 106–07.)
2. Walker, *Anything We Love Can Be Saved:* 5.
3. Hesse, *Demian:* prologue.
4. Havel, Speech to Congress.
5. Havel, "The Need for Transcendence in the Postmodern World."
6. Russell, *The Global Brain:* 18.
7. Ibid.
8. Edge, "Spirituality in the Natural and Social Worlds."
9. Evans, *Spirituality and Human Nature:* 166.
10. Ibid., 266.
11. Campbell, *The Hero's Journey:* 40.
12. Targ, *The Reality of ESP:* 248.
13. Cleary, *The Flower Ornament Scripture.*
14. Targ, *The Reality of ESP:* 248.
15. The phrase is Martin Heidegger's: "A person is neither a thing nor a process, but an opening or clearing through which the Absolute can manifest." University of Arizona Computer Science website. www.cs.arizona.edu/~kece/Personal/quotes.html. Accessed March 24, 2012.
16. Rumi, *Rumi: The Big Red Book:* 28.
17. Rumi, *Rumi: The Book of Love:* 169.

REFERENCES

Aanstoos, Christopher. "Psi and the Phenomenology of the Long Body." *Theta.* 1986; 13–14: 49–51.

Achterberg, J., et al. "Evidence for Correlations Between Distant Intentionality and Brain Function in Recipients: A Functional Magnetic Resonance Imaging Analysis." *Journal of Alternative and Complementary Medicine.* 2005; 11(6): 965–71.

Ainsworth, Mary D. "Deprivation of Maternal Care: A Reassessment of its Effects." *Public Health Papers.* No. 14. Geneva; World Health Organization; 1962; 14: 97–165.

Akashic Records. Wikipedia. http://en.wikipedia.org/wiki/Akashic_records. Accessed December 3, 2011.

Albert, David Z. and Rivka Galchen. "Was Einstein Wrong? A Quantum Threat to Special Relativity." *Scientific American.* www.scientificamerican.com/article.cfm?id=was -einstein-wrong-about-relativity. February 18, 2009. Accessed January 21, 2012.

Alderton, David. *Animal Grief: How Animals Mourn.* Dorcester, U.K.: Hubble & Hattie; 2011.

Alexander, Charles D. *Bobbie, A Great Collie.* New York: Dodd, Mead and Company; 1926.

Alexander III, Eben. "Life Beyond Death: Consciousness is the Most Profound Mystery in the Universe." www.lifebeyonddeath.net. Accessed December 1, 2011.

———. "Neurosurgeon Eben Alexander's Near-Death Experience Defies Medical Model of Consciousness." Interview by Alex Tsakaris. Skeptiko.com. www.skeptiko .com/154-neurosurgeon-dr-eben-alexander-near-death-experience/. Accessed December 2, 2011.

———. *Proof of Heaven: A Neurosurgeon's Journey into the Afterlife.* New York: Simon & Schuster; 2012.

Al-Hallaj, Mansur. Wikipedia. http://en.wikipedia.org/wiki/Mansur_Al-Hallaj. Accessed December 5, 2011.

Allen, Arthur. "The Mysteries of Twins." *The Washington Post.* January 11, 1998. www .washingtonpost.com/wp-srv/national/longterm/twins/twins1.htm. Accessed December 23, 2010.

Almeder, Robert. *Death and Personal Survival: The Evidence for Life after Death.* Lanham, MD: Rowman & Littlefield; 1992.

"Amazing Moment Mila the Beluga Whale Saved a Stricken Diver's Life by Pushing Her to the Surface." Daily Mail online. www.dailymail.co.uk/news/worldnews/article -1202941/Pictured-The-moment-Mila-brave-Beluga-whale-saved-stricken-divers-life -pushing-surface.html. Accessed May 16, 2011.

Andrews, Robert. "Misery Loves (Cyber) Company." Wired.com, June 30, 2005. http://www.wired.com/culture/lifestyle/news/2005/06/68010. Accessed November 24, 2011.

Anonymous. "Telling the Bees." Dailygrail.com. www.dailygrail.com/blogs/shadow /2005/7/Telling-Bees. Accessed January 10, 2011.

Apollo 14. Wikipedia. http://en.wikipedia.org/wiki/Apollo_14. Accessed December 26, 2011.

Armstrong, Susan J. "Souls in Process: A Theoretical Inquiry into Animal Psi." In Michael Stoeber and Hugo Meynell (eds.). *Critical Reflections on the Paranormal.* Albany, NY: SUNY Press; 1996.

Autrey, Wesley. Wikipedia. http://en.wikipedia.org/wiki/Wesley_Autrey. Accessed January 1, 2012.

Ayer, A. J. "Ayer's Intimations of Immortality: What Happens When the World's Most Eminent Atheist Dies." *National Review.* October 14, 1988.

———. "Postscript to a Postmortem." London: *The Spectator.* October 15, 1988.

———. "What I Saw When I Was Dead." London: *Sunday Telegraph.* August 28, 1988.

———. "What I Saw When I Was Dead." In Paul Edwards (ed.). *Immortality.* Amherst, NY: Prometheus; 1997.

Baggini, Julian. *The Ego Trick.* London: Granta; 2012.

———. "The Self: Why Science Is Not Enough." *New Scientist.* March 12, 2011; 209(2803): 34–35.

Baker, Carlos. *Emerson Among the Eccentrics.* New York: Penguin; 1996.

Baldwin, Neil. *Edison: Inventing the Century.* New York: Hyperion; 1995.

Banville, John. "The Most Entertaining Philosopher." *The New York Review of Books.* October 27, 2011: 40–42.

Barasch, Marc. Green World Campaign. http://greenworld.org. Accessed January 2, 2013.

Bardens, Dennis and David Bellamy. *Psychic Animals.* New York: Holt; 1989.

Barnum, Barbara S. "Expanded Consciousness: Nurses' Experiences." *Nursing Outlook.* 1989; 37(6): 260–66.

Barrington, Mary Rose, Peter Mulacz, and Titus Rivas. "The Case of Iris Farczáday—a Stolen Life." *Journal of the Society for Psychical Research.* 2005; 69(879): 49–77.

Bartal, Inbal Ben-Ami, Jean Decety, and Peggy Mason. "Empathy and Pro-Social Behavior in Rats." *Science.* December 9, 2011; 334 (6061): 1427–30.

Bateson, Gregory. *Steps to an Ecology of Mind.* San Francisco: Chandler Press; 1972.

Beauregard, Mario. *Brain Wars: The Scientific Battle Over the Existence of the Mind and the Proof That Will Change the Way We Live Our Lives.* New York: HarperOne; 2012.

Becker, Carl. *Paranormal Experience and the Survival of Death.* Albany, NY: State University of New York Press; 1993.

Bee. Wikipedia. http://en.wikipedia.org/wiki/Bee_(mythology). Accessed January 9, 2011.

Beischel, Julie and A. J. Rock. "Addressing the Survival vs. Psi Debate Through Process-Focused Mediumship Research." *Journal of Parapsychology.* 2009; 73: 71–90.

Beischel, Julie and Gary E. Schwartz. "Anomalous Information Reception by Research Mediums Demonstrated Using a Novel Triple-Blind Protocol." *Explore: The Journal of Science and Healing.* 2007; 3(1): 23–27.

Bell, Eva. "Ways of Overcoming Loneliness." Ezinearticles.com. http://ezinearticles.com/?Ways-of-Overcoming-Loneliness&id=4417336. Accessed November 24, 2011.

Bell, Michael. *D. H. Lawrence: Language and Being.* New York: Cambridge University Press; 1992.

Bell, Thia. Interview with David Bohm. *Ojai Valley News.* December 30, 1987.

Belluck, Pam. "Strangers May Cheer You Up, Study Shows." *The New York Times* online. www.nytimes.com/2008/12/05/health/05happy-web.html. December 4, 2008. Accessed January 17, 2012.

Beloff, John. *Parapsychology: A Concise History.* New York: St. Martin's Press; 1993.

Bem, Daryl J. and Charles Honorton. "Does Psi Exist? Replicable Evidence for an Anomalous Process of Information Transfer." *Psychological Bulletin.* 1994; 115: 4–8.

Benedict, Mellen-Thomas. Interview by E. W. Moser. *Wisdom.* http://wisdom-magazine.com/Article.aspx/1164. Accessed January 5, 2011.

———. "Insights from the Other Side: Mellen-Thomas Benedict's Near-Death Experience." http://www.near-death.com/experiences/reincarnation04.html. Accessed January 20, 2011.

Bengston, William F. *The Energy Cure.* Louisville, CO: Sounds True; 2010.

Bengston, William F. and David Krinsley. "The Effect of the 'Laying-on of Hands' on Transplanted Breast Cancer in Mice." *Journal of Scientific Exploration.* 2000; 14 (3): 353–64.

Benson, Herbert, et al. "Study of the Therapeutic Effects of Intercessory Prayer (STEP) in Cardiac Bypass Patients: A Multicenter Randomized Trial of Uncertainty and Certainty of Receiving Intercessory Prayer." *American Heart Journal.* 2006; 151: 934–42.

Benson, Michael. *Beyond: Visions of the Interplanetary Probes.* New York: Abrams; 2008.

———. *Far Out: A Space-Time Chronicle.* New York: Abrams; 2009.

Berg, Elizabeth. *The Sun.* November 1995; 239: 40.

Berger, Hans. *Psyche.* Jena: Gustav Fischer; 1940.

———. Wikipedia. http://en.wikipedia.org/wiki/Hans_Berger. Accessed December 12, 2011.

Bergson, Henri-Louis. *The Creative Mind.* New York: Citadel Press; 1946.

———. Presidential address. *Proceedings of the Society for Psychical Research.* 1913; 26: 462–79.

Bernstein, Jeremy. *Quantum Profiles.* Princeton, NJ: Princeton University Press; 1990.

Best, Nicholas. *Five Days That Shocked the World.* New York: Thomas Dunne Books; 2011.

Bischof, M. "Introduction to Integrative Biophysics." In Fritz-Albert Popp and Lev Be-loussov (eds.). *Integrative Biophysics: Biophotonics.* Dordrecht, The Netherlands: Kluwer Academic Publishers; 2003.

Black, Edwin. "Eugenics and the Nazis—the California Connection." *San Francisco Chronicle.* November 9, 2003. http://articles.sfgate.com/2003-11-09/opinion /17517477_1_eugenics-ethnic-cleansing-master-race. Accessed January 18, 2011.

Blackburn, Simon. *The Oxford Dictionary of Philosophy.* Oxford, U.K.: Oxford University Press; 1994.

Blum, Deborah. *Ghost Hunters: William James and the Search for Scientific Proof of Life after Death.* New York: Penguin; 2006.

Bobrow, Robert S. "Evidence for a Communal Consciousness." *Explore: The Journal of Science and Healing.* 2011; 7(4): 246–48.

———. *The Witch in the Waiting Room.* New York: Thunder's Mouth Press; 2006.

Bohm, David. *Wholeness and the Implicate Order.* London: Routledge and Kegan Paul; 1980.

———. Interview by John Briggs, F. David Peat. *Omni.* January 1987; 9(4): 68.

Bohm, David and Basil Hiley. *The Undivided Universe.* London: Routledge; 1993.

Bohm, David and Jiddu Krishnamurti. *The Limits of Thought: Discussions between J. Krishnamurti and David Bohm.* London: Routledge; 1999.

Bond, Michael. "Three Degrees of Contagion." *New Scientist.* 2009; 201(2689): 24–27.

Borysenko, Joan. "Shared Deathbed Visions." Near-death.com. www.near-death.com /experiences/evidence09.html. Accessed March 6, 2012.

Boswell, James. *Life of Samuel Johnson.* London, 1777.

Boulding, Kenneth. "The Practice of the Love of God." William Penn Lecture. Deliv-ered at Arch Street Meetinghouse, Philadelphia, 1942.

Boycott, B. B. "Learning in the Octopus." *Scientific American.* 1965; 212(3): 42–50.

Braud, William. "Wellness Implications of Retroactive Intentional Influence: Exploring an Outrageous Hypothesis." *Alternative Therapies in Health & Medicine.* 2000; 6(1): 37–48. http://inclusivepsychology.com/uploads/WellnessImplicationsOfRetroactive IntentionalInfluence.pdf. Accessed January 5, 2011.

Braud, William and Marilyn Schlitz. "A Methodology for the Objective Study of Transpersonal Imagery." *Journal of Scientific Exploration.* 1989; 3(1): 43–63.

Braud, William, D. Shafer, and S. Andrews. "Electrodermal Correlates of Remote At-tention: Autonomic Reactions to an Unseen Gaze." *Proceedings of the Presented Papers, Parapsychology Association 33rd Annual Convention,* Chevy Chase, MD; 1990: 14–28.

———. "Possible Role of Intuitive Data Sorting in Electrodermal Biological Psychoki-nesis (bio-PK)." In *Research in Parapsychology 1987.* Metuchen, NJ: Scarecrow Press; 1988.

Braude, Stephen E. "The Creativity of Dissociation." *Journal of Trauma and Dissociation.* 2002; 3(5): 5–26.

———. *Immortal Remains: The Evidence for Life after Death.* Lanham, MD: Rowman & Littlefield; 2003.

Brazier, G. F. "Bobbie: The Wonder Dog of Oregon." In Curtis Wager-Smith (ed.). *Animal Pals*. Philadelphia: Macrae Smith Company; 1924. See http://silvertonor.com /murals/bobbie/bobbie_wonder_dog2.htm. Accessed January 7, 2011.

Breton, André. Quoted in Adolf Wölfli. Adolf Wölfli Foundation. www.adolfwoelfli.ch /index.php?c=e&level=17&sublevel=0. Accessed March 24, 2011.

Brian, Dennis. *Genius Talk: Conversations with Nobel Scientists and Other Luminaries.* Dordrecht, Netherlands: Kluwer Academic Publishers; 1995.

Briggs, John. *Fire in the Crucible.* Los Angeles: Jeremy P. Tarcher; 1990.

Broad, C. D. *Lectures in Psychical Research.* Routledge revival edition. London: Routledge; 2010.

Brown, Arthur. "The Man from Whom God Hid Nothing." www.philosophos.com /philosophy_article_105.html. Accessed December 4, 2011.

Brown, Dan. *The Lost Symbol.* New York: Doubleday; 2009.

Brunton, Paul. Quoted in *Network Newsletter* (of the Scientific and Medical Network, U.K.). April 1987; 33: 18.

Bryson, Bill. *Notes from a Small Island.* New York: William Morrow; 1997.

Buchmann, Stephen. *Letters from the Hive: An Intimate History of Bees, Honey, and Humankind.* New York: Bantam; 2006.

Bucke, R. M. *Cosmic Consciousness.* Philadelphia: Innes & Sons; 1901.

Buckley, Cara. "Man is Rescued by Stranger on Subway Tracks." *The New York Times* online. January 3, 2007. www.nytimes.com/2007/01/03/nyregion/03life.html. Accessed January 8, 2012.

Bull, Emma. *Bone Dance: A Fantasy for Technophiles.* Reprint edition. New York: Orb; 2009.

———. Thinkexist.com. http://69.59.157.161/quotes/emma_bull. Accessed December 14, 2011.

Burkeman, Oliver. "Anybody There?" *The Guardian* online. http://www.guardian.co .uk/technology/2005/aug/30/g2.onlinesupplement. August 29, 2005. Accessed November 25, 2011.

Burt, Cyril. *Psychology and Psychical Research. The Seventeenth Frederick W. H. Myers Memorial Lecture.* London; 1968; 50: 58–59.

Campbell, Joseph. Phil Cousineau (ed.).*The Hero's Journey: Joseph Campbell on His Life and Work.* Third edition. Novato, CA: New World Library; 2003.

———. *The Inner Reaches of Outer Space.* Novato, CA: New World Library. Third (revised) edition; 2002.

Campbell, Joseph and Michael Toms. *An Open Life: Joseph Campbell in Conversation with Michael Toms.* Burdett, NY: Larson Publications; 1988.

Cardeña, Etzel, S. J. Lynn, and S. Krippner (eds.). *Varieties of Anomalous Experience: Examining the Scientific Evidence.* Washington, DC: American Psychological Association; 2000.

Carey, Benedict. "Journal's Paper on ESP Expected to Prompt Outrage." *The New York Times* online. http://www.nytimes.com/2011/01/06/science/06esp. html?pagewanted=all&_r=0. Accessed January 22, 2012.

Caribou. U. S. Fish and Wildlife Service. Arctic National Wildlife Refuge. http://arctic .fws.gov/caribou.htm. Accessed December 5, 2010.

Carpenter, James C. *First Sight: ESP and Parapsychology in Everyday Life.* Latham, MD: Rowman & Littlefield; 2012.

———. "First Sight: Part One. A Model of Psi and the Mind." *Journal of Parapsychology.* 2004; 68(2): 217–54.

———. "First Sight: Part Two. Elaboration of Model of Psi and the Mind." *Journal of Parapsychology.* 2004; 69(1): 63–112.

Carter, Chris. *Parapsychology and the Skeptics.* Pittsburgh, PA: Sterlinghouse; 2007.

———. *Science and the Afterlife Experience.* Rochester, VT: Inner Traditions; 2012.

———. *Science and the Near-Death Experience: How Consciousness Survives Death.* Rochester, VT: Inner Traditions; 2010.

"Cat heroes." Squidoo.com. www.squidoo.com/catheroes#module9861309. Accessed February 6, 2013.

Cellzic, M. "Dolphins Save Surfer from Becoming Shark's Bait." Today.com. http://today.msnbc.msn.com/id/21689083/. Accessed May 14, 2011.

Chang, Richard S. "Texting is More Dangerous Than Driving Drunk." *The New York Times* online. July 25, 2009. http://wheels.blogs.nytimes.com/2009/06/25/texting-is -more-dangerous-than-driving-drunk/. Accessed March 20, 2011.

Charman, R. A. "Minds, Brains and Communication." *Network Review* (UK). Spring 2007: 11–15.

Chauvois, Louis. *William Harvey: His Life and Times, His Discoveries, His Methods.* New York: Philosophical Library; 1957.

Chesterman, J. *An Index of Possibilities: Energy and Power.* New York: Pantheon; 1975.

Christakis, Nicholas A. and James H. Fowler. *Connected: The Surprising Power of Our Social Networks and How They Shape Our Lives.* Boston: Little, Brown; 2009.

———. "The Spread of Obesity in a Large Social Network over 32 Years." *New England Journal of Medicine.* 2007; 357: 370–79.

Churchill, Winston. Wikiquote. http://en.wikiquote.org/wiki/Winston_Churchill. Accessed February 2, 2012.

Clark, Glenn. *The Man Who Tapped the Secrets of the Universe.* Minneapolis: Filiquarian Publishing; 2007.

Clark, Nancy. *Divine Moments.* Fairfield, IA: 1st World Publishing; 2012.

Cleary, Thomas (ed.). *The Flower Ornament Scripture.* Boston: Shambhala; 1993.

Clive, Sophie Windsor. Murmuration. http://vimeo.com/31158841. Accessed December 29, 2011.

Cole, David (ed.). *The Torture Memos: Rationalizing the Unthinkable.* New York: The New Press; 2009.

Combs, Allan and Mark Holland. *Synchronicity: Through the Eyes of Science, Myth and the Trickster.* New York: Marlowe/Avalon; 1996.

Conrad, Joseph. *Typhoon and Other Tales.* New York: New American Library; 1925.

Cook, Edward. *The Life of Florence Nightingale.* Volume 1. London: Macmillan; 1913.

Cook, Francis H. *Hua-Yen Buddhism: The Jewel Net of Indra.* University Park, PA: Penn State University Press; 1977.

Cottrell, J. E., G. A. Winer, and M. C. Smith. "Beliefs of Children and Adults about Feeling Stares of Unseen Others." *Developmental Biology.* 1996; 32: 50–61.

Cox, Craig. "If You Market 'Nothing,' Everyone Will Want It." *Utne Reader.* July–August 1999. www.utne.com/1999-07-01/NothingQuiteLikeIt.aspx. Accessed November 12, 2011.

Crick, Francis. *The Astonishing Hypothesis: The Scientific Search for the Soul.* New York: Simon & Schuster; 1994.

Da Vinci, Leonardo. Quoted at Goodreads.com. www.goodreads.com/quotes/tag /cats. Accessed November 24, 2012.

Darling, David. *Soul Search.* New York: Villard; 1995.

———. "Supposing Something Different: Reconciling Science and the Afterlife." *OMNI.* 1995; 17(9): 4.

Davenport, Richard. *An Outline of Animal Development.* Reading, MA: Addison-Wesley; 1979.

Dawkins, Richard. *The God Delusion.* New York: Mariner; 2008.

———. *The Selfish Gene.* 30th anniversary edition. Oxford, U.K.: Oxford University Press; 2006.

De Beauregard, O. Costa. Address to the Third Annual Meeting of the Society for Scientific Exploration, October 11–13, 1996, Freiburg, Germany.

De Becker, Raymond. *The Understanding of Dreams and Their Influence on the History of Man.* New York: Hawthorn Books; 1968.

De Chardin, Pierre Teilhard. *The Future of Man.* New York: HarperCollins; 1964.

De Gaulle, Charles. Quoted at Goodreads.com. www.goodreads.com/quotes/tag /dogs. Accessed November 24, 2012.

Dean, Douglas and John Mihalasky. *Executive ESP.* Englewood Cliffs, NJ: Prentice-Hall; 1974.

Dean, Stanley R., C. O. Plyler, Jr., and M. L. Dean. "Should Psychic Studies Be Included in Psychiatric Education? An Opinion Survey." *American Journal of Psychiatry.* 1980; 137(10): 1247–49.

Dennett, Daniel C. *Breaking the Spell: Religion As a Natural Phenomenon.* New York: Penguin; 2007.

———. *Consciousness Explained.* Boston: Back Bay Books; 1992.

Deonna, Waldemar. *De la Planète Mars en Terre Sainte: Art et Subconscient, Un Médium Peintre: Hélène Smith.* Paris: De Boccard; 1932.

Devorkin, David and Robert Smith. *Hubble: Imaging Space and Time.* Washington, DC: National Geographic; 2008.

Diamond, Jared. *Collapse: How Societies Choose to Fail or Succeed.* New York: Penguin; 2005.

Dickinson, Emily. Thomas H. Johnson (ed.). *The Complete Poems of Emily Dickinson.* Boston: Little, Brown; 1960.

————. Thomas H. Johnson (ed.). "There's a Certain Slant of Light." In *Final Harvest: Emily Dickinson's Poems*. Boston: Little, Brown; 1961.

Diekman, Arthur J. "'I' = Awareness." *Journal of Consciousness Studies*. 1996; 3(4): 350–56.

Dobzhansky, Theodosius. *Genetics and the Origin of Species*. 3rd ed. New York: Columbia University Press; 1951.

"Dolphins Save Lifeguards from Circling Great White Shark." www.joe-ks.com. http://joe-ks.com/archives_nov2004/Dolphins_Save_Lifeguards.htm. Accessed May 15, 2011.

Donne, John. John Carey (ed.). *John Donne: The Major Works*. Oxford, U.K.: Oxford University Press; 1990.

Doore, Gary (ed.). *What Survives?* Los Angeles: Jeremy P. Tarcher; 1990.

Dosa, David. "A Day in the Life of Oscar the Cat." *New England Journal of Medicine*. 2007; 357(4): 328–29.

Dossey, Barbara and Lynn Keegan. *Holistic Nursing: A Handbook for Practice*. 6th edition. Burlington, MA: Jones & Bartlett Learning; 2013.

Dossey, Larry. "All Tangled Up: Life in a Quantum World." *Explore: The Journal of Science and Healing*. 2011; 7(6): 335–44.

————. "Distance Healing: Evidence." In R. M. Schoch, L.Yonavjak (eds.). *The Parapsychology Revolution: A Concise Anthology of Paranormal and Psychical Research*. New York: Tarcher/Penguin; 2008: 216–23.

————. *Healing Beyond the Body*. Boston: Shambhala; 2003.

————. "Healing Research: What We Know and Don't Know." *Explore: The Journal of Science and Healing*. 2008; 4(6): 341–52.

————. "Lessons from Twins: Of Nature, Nurture, and Consciousness." *Alternative Therapies in Health and Medicine*. 1997; 3(3): 8–15.

————. *The Power of Premonitions*. New York: Dutton; 2009.

————. *Recovering the Soul*. New York: Bantam; 1989.

————. *Space, Time & Medicine*. Boston: Shambhala; 1982.

————. "Strange Contagions: Of Laughter, Jumps, Jerks, and Mirror Neurons." *Explore: The Journal of Science and Healing*. May 2010; 6(3): 119–28.

————. "Why Are Scientists Afraid of Daryl Bem?" *Explore: The Journal of Science and Healing*. 2011; 7(3): 127–37.

Duane, T. D., and T. Behrendt. "Extrasensory Electroencephalographic Induction Between Identical Twins." *Science*. 1965; 150(3694): 367.

Duckett, Jane. "Adaptive and Maladaptive Behavior of Idiot Savants." *American Journal of Mental Deficiency*. 1977; 82: 308–11.

————. "Idiot Savants: Super-Specialization in Mutually Retarded Persons." Unpublished doctoral dissertation. University of Texas at Austin, Department of Special Education; 1976.

Dutton, Diane and Carl Williams. "Clever Beasts and Faithful Pets: A Critical Review of Animal Psi Research." *Journal of Parapsychology*. 2009; 73(1): 43. Available at: Thefreelibrary.com. www.thefreelibrary.com/Clever+beasts+and+faithful+pets%3A+a+critical+review+of+animal+psi-a0219588957. Accessed January 22, 2011.

Dyson, Freeman. *Infinite in All Directions.* New York: Harper and Row; 1988.

Eccles, Sir John and Daniel N. Robinson. *The Wonder of Being Human.* Boston: Shambhala; 1985.

Eckhart, Meister. Raymond B. Blakney (trans.). *Meister Eckhart: A Modern Translation.* New York: Harper & Row; 1941.

———. Quoted at Goodreads.com. www.goodreads.com/author/quotes/73092 .Meister_Eckhart. Accessed December 3, 2011.

———. Edmund Colledge and Bernard McGinn (trans.). *Meister Eckhart: The Essential Sermons.* Mahwah, NJ: Paulist Press; 1981: 204–5.

———. "Spiritual Practices: Silence." www.spiritualityandpractice.com/practices /practices.php?id=28&g=1. Accessed January 7, 2012.

Eddington, Sir Arthur. *The Nature of the Physical World.* New York: Macmillan; 1928.

Edge, Hoyt L. "Spirituality in the Natural and Social Worlds." In Charles T. Tart, (ed.). *Body, Mind, Spirit: Exploring the Parapsychology of Spirituality.* Charlottesville, VA: Hampton Roads; 1997.

Edwards, Paul (ed.). *Immortality.* Amherst, NY: Prometheus Books; 1997.

Einstein, Albert. *Ideas and Opinions.* New York: Crown; 1954: 12.

———. Quoted in *The New York Times.* March 29, 1972.

———. Wikiquote. http://en.wikiquote.org/wiki/Albert_Einstein. Accessed February 4, 2012.

Einstein, Albert, Boris Podolsky, and Nathan Rosen. "Can Quantum-Mechanical Description of Physical Reality Be Considered Complete?" *Physical Review.* 1935; 47 (10): 777–80.

Emerson, Ralph Waldo. *Essays: First Series.* Reprint edition. Seattle, WA: CreateSpace; 2011.

———. *Essays and Lectures.* Lawrence, KS: Digireads.com Publishing; 2009.

———. Stanley Applebaum (ed.). *Self-Reliance and Other Essays.* New York: Dover; 1993.

———. David M. Robinson (ed.). *The Spiritual Emerson: Essential Writings .* Boston: Beacon Press; 2004.

Ensisheim meteorite. Encyclopedia of Science. www.daviddarling.info/encyclopedia/E /Ensisheim_meteorite.html. Accessed February 17, 2012.

Erdoes, Richard. *Lame Deer—Seeker of Visions.* New York: Simon & Schuster; 1972.

Evans, Christopher. "Parapsychology—What the Questionnaire Revealed." *New Scientist.* January 25, 1973; 57(830): 209.

Evans, Donald. *Spirituality and Human Nature.* Albany, NY: SUNY Press; 1993.

Falk, Geoffrey D. *The Science of the Soul.* Nevada City, CA: Blue Dolphin Publishing; 2004.

Feinstein, David. "At Play in the Fields of the Mind: Personal Myths as Fields of Information." *Journal of Humanistic Psychology.* Summer 1998; 38(3): 71–109.

Fenwick, Peter and Elizabeth Fenwick. *The Truth in the Light.* New York: Berkley; 1997.

Feynman, Richard P. *Six Easy Pieces.* Fourth edition. New York: Basic Books: 2011.

"Final Report of the Tuskegee Syphilis Study Legacy Committee—May 20, 1996." Claude Moore Health Sciences Library, University of Virginia Health System. www.hsl .virginia.edu/historical/medical_history/bad_blood/report.cfm. Accessed January 5, 2011.

Finocchiaro, Maurice A. (ed. and trans.). *The Galileo Affair: A Documentary History.* Available online at: http://web.archive.org/web/20070930013053/http://astro.wcupa .edu/mgagne/ess362/resources/finocchiaro.html#sentence. Accessed January 1, 2011.

Fiol, C. Marlene and Edward J. O'Connor. "The Power of Mind: What If the Game Is Bigger than We Think?" *Journal of Management Inquiry.* 2004; 13(4): 342–52.

Flat Earth Society. www.theflatearthsociety.org/forum/index.php. Accessed December 10, 2011.

Flutterofwings. www.yourghoststories.com/real-ghost-story.php?story=2832. Accessed December 25, 2011.

Fodor, Jerry A. "The Big Idea: Can There Be a Science of Mind?" *Times Literary Supplement.* July 3, 1992.

Fodor, Nandor and Oliver Lodge. *Encyclopedia of Psychic Science.* Whitefish, MT: Kessinger Publishing; 2003.

Forman, Robert. *Enlightenment Ain't What It's Cracked Up To Be.* Alresford, Hants, U.K.: O-Books/John Hunt Publishing; 2011.

Foster, Charles. *The Selfless Gene: Living with God and Darwin.* Nashville, TN: Thomas Nelson, Inc.; 2010.

Fowler, James H. and Nicholas Christakis. "Dynamic Spread of Happiness in a Large Social Network: Longitudinal Analysis Over 20 Years in the Framingham Heart Study." *British Medical Journal.* 2008; 337: a2338.

French, Roger. *William Harvey's Natural Philosophy.* Cambridge, U.K.: Cambridge University Press; 1994.

Fromm, Erich. *Creativity and Its Cultivation.* New York: Harper & Row; 1959.

Frost, Robert. From "Mending Wall." *The Poetry of Robert Frost.* New York: Henry Holt; 1979.

Gallagher, N. "Psychoanalyst and Clinical Professor Elizabeth 'Lisby' Mayer Dies Jan. 1 at Age 57." *UC Berkeley News.* January 6, 2005. www.berkeley.edu/news/media /releases/2005/01/06_lisby.shtml. Accessed February 21, 2007.

Gallup, Jr., George and W. Proctor. *Adventures in Immortality: A Look Beyond the Threshold of Death.* New York: McGraw-Hill; 1982.

Gallup Poll. "New Poll Gauges Americans' General Knowledge Levels." www.gallup .com/poll/3742/new-poll-gauges-americans-general-knowledge-levels.aspx. Accessed December 10, 2011.

Galton, Francis. *Memories of My Life.* London: Methuen; 1908.

———. Vox populi. *Nature.* 1907; 75: 450–51.

Gandhi, Kishore (ed.).*The Evolution of Consciousness.* New York: Paragon House; 1986.

Garrison, Fielding H. *An Introduction to the History of Medicine.* Fourth edition. Philadelphia: W. B. Saunders; 1929.

Geber, Marcelle. "The Psycho-motor Development of African Children in the First Year and the Influence of Maternal Behavior." *Journal of Social Psychology.* 1958; 47: 185–95.

Gefter, Amanda. "Near-Death Neurologist: Dreams on the Border of Life." *New Scientist.* December 22, 2010; 2792: 80–81.

George, Marianne. "Dreams, Reality, and the Desire and Intent of Dreamers as Experienced by a Fieldworker." *Anthropology of Consciousness.* 1995; 6(3): 17–33.

Gersi, Douchan. *Faces in the Smoke.* New York: Tarcher; 1991.

Gessler, Paul. "Couple Alerted by Dolphins about Tired Dog Tells Story." ABC7 News online. www.abc-7.com/Global/story.asp?S=14145484. Accessed May 16, 2011.

Giberson, Karl. "The Man Who Fell to Earth." Interview with Sir Roger Penrose. *Science & Spirit.* March/April; 2003: 34–41.

Gibson, Arvin. *Fingerprints of God.* Bountiful, UT: Horizon Publishers; 1999.

Gizzi, Martin S. and Bernard Gitler. "Coronary Risk Factors: The Contemplation of Bigamy. Letter." *Journal of the American Medical Association.* 1986; 256: 1138.

Goethe, J. W. V. *Maximen und Reflexionen.* Köln, Germany: Anaconda Verlag GmbH; 2008.

Golden, R. L. "William Osler at 150: An Overview of a Life." *Journal of the American Medical Association.* December 15, 1999; 282(23): 2252–58.

Goleman, Daniel. *Vital Lies, Simple Truths.* New York: Simon & Schuster; 1996.

Gonin, Mervin Willett. "Extract from the Diary of Lieutenant Colonel Mervin Willett Gonin." www.bergenbelsen.co.uk/pages/Database/ReliefStaffAccount.asp?Heroes ID=17&=17. Accessed July 1, 2012.

"Gorilla at an Illinois Zoo Rescues a 3-Year-Old Boy." *The New York Times* online. August 17, 1996. www.nytimes.com/1996/08/17/us/gorilla-at-an-illinois-zoo -rescues-a-3-year-old-boy.html. Accessed June 7, 2011.

"Gorilla Rescues Child: The World Goes Ape." Year in Review: 1996. www.cnn.com /EVENTS/1996/year.in.review/talk/gorilla/gorilla.index.html. Accessed June 7, 2011.

"Gorilla's Maternal Instinct Saves Baby Boy Who Fell into Zoo Enclosure from Coming to Harm." *The Independent* online. August 19, 1996. www.independent.co.uk/news /world/gorillas-maternal-instinct-saves-baby-boy-who-fell-into-zoo-enclosure-from -coming-to-harm-1310456.html. Accessed June 7, 2011.

Gottlieb, Anthony. "A Miracle, If True." *The New York Times* online. www.nytimes.com /roomfordebate/2011/01/06/the-esp-study-when-science-goes-psychic/esp-findings -a-miracle-if-true. January 7, 2011. Accessed February 6, 2012.

Govinda, Anagarika Brahmacari. *Creative Meditation and Multi-Dimensional Consciousness.* Wheaton, IL: Theosophical Publishing House; 1976.

Graham, John. *Sit Down Young Stranger: One Man's Search for Meaning.* Langley, WA: Packard Books; 2008.

Grann, David. *The Lost City of Z.* New York: Vintage; 2010.

Graves, Robert James. "Newly Observed Affection of the Thyroid Gland in Females." *London Medical & Surgical Journal.* 1835; 8(2): 516–17.

Greene, M. (ed.) "Toward a Unity of Knowledge." *Psychological Issues.* 1969; 22: 45.

Greenhalgh, Trisha. *How to Read a Paper: The Basics of Evidence-Based Medicine.* Fourth edition. London: BMJ Books; 2001.

Grellet, Stephen. Wikipedia. http://en.wikipedia.org/wiki/Stephen_Grellet. Accessed March 1, 2012.

Greyfriars Bobby. www.imdb.com/title/tt0435597/. Accessed January 9, 2011.

Greyson, Bruce. "Incidence and Correlates of Near-Death Experiences in a Cardiac Care Unit." *General Hospital Psychiatry.* 2003; 25: 269–76.

———. "Increase in Psychic Phenomena Following Near-Death Experiences." *Theta.* 1983; 11: 26–29.

Grinberg-Zylberbaum, J., M. Delaflor, L. Attie, and A. Goswami. "The Einstein-Podolsky-Rosen Paradox in the Brain: The Transferred Potential." *Physics Essays.* 1994; 7(4): 422–28.

Grinberg-Zylberbaum, J., M. Delaflor, M.E. Sanchez, and M. A. Guevara. "Human Communication and the Electrophysiological Activity of the Brain." *Subtle Energies and Energy Medicine.* 1993; 3: 25–43.

Grinberg-Zylberbaum, J. and J. Ramos. "Patterns of Interhemispheric Correlation During Human Communication." *International Journal of Neuroscience.* 1987; 36(101502): 41–53.

Grof, Stanislav. *The Holotropic Mind: The Three Levels of Human Consciousness and How They Shape Our Lives.* San Francisco: HarperCollins; 1992.

Grosso, Michael. "The Advantages of Being Multiplex." *Journal of Scientific Exploration.* 2010; 24(2): 225–46.

———. "Miracles: Illusions, Natural Events, or Divine Intervention?" *Journal of Religion and Psychical Research.* October 1997; 20(4): 182.

"Group Near-Death Experiences: People Sharing the Same NDE." Near-death.com. www.near-death.com/group.html. Accessed February 20, 2012.

Groupthink. Wikipedia. http://en.wikipedia.org/wiki/Groupthink. Accessed July 27, 2011.

Guiley, Rosemary Ellen. *Harper's Encyclopedia of Mystical and Paranormal Experience.* Edison, NJ: Castle; 1991.

Gurney, Edmund, F. W. H. Myers, and F. Podmore. *Phantasms of the Living.* Volume 1. London: Trübner; 1886.

Haanel, Charles. Anthony R. Michalski, ed. *The Master Key System.* Volume I. Wilkes-Barre, PA: Kallisti Publishing; 2000.

Hadamard, Jacques. *The Psychology of Invention in the Mathematical Field.* Princeton, NJ: Princeton University Press; 1949.

Hafiz. Daniel Ladinsky (trans). *I Heard God Laughing: Renderings of Hafiz.* Oakland, CA: Mobius Press; 1996.

Haisch, Bernard. *The Purpose-Guided Universe: Believing in Einstein, Darwin, and God.* Franklin Lakes, NJ: New Page Books; 2010.

Haldane, J. B. S. Wikiquote. http://en.wikiquote.org/wiki/J._B._S._Haldane. Accessed January 17, 2012.

Hall, Michael D. and Eugene Metcalf (eds.). *The Artist Outsider: Creativity and the Boundaries of Culture.* Washington, DC: Smithsonian Institute Press; 1992.

Hameroff, Stuart. "Quantum Coherence in Microtubules: A Neural Basis for Emergent Consciousness?" *Journal of Consciousness Studies.* 1994; 1(1): 91–118.

Hamilton, Craig. "Come Together." EnlightenNext.org. www.enlightennext.org /magazine/j25/collective.asp. Accessed March 27, 2011.

Hanh, Thich Nhat. "Interrelationship." Poetry-chaikhana.com. www.poetry-chaikhana .com/H/HanhThichNha/Interrelatio.htm. Accessed December 1, 2011.

Hansen, George P. "CSICOP and the Skeptics: An Overview." *Journal of the Society for Psychical Research.* 1992; 86:19–63.

———. *The Trickster and the Paranormal.* Philadelphia: Xlibris; 2001.

Haraldsson, Erlundur. *The Departed Among the Living.* Guilford, Surrey, U.K.: White Crow Press; 2012.

Harness, Jill. "The Most Famous Mutts Ever." Neatorama.com. http://www.neatorama .com/2012/07/31/the-most-famous-mutts-ever/. July 31, 2012. Accessed March 29, 2013.

Harris, Sam. *The End of Faith.* New York: Norton; 2005.

Harrison, Jim. *Off to the Side: A Memoir.* New York: Grove Press; 2002.

Hartong, Leo. *Awakening to the Dream.* Salisbury, Wiltshire, U.K.: Non-Duality Press; 2003. E-book available at www.awakeningtothedream.com.

Hastings, Arthur. *With the Tongues of Men and Angels: A Study of Channeling.* San Francisco: Holt, Rinehart and Winston; 1991.

Havel, Vaclav. "The Need for Transcendence in the Postmodern World." *The Futurist.* 1995; 29(4): 46. Available at: www.worldtrans.org/whole/havelspeech.html. Accessed March 24, 2012.

———. Speech to Congress, February 21, 1990. In Jackson J. Spielvogel. *Western Civilization. Volume C: Since 1789.* Eighth Edition. Boston: Wadsworth; 2012: 953. Speech available at Everything2.com. http://everything2.com/title/Vaclav+Havel%2527s+addr ess+to+the+US+Congress%252C+21+February+1990. Accessed March 24, 2012.

Hawkes, Joyce W. *Cell-Level Healing: The Bridge from Soul to Cell.* New York: Atria Books: 2006.

———. Website. www.celllevelhealing.com/Author.html. Accessed March 30, 2011.

Hearne, Keith. "Visually Evoked Responses and ESP." *Journal of the Society for Psychical Research.* 1977; 49, 648–57.

Heidt, John. "The King of Terrors: The Theology of Henry Scott Holland." *Contemporary Review.* March 2000. http://www.questia.com/library/1G1-61947811/the-king-of -terrors-the-theology-of-henry-scott-holland. Accessed March 27, 2011.

Heisenberg, Werner. *Physics and Beyond.* New York: Harper & Row; 1971.

Helfand, David. "An Assault on Rationality." *The New York Times* online. www.nytimes .com/roomfordebate/2011/01/06/the-esp-study-when-science-goes-psychic/esp-and -the-assault-on-rationality. January 7, 2011. Accessed February 2, 2012.

Hellman, Hal. *Great Feuds in Medicine.* New York: Wiley; 2002.

———. *Great Feuds in Science.* New York: Wiley; 1999.

Henkel, Linda A. and Rick E. Berger (eds.). *Research in Parapsychology 1988*. Metuchen, NJ: Scarecrow Press; 1989.

Herbert, Nick. *Elemental Mind*. New York: Dutton; 1993.

———. *Quantum Reality*. Garden City, NY: Anchor/Doubleday; 1987.

Herbert, Robert L. (ed.).*Modern Artists on Art*. Englewood, NJ: Prentice-Hall; 1964.

"Heroic Horse Halted Cow's Attack." BBC News online. http://news.bbc.co.uk/2/hi /uk_news/scotland/south_of_scotland/6945914.stm. Accessed May 16, 2011.

Hesse, Hermann. *Demian*. Berlin: S. Fischer Verlag; 1919.

Highwater, Jamake. *The Primal Mind*. Seattle: Replica Books; 2001.

Hillenbrand, Laura. *Unbroken*. New York: Random House; 2010.

Hippocrates. W. H. S. Jones (trans.). *Hippocrates*. Volume 2. The Loeb Classical Library. Cambridge, MA: Harvard University Press; 1952.

Hirshberg, Caryle and Marc I. Barasch. *Remarkable Recovery: What Extraordinary Healings Tell Us About Getting Well and Staying Well*. New York: Riverhead; 1995.

Hirshberg, Caryle and Brendan O'Regan. *Spontaneous Remission: An Annotated Bibliography*. Petaluma, CA: Institute of Noetic Sciences; 1993.

"History of Meteoritics." Meteorite.fr. www.meteorite.fr/en/basics/meteoritics.htm. Accessed March 3, 2010

"History of the Grandfather Clock." The Clock Depot. www.theclockdepot.com /history_of_the_grandfather_clock.html. Accessed March 27, 2008.

Hitchens, Christopher. *God Is Not Great: How Religion Poisons Everything*. New York: Twelve; 2009.

———. *The Portable Atheist*. New York: Da Capo; 2007.

Hobling, Hugo. "Refusing to Look Through Galileo's Telescope." The Galilean Library. http://academy.galilean-library.org/archive/index.php/t-6131.html. Accessed January 2, 2011.

Hoffman, Donald "Conscious Realism and the Mind-Body Problem." *Mind & Matter.* 2008; 6(1): 87–121.

Hoffman, R. M. "Disclosure Needs and Motives after Near-Death Experiences: Influences, Obstacles, and Listener Selection." *Journal of Near-Death Studies*. 1995; 14: 29–48.

Hofstadter, Douglas. "A Cutoff for Craziness." *The New York Times* online. www .nytimes.com/roomfordebate/2011/01/06/the-esp-study-when-science-goes -psychic/a-cutoff-for-craziness. January 7, 2011. Accessed February 2, 2012.

Holden, Constance. "Identical Twins Reared Apart." *Science*. 1980; 207:1323–28.

Holden, Janice Miner, Bruce Greyson, and Debbie James (eds.). *Handbook of Near-Death Experiences: Thirty Years of Investigation*. New York: Praeger; 2009.

Hollander, Lorin. In "Child's Play: Prodigies and Possibilities." *Nova*. Boston: WGBH television; 1985.

———. Personal communication from Lorin Hollander to Larry Dossey, June 1983.

Hornaday, William Temple. *Our Vanishing Wild Life. Its Extermination and Preservation*. Original edition 1913. Reprint edition: Whitefish, MT: Kessinger Publishing; 2009.

"How Old Is the Universe?" Universe 101. http://map.gsfc.nasa.gov/universe/uni_age
.html. Accessed July 13, 2011.

Howes, David. *The Sixth Sense Reader.* London: Berg; 2009.

Hu, Mu. "Social Use of the Internet and Loneliness." Doctoral dissertation 2007, Ohio State University. Ohiolink.edu. http://etd.ohiolink.edu/view.cgi/Hu%20Mu.pdf?osu 1186168233. Accessed November 25, 2011.

———. "Will Online Chat Help Alleviate Mood Loneliness?" *Cyberpsychology and Behavior.* 2009; 12(2): 219–223.

Hummer, R., R. Rogers, C. Nam, and C. G. Ellison. "Religious Involvement and U. S. Adult Mortality." *Demography.* 1999; 36(2): 273–85.

Huxley, Aldous. *The Doors of Perception.* New York: Harper Perennial Modern Classics; 2004. Original publication: New York: Harper & Row; 1954.

———. *The Doors of Perception.* London: Chatto and Windus; 1954. Reprint: London: Granada Publishing; 1984.

———. *The Perennial Philosophy.* New York: Harper & Row; 1945.

———. *Tomorrow and Tomorrow and Tomorrow.* New York: Signet; 1964.

———. Wikiquote.com. Accessed January 18, 2011. http://en.wikiquote.org/wiki /Aldous_Huxley. Accessed January 28, 2011.

"I Am Lonely Will Anyone Speak to Me." The thread is now available at "A Lonely Life" at: http://lounge.moviecodec.com/on-topic/i-am-lonely-will-anyone-speak-to -me-2420/. Accessed November 24, 2011.

Inglis, Brian. *Natural and Supernatural: A History of the Paranormal.* Bridport, Dorset, U.K.: Prism Press; 1992.

Jack, Fiona. "Nothing." http://fionajack.net/projects/nothing/. Accessed November 12, 2011.

———. "Nothing billboard." www.adbusters.org/content/nothing-you-want. Accessed November 12, 2011.

Jackson, Donald Dale. "Reunion of Identical Twins, Raised Apart, Reveals Some Astonishing Similarities." *Smithsonian.* October 1980; 48–56.

Jahn, Robert G. "Report on the Academy of Consciousness Studies." *Journal of Scientific Exploration.* 1995; 9(3): 393–403.

Jahn, Robert G., and Brenda J. Dunne. *Consciousness and the Source of Reality.* Princeton, NJ: ICRL Press; 2011.

———. *Margins of Reality: The Role of Consciousness in the Physical World.* New York: Harcourt Brace Jovanovich; 1987.

James, William. "The Confidences of a Psychical Researcher." In F. H. Burkhardt (ed.). *Essays in Psychical Research.* Cambridge, MA: Harvard University Press; 1986. Original publication 1909.

———. *Human Immortality.* New York: Dover; 1956. Original publication 1897.

———. *Principles of Psychology.* New York: Holt; 1890.

———. *The Varieties of Religious Experience.* New York: Library of America; 1987.

———. *The Will to Believe and Other Essays in Popular Philosophy.* London: Longmans, Green; 1910 (composed of segments originally published in 1890, 1892, and 1896).

Jameson, Robert. "Scientific Intelligence: Passenger Pigeon." *Edinburgh New Philosophical Journal.* October 1835; XX: 209.

Janis, Irving L. *Victims of Groupthink: A Psychological Study of Foreign-Policy Decisions and Fiascoes.* Boston: Houghton Mifflin; 1972.

Jauregui, Ann. *Epiphanies: Where Science and Miracles Meet.* New York: Atria; 2007.

Jayakar, Pupul. *Krishnamurti: A Biography.* San Francisco: Harper & Row; 1986.

Jeans, Sir James. *Physics and Philosophy.* New York: Dover; 1981.

Johnson, M. Alex. "The Culture of Einstein." MSNBC.com. www.msnbc.msn.com /id/7406337/#.Ty2tbRxZ2jQ. April 18, 2005. Accessed February 4, 2012.

Jordan. "In the Footnotes of Library Angels: A Bi(bli)ography of Insurrectionary Imagination." www.thisisliveart.co.uk/pdf_docs/SRG_Jordan.pdf. Accessed December 14, 2011.

Josephson, Brian. "Pathological Disbelief." Lecture given at the Nobel Laureates' meeting, Lindau, Germany, June 30, 2004. www.lenr-canr.org/acrobat/Josephson Bpathologic.pdf. Accessed December 26, 2011. See also: www.lenr-canr.org/acrobat /JosephsonBabstractfo.pdf. Accessed December 26, 2011.

Julian of Norwich. Father John-Julian. (trans.). *Revelations of Divine Love.* Brewster, MA: Paraclete Press; 2011.

Jung, C. G.; G. Adler and R. F. C. Hull (trans.).*The Archetypes and the Collective Unconscious.* Volume 9, Part 1, of *The Collected Works of C. G. Jung* Princeton, NJ: Princeton University Press; 1981.

———. R. F. C. Hull (trans.). *The Archetypes and the Collective Unconscious.* Bollingen Series XX. *The Collected Works of C. G. Jung.* Volume 9, Part I. Princeton, NJ: Princeton University Press; 1969.

———. *Jung on Death and Immortality.* Jenny Yates, introduction. Princeton, NJ: Princeton University Press; 1999.

———. Aniela Jaffé (ed.). Richard and Clara Winston (trans.). *Memories, Dreams, Reflections.* New York: Random House; 1961.

———. Joseph Campbell (ed.). *The Mysteries: Papers from the Eranos Yearbooks.* Volume 2. Princeton, NJ: Princeton University Press; 1978.

———. Sir Herbert Read and Gerhard Adler (eds.), R.F.C. Hull (trans.). *Psychology and Religion: West and East.* Volume 11. *The Collected Works of C. G. Jung.* Princeton, NJ: Princeton University Press; 1975.

———. Joseph Campbell (ed.), R.F.C. Hull (trans.). "The Stages of Life." In *The Portable Jung.* New York: Penguin; 1976.

———. R. F. C. Hull (trans.). *The Symbolic Life. Collected Works.* Princeton, NJ: Princeton University Press; 1977.

———. R. F. C. Hull (trans.). *Synchronicity: An Acausal Connecting Principle.* 2nd edition. Bollingen Series XX. Princeton, NJ: Princeton University Press; 1973.

Kafatos, Menas and Robert Nadeau. *The Conscious Universe: Parts and Wholes in Physical Reality.* New York: Springer; 1991.

Kane, Muriel. "Study Shows Lab Rats Would Rather Free a Friend than Eat Chocolate." Rawstory.com. www.rawstory.com/rs/2011/12/09/study-shows-lab-rats-would-rather -free-a-friend-than-eat-chocolate/. December 9, 2011. Accessed February 5, 2012.

Kane, Naomi. "Do Dogs Mourn?" Dogsincanada.com. http://www.lewenhart.com /mourning.htm. Accessed January 9, 2011.

Kaplan, Karen. "Happiness Is Contagious, Research Finds." *Los Angeles Times* online. http://articles.latimes.com/2008/dec/05/science/sci-happy5. December 5, 2008. Accessed January 19, 2021.

Kaptchuk, Ted J. "The Double-Blind, Randomized, Placebo-Controlled Trial: Gold Standard or Golden Calf?" *Journal of Clinical Epidemiology.* 2001; 54(6): 541–49.

Karpf, Anne. "Climate Change: You Can't Ignore It." *The Guardian.* November 20, 2012. www.guardian.co.uk/environment/2012/nov/30/climate-change-you-cant -ignore-it. Accessed December 14, 2012.

———. *The Human Voice.* New York: Bloomsbury USA; 2006.

Kauffman, Stuart. "God Enough." Interview of Stuart Kauffman by Steve Paulson. Salon.com. www.salon.com/env/atoms_eden/2008/11/19/stuart_kauffman/index1 .html. Accessed January 30, 2010.

Keating. Thomas. "Spiritual Practices: Silence." www.spiritualityandpractice.com /practices/practices.php?id=28&g=1. Accessed January 7, 2012.

Kedrov, K. "On the Question of Scientific Creativity." *Voprosy Psikologii.* 1957; 3: 91–113

Keller, Evelyn Fox. *A Feeling for the Organism.* New York: Times Books; 1984.

Kelly, Edward F., et al. *Irreducible Mind: Toward a Psychology for the 21st Century.* Lanham, MD: Rowman and Littlefield; 2009.

Kelly, E. F. and J. Lenz. "EEG Changes Correlated with a Remote Stroboscopic Stimulus: A Preliminary Study." In J. Morris, W. Roll, R. Morris (eds.). *Research in Parapsychology 1975.* Metuchen, NJ: Scarecrow Press; 1975 (abstracted in *Journal of Parapsychology.* 1975; 39: 25).

Kerouac, Jack. *Scattered Poems.* San Francisco: City Lights Books; 1971.

"Key Facts about Near-Death Experiences." Prevalence of NDEs. IANDS.org. http: //iands.org/about-ndes/key-nde-facts.html?showall=1. Accessed March 3, 2012.

Kiecolt-Glaser, Janice, et al. "Hostile Marital Interactions, Proinflammatory Cytokine Production, and Wound Healing." *Archives of General Psychiatry.* 2005; 62(12): 1377–84.

Kincheloe, Lawrence. "Intuitive Obstetrics." *Alternative Therapies in Health & Medicine.* 2003; 9(6): 16–17.

King, Jr., Martin Luther. Commencement address for Oberlin College. www.oberlin .edu/external/EOG/BlackHistoryMonth/MLK/CommAddress.html. Accessed November 28, 2011.

Kittenis, M., P. Caryl, and P. Stevens. "Distant Psychophysiological Interaction Effects Between Related and Unrelated Participants." *Proceedings of the Parapsychological Association Convention 2004*: 67–76. Meeting held in Vienna, Austria, August 5–8, 2004.

Knoblauch, H., et al. "Different Kinds of Near-Death Experience: A Report on a Survey of Near-Death Experiences in Germany." *Journal of Near-Death Studies;* 2001; 20: 15–29.

Knox, Sarah S. *Science, God and the Nature of Reality.* Boca Raton, FL: Brown Walker Press; 2010.

Koestler, Arthur. *The Act of Creation.* New York: Macmillan; 1964.

———. *Janus: A Summing Up.* New York: Vintage 1979.

———. *The Roots of Coincidence.* New York: Random House; 1972.

Kohut, Heinz. Paul Ornstein (ed.). *The Search for the Self: Selected Writings of Heinz Kohut: 1950–1978.* Volume 1. New York: International Universities Press; 1978.

Krauss, Lawrence M. "No Sacred Mantle." *The New York Times* online. www.nytimes.com/roomfordebate/2011/01/06/the-esp-study-when-science-goes-psychic/publication-is-not-a-sacred-mantle. January 7, 2011. Accessed February 6, 2012.

———. *Quantum Man: Richard Feynman's Life in Science.* New York: Norton; 2011.

Krippner, Stanley. "A Psychic Dream? Be Careful Whom You Tell!" *Dream Network.* 1995; 14(3): 35–36.

Krippner, Stanley, Fariba Bogzaran, and André Percia de Carvalho. *Extraordinary Dreams and How to Work with Them.* Albany, NY: SUNY Press; 2002.

Krippner, Stanley and L. Faith. "Exotic Dreams: A Cross-Cultural Survey." *Dreaming.* 2000; 11: 72–83.

Krishna, Gopi. *The Biological Basis of Religion and Genius.* New York: Harper and Row; 1972.

Kuhn, Thomas. *The Structure of Scientific Revolutions.* Third edition. Chicago: University of Chicago Press; 1996.

Kundera, Milan. Quoted at Goodreads.com. www.goodreads.com/quotes/tag/dogs. Accessed November 24, 2012.

Kurtz, Paul (ed.). *A Skeptic's Handbook of Parapsychology.* Buffalo, NY: Prometheus Books, 1985.

Lachman, Roy, Janet L. Lachman, and Earl C. Butterfield. *Cognitive Psychology and Information Processing: An Introduction.* Hillsdale, NJ: Lawrence Erlbaum Associates; 1979.

Langworth, Richard (ed.). *Churchill by Himself: The Definitive Collection of Quotations.* Reprint edition. New York: PublicAffairs; 2011.

Lanier, Jean. "From Having a Mystical Experience to Becoming a Mystic." *ReVision.* 1989; 12(1): 41–44.

Lanza, Robert with Bob Berman. *Biocentrism: How Life and Consciousness are the Keys to Understanding the True Nature of the Universe.* Dallas, TX: BenBella Books, Inc.; 2009.

Laozi. Wikiquote. http://en.wikiquote.org/wiki/Laozi. Accessed March 18, 2012.

Lara, Adair. *The Sun.* June 1994; Issue 222: 40.

Larson, E. "Did Psychic Powers Give Firm a Killing in the Silver Market?" *Wall Street Journal.* October 22, 1984.

Lashley, Karl S. "In Search of the Engram." *Symposia of the Society for Experimental Biology.* 1950; 4: 454–82.

Laszlo, Ervin. *The Akashic Experience: Science and the Cosmic Memory Field.* Rochester, VT: Inner Traditions; 2009.

———. *The Interconnected Universe.* River Edge, NJ: World Scientific; 1995.

———. *Science and the Akashic Field: An Integral Theory of Everything.* Rochester, VT: Inner Traditions; 2007.

Laughlin, Charles D. *Communing with the Gods.* Brisbane, Australia: Daily Grail Publishing; 2011.

———. "Transpersonal Anthropology: Some Methodological Issues." *Western Canadian Anthropologist.* 1989; 5: 29–60.

———. "Transpersonal Anthropology, Then and Now." *Transpersonal Review.* 1994; 1(1): 7–10.

Lawrence, Tony. "Bringing Home the Sheep: A Meta-Analysis of Sheep/Goat Experiments." In *Proceedings of Presented Papers,* 36th Annual Parapsychological Association Convention. M. J. Schlitz (ed.). Fairhaven, MA: Parapsychological Association; 1993.

Lemke, Leslie. Wikipedia. http://en.wikipedia.org/wiki/Leslie_Lemke. Accessed January 4, 2011.

LeShan, Lawrence. *Landscapes of the Mind.* Guilford, CT: Eirini Press; 2012

———. *A New Science of the Paranormal: The Promise of Psychical Research.* Wheaton, IL: Quest; 2009.

Lessing, Doris. *The Making of the Representative for Planet 8.* London: Flamingo/HarperCollins; 1994.

Levin, Jeffrey S. *God, Faith, and Health.* New York. Wiley; 2001.

Lewis, C. S. Quoted at Thinkexist.com. http://thinkexist.com/quotation/you_don-t _have_a_soul-you_are_a_soul-you_have_a/202051.html. Accessed November 22, 2011.

Libet, Benjamin. "A Testable Field Theory of Mind-Brain Interaction." *Journal of Consciousness Studies.* 1994; 1(1): 119–26.

"Life of the Party: Study Shows that Socializing Can Extend Your Life." MedicineNet. com. www.medicinenet.com/script/main/art.asp?articlekey=50788. Accessed January 12, 2011.

Lindsay, E. M. "Maskelyne and Meteors." *The Irish Astronomical Journal.* 1967; 8(3): 69.

List of social networking websites. Wikipedia. http://en.wikipedia.org/wiki/List_of _social_networking_websites. Accessed December 1, 2011.

Lloyd, D. H. "Objective Events in the Brain Correlating with Psychic Phenomena." *New Horizons.* 1973; 1: 69–75.

Lombardo, Paul. "Eugenic Sterilization Laws." Dolan DNA Learning Center, Cold Spring Harbor Laboratory. www.eugenicsarchive.org. Accessed January 3, 2011.

Loneliness. Wikipedia. http://en.wikipedia.org/wiki/Loneliness#cite_note-19. Accessed November 28, 2011.

Long, William J. *How Animals Talk: And Other Pleasant Studies in Birds and Beasts.* Rochester, VT: Bear & Company; 2005.

Lorber, John. "Is Your Brain Really Necessary?" *Science.* 1980; 210:1232–34.

Lorimer, David. *Whole in One.* London: Arkana/Penguin; 1990.

Lovejoy, Arthur. *The Great Chain of Being.* Cambridge, MA: Harvard University Press; 1936.

Luke, David. "Experiential Reclamation and First Person Parapsychology." *Journal of Parapsychology.* 2011; 75(2): 185–99.

Mackay, Charles. *Extraordinary Popular Delusions and the Madness of Crowds.* New York: Crown; 1980.

Maddox, Sir John. "The Unexpected Science to Come." *Scientific American.* December 1999; 281(6): 62–67.

Maeterlink, Maurice. *The Unknown Guest.* New York: Cosimo, Inc.; 2005.

Maharshi, Ramana. "The End of Seeking: Quotations from the Teachings of Ramana Maharshi." Theendofseeking.net. www.theendofseeking.net/E%20-%20Is%20 there%20Enlightenment.html. Accessed January 3, 2011.

Major, Ralph H. (ed.). *Classic Descriptions of Disease.* Third edition. Springfield, IL: Charles C. Thomas; 1945.

Mann, Charles C. *1491: New Revelations of the Americas Before Columbus.* Second edition. New York: Vintage; 2011.

Marano, Hara Estroff. "The Dangers of Loneliness." Psychologytoday.com. www.psychologytoday.com/articles/200308/the-dangers-loneliness. July 1, 2003. Accessed November 24, 2011.

Margenau, Henry. *The Miracle of Existence.* Woodbridge, CT: Ox Bow Press;1984.

Martin, Barclay, letter to the editor. Reply by John Searle. *The New York Review of Books.* September 29, 2011: 101.

Martin, Joel and William J. Birnes. *The Haunting of the Presidents.* New York: New American Library; 2003.

Mason, Herbert W. *Al-Hallaj.* London: Routledge; 1995.

Matthew, R. "Sixth Sense Helps You Watch Your Back." *Sunday Telegraph.* April 14, 1996.

May, E. C., R. Targ, and H. E. Puthoff. "EEG Correlates to Remote Light Flashes under Conditions of Sensory Shielding." In Charles Tart, Hal E. Puthoff, Russell Targ (eds.). *Mind at large: IEEE Symposia on the Nature of Extrasensory Perception.* Charlottesville, VA: Hampton Roads; 1979 and 2002.

Mayer, Elizabeth Lloyd. *Extraordinary Knowing: Science, Skepticism, and the Inexplicable Powers of the Human Mind.* New York: Bantam/Random House; 2007.

McCoy, Harold. *Power of Focused Mind Healing.* Fayetteville, AR: JTG Publishing: 2011.

McDermott, John J. (ed.). *The Writings of William James: A Comprehensive Edition.* Chicago: University of Chicago Press; 1977.

McDermott, Robert A. (ed.). *The Essential Steiner.* San Francisco: Harper & Row; 1984.

McEneaney, Bonnie. *Messages: Signs, Visits, and Premonitions from Loved Ones Lost on 9/11.* New York: Morrow; 2010.

McTaggart, Lynne. *The Field.* New edition. New York: HarperCollins; 2008.

Mead, Margaret. Quotationspage.com. www.quotationspage.com/quote/33522.html. Accessed December 12, 2012.

Merleau-Ponty, Maurice. Quoted in Emilios Bouratinos. "Primordial Wholeness: Hints of Its Non-Local and Non-Temporal Role in the Co-Evolution of Matter, Consciousness, and Civilization." In Zachary Jones, Brenda Dunne, Elissa Hoeger, and Robert Jahn (eds.). *Filters and Reflections: Perspectives on Reality.* Princeton, NJ: ICRL Press; 2009.

Mermin, N. David. "Extreme Quantum Entanglement in a Superposition of Macroscopically Distinct States." *Physical Review Letters.* 1990; 65(15): 1838–40.

Merrill, James and Helen Vendler. "James Merrill's Myth: An Interview." *The New York Review of Books.* May 3, 1979. www.nybooks.com/articles/archives/1979/may/03 /james-merrills-myth-an-interview. Accessed March 23, 2011.

Midgley, Mary. *Science As Salvation: A Modern Myth and Its Meaning.* London: Routledge; 1992.

———. "Thinking Matter." *New Scientist.* 2009; 201 (2689): 16.

Millay, Jean. *Multidimensional Mind: Remote Viewing in Hyperspace.* Berkeley, CA: North Atlantic Books; 2000.

Miller, Jeannie P. (ed.). *Emerging Issues in the Electronic Environment.* Binghamton, NY: Haworth Information Press; 2004.

Miller, Peter. "The Genius of Swarms." *National Geographic.* NGM.com. July 2007. http://ngm.nationalgeographic.com/2007/07/swarms/miller-text. Accessed December 5, 2010.

Millet, David. "The Origins of the EEG." www.bri.ucla.edu/nha/ishn/ab24-2002.htm. Accessed December 12, 2010.

Milton, John. Arthur Thomas Quiller-Couch (ed.). *The Oxford Book of English Verse: 1250–1900.* Oxford, U.K.: Clarendon; 1919.

Milton, Richard. *Alternative Science: Challenging the Myths of the Scientific Establishment.* Rochester, VT: Park Street Press; 1996.

Mirandola, Pico della. *Opera Omnia.* Basel; 1557: 40.

Mitchell, Edgar. *The Way of the Explorer: An Apollo Astronaut's Journey Through the Material and Mystical Worlds.* Revised edition. Franklin Lakes, NJ: New Page Books; 2008.

Mitchell, Weir. "The Case of Mary Reynolds." *Transactions of the College of Physicians of Philadelphia.* Volume 1; April 1888. Cited in William James. *Principles of Psychology.* New York: Holt; 1890.

Mitchum, Robert. "Rats Free Trapped Companions, Even When Given Choice of Chocolate Instead." UChicagoNews. http://news.uchicago.edu/article/2011/12/08 /helping-your-fellow-rat-rodents-show-empathy-driven-behavior. December 8, 2011. Accessed February 5, 2012.

Moody, Raymond. *Life After Life.* Reprint. New York: HarperOne; 2001.

———. *Paranormal: My Life in Pursuit of the Afterlife.* New York: HarperOne; 2012.

Moore, Walter. *Schrödinger: Life and Thought.* Cambridge, U.K.: Cambridge University Press; 1989.

Morris, J. D., W. G. Roll, and R. L. Morris (eds.). *Research in Parapsychology 1975.* Metuchen, NJ: Scarecrow Press; 1975.

Moss, Lyndsay. "Simple MRI Brain Scan Offers Autism Diagnosis in 15 Minutes." News.csotsman.com. August 11, 2010. http://news.scotsman.com/health/Simple -MRI-brain-scan-offers.6467791.jp. Accessed January 3, 2011.

Muir, John. Wikiquote. http://en.wikiquote.org/wiki/John_Muir. Accessed December 1, 2011.

My Grandfather's Clock. Wikipedia. http://en.wikipedia.org/wiki/My_Grandfather's _Clock. Accessed March 27, 2008.

Myers, Frederic W. H. *Human Personality and Its Survival of Bodily Death.* London: Longman, Green, and Co.; 1906.

Myth of Er. Wikipedia. http://en.wikipedia.org/wiki/Myth_of_Er. Accessed January 27, 2011.

Nadeau, R., and M. Kafatos. *The Non-Local Universe: The New Physics and Matters of the Mind.* New York: Oxford University Press; 1999.

Nan Huaijin. *Basic Buddhism: Exploring Buddhism and Zen.* York Beach, ME: Weiser Books; 1997.

Needleman, Jacob. "The Heart of Philosophy." Interview by Stephan Bodian. *Yoga Journal.* March 1989; 58-61.

Nelson, Roger D., Dean I. Radin, Richard Shoup, and Peter A. Bancel. "Correlations of Continuous Random Data with Major World Events." *Foundations of Physics Letters.* 2002; 15(6). See: http://www.boundary.org/randomness.htm. Accessed June 12, 2007.

Nielsen, K. M., et al. "Danish Singles Have a Twofold Risk of Acute Coronary Syndrome: Data from a Cohort of 138,290 Persons." *Journal of Epidemiology and Community Health.* 2006; 60(8): 721–28.

Nikhilananda, Swami. Description of the Hindu sage Sankaracharya. In Swami Nikhilananda. *Self-Knowledge.* New York: Ramakrishna-Vivekananda Center; 1980. Quoted in Karen Hall Siegel. "Is Fear Inevitable?" *Yoga Journal.* March/April 1988; 16.

Nisargadatta Maharaj. Wikiquote. http://en.wikiquote.org/wiki/Nisargadatta_Maharaj. Accessed November 29, 2011.

Nisbet, Lee. Quoted at Skepticalinvestigations.org. www.skepticalinvestigations.org /Organskeptics/index.html. Accessed January 1, 2011.

Nisker, Wes. Quoted in *Inquiring Mind*; Spring 2005.

Nuland, Sherwin B. *Doctors: The Biography of Medicine.* New York: Vintage: 1995.

Nuremberg Rally. Wikipedia. http://en.wikipedia.org/wiki/Nuremberg_Rally. Accessed July 28, 2010.

"NZ Dolphin Rescues Beached Whales." BBC News online. http://news.bbc.co.uk/2 /hi/7291501.stm. Accessed May 12, 2011.

"Of All the Pigeon Lofts in the World." *Fortean Times.* July 1996; 88: 10. Also reported in the *London Daily Telegraph,* March 23, 1996.

Olson, Geoff. "Is the Universe Friendly?" http://geoffolson.com/page5/page11 /page34/page34.html. Accessed December 1, 2011.

Origen. *Liviticum Homilae.* Quoted in Laurens van der Post. *Jung and the Story of Our Time.* New York: Vintage; 1975.

Orlean, Susan. *Rin Tin Tin: The Life and Legend.* New York: Simon & Schuster; 2011.

Orme-Johnson, D. W., M. C. Dillbeck, R. K. Wallace, and G. S. Landrith. "Intersubject EEG Coherence: Is Consciousness a Field?" *International Journal of Neuroscience.* 1982; (16): 203–09.

Oz2. Dailygrail.com. www.dailygrail.com/blogs/shadow/2005/7/Telling-Bees. Accessed January 12, 2011.

Ozark Research Institute. www.ozarkresearch.org/Site/welcome.html. Accessed December 12, 2011.

Panksepp, Jules B. "Feeling the Pain of Social Loss." *Science*. 2003; 302(5643): 237–39.

Passenger Pigeon. Wikipedia. http://en.wikipedia.org/wiki/Passenger_Pigeon. Accessed November 6, 2011.

Pearce, Joseph Chilton. *Evolution's End*. San Francisco: HarperSanFrancisco: 1993: 3–11, 30, 95, 149, 221.

Peek, Kim. Wikipedia. http://en.wikipedia.org/wiki/Kim_Peek. Accessed January 20, 2011.

Penfield, Wilder. *The Mystery of the Mind: A Critical Study of Consciousness and the Human Brain*. Princeton, NJ: Princeton University Press; 1975.

Perera, M., et al. "Prevalence of Near-Death Experiences in Australia." *Journal of Near-Death Studies*. 2005; 24: 109.

Pew Forum/Pew Research Center. "Many Americans Mix Multiple Faiths." http://pewforum.org/Other-Beliefs-and-Practices/Many-Americans-Mix-Multiple-Faiths.aspx. Accessed December 10, 2011.

Pierce, David (ed.). *Irish Writing in the Twentieth Century*. Cork, Ireland: Cork University Press; 2000.

Pinker, Steven. *How the Mind Works*. New York: Norton; 1997.

Pizzi R., A. et al. "Non-Local Correlation Between Separated Human Neural Networks." In E. Donkor, A. R. Pirick, and H. E. Brandt (eds.) *Quantum Information and Computation II*. Proceedings of SPIE5436. 2004:107–17. Abstract available at: The Smithsonian/NASA Astrophysics Data System. http://adsabs.harvard.edu/abs/2004SPIE.5436.107P. Accessed January 17, 2011.

Planck, Max. *Where is Science Going?* Reprint edition. Woodbridge, CT: Ox Bow Press; 1981. (First published by Allen & Unwin; 1933.)

"Planes, Trains, and Ant Hills: Computer Scientists Simulate Activity of Ants to Reduce Airline Delays." ScienceDaily.com. www.sciencedaily.com/videos/2008/0406-planes_trains_and_ant_hills.htm. Accessed December 5, 2010.

Plato. Benjamin Jowett (trans.). *Collected Dialogues of Plato*. 4th edition. Oxford, U.K.: Oxford University Press; 1953.

———."The Myth of Er." *The Republic*. Davidson.edu. http://www.davidson.edu/academic/classics/neumann/CLA350/ErMyth.html. Accessed March 29, 2013.

Platt, Anthony. "The Frightening Agenda of the American Eugenics Movement." Remarks made before California State Judiciary Committee, June 24, 2003.

Playfair, Guy Lyon. *Twin Telepathy: The Psychic Connection*. London: Vega; 2002.

Pocheptsova A., R. Ferraro, and A. T. Abraham. "The Effect of Mobile Phone Use on Prosocial Behavior." ScienceDaily.com. www.sciencedaily.com/releases/2012/02/120214122038.htm. February 14, 2012. Accessed May 15, 1012.

Posey, T. B. and M. E. Losch. "Auditory Hallucinations of Hearing Voices in 375 Normal Subjects." *Imagination, Cognition and Personality*. 1983–1984; 3(2): 99–113.

Potts, Wayne. "The Chorus-Line Hypothesis of Manoeuvre in Avian Flocks." *Nature.* 1984; 309: 344–45.

Priestley, J. B. *Man & Time.* London: W. H. Allen; 1978.

Project MKULTRA. Wikipedia. http://en.wikipedia.org/wiki/Project_MKULTRA. Accessed December 1, 2011.

"Project MKULTRA, the CIA's Program of Research into Behavioral Modification." Joint Hearing before the Select Committee on Intelligence and the Subcommittee on Health and Scientific Research of the Committee on Human Resources, United State Senate, Ninety-Fifth Congress, First Session. Available at: www.nytimes.com/packages /pdf/national/13inmate_ProjectMKULTRA.pdf. U. S. Government Printing Office. August 8, 1977. Accessed January 2, 2011.

"Project Passenger Pigeon: Lessons from the Past for a Sustainable Future." http://www.passengerpigeon.org/. Accessed November 6, 2011.

"Propaganda in Nazi Germany." History Learning Site. http://www.historylearningsite .co.uk/propaganda_in_nazi_germany.htm. Accessed March 29, 2013.

Psychic Sea Hunt. Pyramid Direct Films. www.pyramiddirect.com/cart/productpage .html?title_id=1951&list=1948,1217,2132,1949,1221,1408,1950,1951,1952&alpha =P. Accessed January 1, 2012.

Puthoff, Hal E. "CIA-Initiated Remote Viewing Program at Stanford Research Institute." *Journal of Scientific Exploration.* 1996; 10(1): 75.

Putnam, Frank W. *A History of Multiple Personality Disorder.* New York: Guilford; 1989: 357.

Quartz clock. Wikipedia. http://en.wikipedia.org/wiki/Quartz_clock. Accessed December 25, 2011.

Radin, Dean. *The Conscious Universe.* San Francisco: HarperSanFrancisco; 1997.

———. *Entangled Minds: Extrasensory Perception in a Quantum Reality.* New York: Simon & Schuster; 2006.

———. "Event-Related Electroencephalographic Correlations Between Isolated Human Subjects." *Journal of Alternative and Complementary Medicine.* 2004; (10): 315–23.

———. "Predicting the Unpredictable: 75 Years of Experimental Evidence." *American Institute of Physics Conference Proceedings.* 2011; Volume 1408: 204–17. Conference title: Quantum Retrocausation: Theory and Experiment. San Diego, CA; June 13–14, 2011. Abstract at: http://proceedings.aip.org/resource/2/apcpcs/1408/1/204_1?is Authorized=no. Accessed January 22, 2012.

Rae, Colleen. *Tales of a Reluctant Psychic.* www.joyflow.com/reluctant-psychic.html. Accessed November 26, 2011.

Raffensperger, Carolyn. "Moral Injuries and the Environment: Healing the Soul Wounds of the Body Politic." SEHN.org. www.sehn.org/blog/?p=749. Accessed December 14, 2012.

Ramachandran, V. S. Interview by Chris Floyd. "The Limbic Fire: Neuroscience and the Soul." *Science & Spirit.* 1999; 10(3): 24–26.

Rao, K. Ramakrishna. *Cognitive Anomalies, Consciousness and Yoga.* Volume XVI, Part 1. *History of Science, Philosophy and Culture in Indian Civilization.* (D. P. Chattopadhyaya, general editor.) New Delhi, India: Centre for Studies in Civilizations and Matrix Publishers (joint publishers): 2011.

Ratliff, Evan. "Hello, Loneliness." NewYorker.com. www.newyorker.com/archive/2005 /08/22/050822ta_talk_ratliff. August 22, 2005. Accessed November 24, 2011.

Rawlence, Christopher (ed.). *About Time.* London: Jonathan Cape; 1985.

Rebert, C. S. and A. Turner. "EEG Spectrum Analysis Techniques Applied to the Problem of Psi Phenomena." *Behavioral Neuropsychiatry.* 1974; (6): 18–24.

Rees, W. D. "The Bereaved and Their Hallucinations." In B. Schoenberg, A. H. Kutscher, and A. C. Carr (eds.). *Bereavement: Its Psychosocial Aspects.* New York: Columbia University Press; 1975.

Rhine, J. B. and S. R. Feather. "The Study of Cases of 'Psi-Trailing' in Animals." *Journal of Parapsychology.* 1962; 26(1): 1–21.

Rhine, Louisa E. "Psychological Processes in ESP Experiences. Part I. Waking Experiences." *Journal of Parapsychology.* 1962; 29: 88–111.

Rifkin, Jeremy. *The Empathic Civilization.* New York: Tarcher/Penguin; 2009.

Rimland, B. "Savant Capabilities of Autistic Children and Their Cognitive Implications." In G. Serban (ed.), *Cognitive Defects in the Development of Mental Illness.* New York: Brunner/Mazel; 1978.

Rin Tin Tin. Wikipedia. http://en.wikipedia.org/wiki/Rin_Tin_Tin. Accessed November 21, 2011.

Ring, Kenneth and Sharon Cooper. *Mindsight: Near-Death and Out-of-Body Experiences in the Blind.* Second edition. New York: iUniverse; 2008.

Rock, A. J., Julie Beischel, and C. C. Cott. "Psi vs. Survival: A Qualitative Investigation of Mediums' Phenomenology Comparing Psychic Readings and Ostensible Communication with the Deceased." *Transpersonal Psychology Review.* 2009; 13: 76–89.

Roe, C. A., C. Sonnex, and E. Roxburgh. "Two Meta-Analyses of Distant Healing Studies." Paper presented at The 55th Annual Convention of The Parapsychological Association, August 9–12, 2012, Durham, North Carolina.

Rogers, Will. Quoted in Dartmouth.org. www.dartmouth.org/classes/53/lighter_fare /FamousPeopleStatements.php. Accessed August 2, 2010.

————. Quoted at Goodreads.com. www.goodreads.com/quotes/tag/dogs. Accessed November 24, 2012.

Roll, William G., et al. "Case Report: A Prototypical Experience of 'Poltergeist' Activity, Conspicuous Quantitative Electroencephalographic Patterns, and sLORETA Profiles— Suggestions for Intervention," *Neurocase.* 2012; DOI:10.1080/13554794.2011.63353 2. Available at: http://dx.doi.org/10.1080/13554794.2011.633532. Accessed January 25, 2012.

"Romania's Murderous Twins." *Fortean Times.* January 2000; 130: 10.

Rominger, Ryan. "An Empathic Near-Death Experience." *The Journal of Spirituality and Paranormal Studies.* 2012; 35(2): 73.

Rose, Ronald. *Primitive Psychic Power.* New York: Signet; 1968.

Rosenberg, Daniel. "Speaking Martian." *Cabinet.* 2000; Issue 1. http://cabinetmagazine.org/issues/1/i_martian.php. Accessed March 24, 2011.

Ross, Stephen David. *Art and Its Significance: An Anthology of Aesthetic Theory.* Albany, NY: State University of New York Press; 1984.

Rowling, J. K. "What Jo says about Albus Dumbledore." www.accio-quote.org/themes /dumbledore.htm. Accessed December 29, 2011.

Rucker, Rudy. *Infinity and the Mind.* New York: Bantam; 1983.

Rumi, Jalal al-Din. Coleman Barks (trans.). *Rumi: The Big Red Book.* New York: Harper-Collins; 2010.

———. Coleman Barks (trans.). *Rumi: The Book of Love.* New York: HarperCollins; 2003.

———. John Moyne and Coleman Barks (trans.). *Open Secret.* Putney, VT: Threshold; 1984.

———. Quoted at Goodreads.com. www.goodreads.com/author/quotes/875661 .Rumi. Accessed December 24, 2013.

Rush, J. H. "New Directions in Parapsychological Research." *Parapsychological Monographs No. 4.* New York: Parapsychological Foundation; 1964.

Russell, Bertrand. *The Basic Writings of Bertrand Russell.* London: Routledge; 1961.

———. *The Collected Papers of Bertrand Russell.* Volume 28. London: Routledge; 2005.

Russell, Peter. *The Global Brain.* 3rd edition. Edinburgh, U.K.: Floris Books; 2008.

Ryder, Richard. *Animal Revolution: Changing Attitudes Towards Speciesism.* Oxford, U.K.: Berg Publishers; 2000.

Sabell, A., C. Clarke, and P. Fenwick. "Inter-Subject EEG Correlations at a Distance— the Transferred Potential." In C. S. Alvarado (ed.). *Proceedings of the 44th Annual Convention of the Parapsychological Association.* New York: Parapsychological Association; 2001.

Sandoz, Mari. *The Buffalo Hunters.* Lincoln, NE: University of Nebraska Press; 1954.

Sato, Rebecca. "Space Euphoria: Do Our Brains Change When We Travel in Outer Space?" Dailygalaxy.com. www.dailygalaxy.com/my_weblog/2008/05/space -euphoria.html. May 20, 2008. Accessed December 18, 2011.

Scheib, R. "Timeline." *Utne Reader.* January–February 1996: 52–61.

Scheltema, Renée. *Something Unknown Is Doing We Don't Know What.* www .somethingunknown.com/about.php. Accessed January 2, 2012.

Schiller, Ferdinand C. S. "The Progress of Psychical Research." *Fortnightly Review.* 1905; 77.1: 70

———. *Riddles of the Sphinx.* London: Swan Sonnenschein; 1891.

Schlitz, Marilyn and William Braud. "Distant Intentionality and Healing: Assessing the Evidence. *Alternative Therapies in Health and Medicine.* 1997; 3(6): 62–73.

Schmeidler, Gertrude. "Predicting Good and Bad Scores in a Clairvoyance Experiment: A Preliminary Report." *Journal of the American Society for Psychical Research.* 1943; 37: 103–10.

Schmicker, Michael. *Best Evidence.* Lincoln, NE: Writers Club Press; 2002.

Schmidt, Stefan. "The Attention-Focusing Facilitation Paradigm: Remote Helping for Meditation? A Meta-Analysis." Paper presented at the Parapsychology Association's 53rd Annual Convention, Paris, France, July 22–25, 2010. Published in *The Journal of Parapsychology.* 2010; 74(2): 259–60. Abstract available at: http://archived.parapsych

.org/convention/2010_PA_Convention_Abstracts_and_Program.pdf. Accessed December 26, 2011.

Schnabel, Jim. "Don't Mess with My Reality." hereticalnotions.com. http://hereticalnotions.com/2011/01/16/dont-mess-with-my-reality. Accessed January 22, 2012.

———. *Remote Viewers: The Secret History of America's Psychic Spies.* New York: Dell; 1997.

Schopenhauer, Arthur. E. F. J. Payne (trans.). *Parerga and Paralipomena,* Volume II. New York: Oxford University Press; 1974.

———. *Sämtliche Werke,* Volume VIII. Stuttgart, Germany; 1850.

———. Quoted at About.com. Hinduism. http://hinduism.about.com/od/reincarnation/a/quotes.htm. Accessed May 25, 2012.

Schrödinger, Erwin. *My View of the World.* Woodbridge, CT: Ox Bow Press; 1983.

———. *What Is Life?* and *Mind and Matter.* London: Cambridge University Press; 1969.

Schul, Bill. *The Psychic Power of Animals.* New York: Fawcett; 1979.

Schulz, Charles M. Quoted at Goodreads.com. www.goodreads.com/quotes/tag/dogs. Accessed November 24, 2012.

Schuman, E. and D. Madison. "Locally Distributed Synaptic Potentiation in the Hypocampus." *Science.* 1994; 263: 532–36.

Schwartz, Gary. *The Afterlife Experiments: Breakthrough Scientific Evidence of Life After Death.* New York: Atria; 2003.

Schwartz, Stephan A. *The Alexandria Project.* Lincoln, NE: iUniverse.com; 2001. Original edition: New York: Delacorte Press; 1983.

———. "An American Profile." *Explore: The Journal of Science and Healing.* 2005; 1(5): 338–39. Available at: http://download.journals.elsevierhealth.com/pdfs/journals/1550-8307/PIIS1550830705002958.pdf. Accessed January 11, 2012.

———. "Nonlocal Awareness and Visions of the Future." Interview of Stephan A. Schwartz by Daniel Redwood. Healthy.net. www.healthy.net/scr/interview.asp?id=305. Accessed November 31, 2011.

———. *Opening to the Infinite: The Art and Science of Nonlocal Awareness.* Buda, Texas: Nemoseen Media; 2007.

———. *The Secret Vaults of Time.* Charlottesville, VA: Hampton Roads. New edition. 2005. Original edition: New York: Grosset & Dunlap; 1978.

Schwartz, Stephan A. and Larry Dossey. "Nonlocality, Intention, and Observer Effects in Healing Studies: Laying a Foundation for the Future." *Explore: The Journal of Science and Healing.* 2010; 6(5): 295–307.

Schwarz, Berthold E. "Possible Telesomatic Reactions." *The Journal of the Medical Society of New Jersey.* 1967; 64(11): 600–03.

Scott, Sam. *Encounters with Beauty.* Albuquerque, NM: Fresco Fine Art Publications; 2007.

Searle, John. Cover quotation. *Journal of Consciousness Studies.* 2(1): 1995.

Seebohm, Benjamin. *Memoirs of the Life and Gospel Labors of Stephen Grellet.* Volume I. Philadelphia: Longstreth; 1867.

Segal, Suzanne. *Collision with the Infinite: A Life Beyond the Personal Self.* 2nd edition. San Diego, CA: Blue Dove Press; 1996.

———. Wikipedia. www.amazon.com/wiki/Suzanne_Segal/ref=ntt_at_bio_wiki#cite _note-7. Accessed December 5, 2011.

Selous, Edmund. *Thought Transference (or What?) in Birds.* London: Constable; 1931.

Setion. Grandfather's clock. www.yourghoststories.com/real-ghost-story.php?story =2832. Accessed December 25, 2011.

Shadow. Dailygrail.com. www.dailygrail.com/blogs/shadow/2005/7/Telling-Bees. Accessed January 12, 2011.

Sheldrake, Rupert. "Commentary on a Paper by Wiseman, Smith and Milton on the 'psychic pet' phenomenon." *Journal of the Society for Psychical Research.* 1999; 63: 306–11. Abstract available at www.sheldrake.org/D&C/controversies/wiseman.html. Accessed December 1, 2011.

———. *Dogs That Know When Their Owners Are Coming Home.* Reprint edition. New York: Three Rivers Press; 1999.

———. *Morphic Resonance: The Nature of Formative Causation* (Revised and Expanded Edition of *A New Science of Life*). Rochester, VT: Park Street Press; 2009.

———. *A New Science of Life: The Nature of Formative Causation.* Fourth edition. Rochester, VT: Park Street Press; 2009.

———. *The Presence of the Past: Morphic Resonance and the Habits of Nature.* New York: Time/Life; 1988.

———. *The Science Delusion.* London: Coronet; 2012.

———. *Science Set Free.* New York: Crown; 2012.

———. *The Sense of Being Stared At: And Other Aspects of the Extended Mind.* New York: Random House; 2003.

Sheldrake, Rupert, Terence McKenna, and Ralph Abraham. *The Evolutionary Mind: Trialogues at the Edge of the Unthinkable.* Santa Cruz, CA: Trialogue Press; 1998.

Sheldrake, Rupert and A. Morgana. "Testing a Language—Using a Parrot for Telepathy." *Journal of Scientific Exploration.* 2003; 17: 601–15. Abstract available at: www .sheldrake.org/Articles&Papers/papers/animals/parrot_telepathy_abs.html. Accessed March 13, 2011.

Sheldrake, Rupert and Pam Smart. "Psychic Pets: A Survey in Northwest England." *Journal of the Society for Psychic Research.* 1997; 61: 353–64.

Sheldrake, Rupert and Lewis Wolpert. "Telepathy Debate." Royal Society of the Arts. London, January 15, 2005. Available online at SkepticalInvestigations.org. http://www .skepticalinvestigations.org/New/Mediaskeptics/telepathy_RSA.html. Accessed October 2, 2007.

Sherrington, Sir Charles. *The Integrative Action of the Nervous System.* New Haven, CT: Yale University Press. First published in 1906.

———. Quoted in Erwin Schrödinger. *What Is Life?* and *Mind and Matter.* London: Cambridge University Press; 1969.

Shoup, Richard. "Physics Without Causality—Theory and Evidence." Paper presented to the Society for Scientific Exploration, 26th Annual Meeting, East Lansing, Michigan, May 30–June 2, 2007:13.

Silverton, Bobbie. Wikipedia. http://en.wikipedia.org/wiki/Silverton_Bobbie. Accessed January 7, 2011.

Simeon, Daphne and Jeffrey Abugel. *Feeling Unreal: Depersonalization Disorder and the Loss of the Self.* New York: Oxford University Press; 2008.

Simons, Daniel. *The Invisible Gorilla: And Other Ways Our Intuitions Deceive Us.* New York: Crown; 2010.

———. Interview. http://neuronarrative.wordpress.com/2010/07/27/did-you-see-the -gorilla-an-interview-with-psychologist-daniel-simons/. Accessed March 20, 2011.

Simpson, George Gaylord. *Life of the Past.* New Haven, CT: Yale University Press; 1953.

Sinel, Joseph. *The Sixth Sense.* London; T. W. Laurie; 1927.

Smith, Huston. *Beyond the Post-Modern Mind.* Wheaton, IL: Theosophical Publishing House; 1982.

———. *Forgotten Truth: The Primordial Tradition.* New York: Harper Colophon; 1976.

Socrates. Quoted in Wisdom. Wikiquote. http://en.wikiquote.org/wiki/Wisdom. Accessed November 28, 2011.

Socrates. QuotesEverlasting.com. http://quoteseverlasting.com/author.php?a =Socrates. Accessed March 29, 2013.

Splane, Lily. *Quantum Consciousness.* San Diego, CA: Anaphase II Publishing; 2004.

Standish, L., L. Kozak, L. C. Johnson, and T. Richards. "Electroencephalographic Evidence of Correlated Event-Related Signals Between the Brains of Spatially and Sensory Isolated Human Subjects." *Journal of Alternative and Complementary Medicine.* 2004: 10(2): 307–14.

Standish, L., L. C. Johnson, T. Richards, and L. Kozak. "Evidence of Correlated Functional MRI Signals Between Distant Human Brains. *Alternative Therapies in Health and Medicine.* 2003; 9: 122–25.

Stein, Gertrude. *Everybody's Autobiography.* New York: Random House; 1937.

Stein, Rob. "Happiness Can Spread among People Like a Contagion, Study Indicates." *Washington Post* online. www.washingtonpost.com/wp-dyn/content/story/2008 /12/04/ST2008120403608.html. December 5, 2009. Accessed January 18, 2012.

Steinbeck, John. *The Grapes of Wrath.* New edition. New York: Penguin; 2002.

Stelljes, Susan. *Wonder Dog, the Story of Silverton Bobbie.* Portland, OR: For the Love of Dogs Books; 2005.

Stevens, E. W. *The Watseka Wonder.* Chicago: Religio-Philosophical Publishing House; 1878.

Stevenson II, Adlai E. Speech at the University of Wisconsin; Madison, Wisconsin; October 8, 1952.

———. *Children Who Remember Previous Lives: A Question of Reincarnation.* Revised edition. Jefferson, NC: McFarland; 2001.

———. *Telepathic Impressions: A Review and Report of Thirty-five New Cases.* Charlottesville, VA: University of Virginia Press; 1970.

———. *Where Reincarnation and Biology Intersect.* Westport, CT: Praeger, 1997.

Stoeber, Michael and Hugo Meynell (eds.) *Critical Reflections on the Paranormal.* Albany, NY: SUNY Press; 1996.

Sturrock, Peter A. *A Tale of Two Sciences: Memoirs of a Dissident Scientist.* Palo Alto, CA: Exoscience; 2009.

Surowiecki, James. *The Wisdom of Crowds.* New York: Anchor; 2005.

Survey of Physicians' Views on Miracles. The Louis Finkelstein Institute for Religious and Social Studies of the Jewish Theological Seminary, New York. December 2004.

Sutherland, Cherie. "Psychic Phenomena Following Near-Death Experiences: An Australian Study." *Journal of Near-Death Experiences.* 1989; 8: 99.

Swanson, Claude. *The Synchronized Universe: The Science of the Paranormal.* Tucson, AZ: Poseidia Press; 2003.

Swarm Intelligence. Wikipedia. http://en.wikipedia.org/wiki/Swarm_intelligence. Accessed December 3, 2010.

Swinburne, Algernon Charles. "The Higher Pantheism in a Nutshell." *Heptalogia.* Reprint edition. Whitefish, MT: Kessinger Publishing; 2005.

Syfransky, Sy (ed.). *Sunbeams: A Book of Quotations.* Berkeley, CA: North Atlantic; 1990.

Targ, Russell. *Do You See What I See?* Charlottesville, VA: Hampton Roads; 2008.

———. *Limitless Mind: A Guide to Remote Viewing and Transformation of Consciousness.* Novato, CA: New World Library; 2004.

———. *The Reality of ESP.* Wheaton, IL: Theosophical Publishing House; 2012.

———. "Remote Viewing at Stanford Research Institute in the 1970s: A Memoir." *Journal of Scientific Exploration.* 1996; 10(1): 77–88.

———. "Why I Am Absolutely Convinced of the Reality of Psychic Abilities and Why You Should Be Too." Invited address. Annual convention of the Parapsychological Association. Paris, France, July 22–25, 2010. http://thescienceofreincarnation.com /pages/Russell-Targ-Parapsychological-PA-Talk-Intro.pdf. Accessed December 28, 2011.

Targ, Russell and Jane Katra. *Miracles of Mind.* Novato, CA: New World Library; 1998.

Targ, Russell and Hal Puthoff. "Information Transmission under Conditions of Sensory Shielding." *Nature.* 1974; 252: 602–07.

———. *Mind-Reach. Scientists Look at Psychic Ability.* New York: Delacorte; 1977. Also: Editorial, "Scanning the issue." *Proceedings of the IEEE.* March 1976; LXIV(3): 291.

Tart, Charles T. *The End of Materialism: How Evidence of the Paranormal is Bringing Science and Spirit Together.* Oakland, CA: New Harbinger, 2009.

———. *Body Mind Spirit: Exploring the Parapsychology of Spirituality.* Charlottesville, VA: Hampton Roads; 1997.

Taylor, D. J. *Orwell: The Life.* New York: Henry Holt; 2003.

Teixeira, P. C. N., H. Rocha, and J. A. C. Neto. "Johrei, a Japanese Healing Technique, Enhances the Growth of Sucrose Crystals." *Explore: The Journal of Science and Healing.* 2010; 6(5): 313–23.

"Telepathy." *Gale Encyclopedia of Occultism and Parapsychology.* Cited material available at: Answers.com. http://www.answers.com/topic/telepathy. Accessed January 9, 2011.

"Telling the Bees." SacredTexts.com. www.sacred-texts.com/neu/eng/osc/osc69.htm. Accessed January 9, 2011.

Thaheld, Fred H. "Biological Nonlocality and the Mind-Brain Interaction Problem: Comments on a New Empirical Approach." *BioSystems*. 2003; 70: 35–41.

———. "A Method to Explore the Possibility of Nonlocal Correlations Between Brain Electrical Activities of Two Spatially Separated Animal Subjects." *BioSystems*. 2004; 73: 205–16.

Thomas, Lewis. *The Lives of a Cell*. New York: Penguin; 1978.

———. "The Long Habit." *New England Journal of Medicine*. 1972; 286: 825–26.

———. *The Medusa and the Snail*. New York: Penguin; 1995.

Thompson, Andrea. "Mystery Flash Traced to Russian Space Junk." MSNBC.com. www.msnbc.msn.com/id/29958635/#.TukqtBxZ2jQ. Accessed December 14, 2011.

Thomson, Ainsley. "Dolphins Saved Us from Shark, Lifeguards Say." European Cetacean Bywatch Campaign. November 23, 2004. www.eurocbc.org/dolphins_protect_lifeguards_from_shark_nz_23nov2004page1802.html. Accessed May 15, 2011.

Thoreau, Henry David. *The Journal of Henry David Thoreau*. Volume V. New York: Dover: 1962.

———. *Walden*. New York: Cosimo, Inc.; 2009.

Tiller, William. "What Are Subtle Energies?" *Journal of Scientific Exploration*. 1993; 7: 293–304.

Tillich, Paul. *The Courage to Be*. New Haven, CT: Yale University Press; 1952.

Trapman, A. H. *The Dog, Man's Best Friend*. London: Hutchinson & Co.; 1929.

Treffert, Darold A. *Extraordinary People: Understanding Savant Syndrome*. Lincoln, NE: iUniverse, Inc.; 2006.

Treffert, Darold A. and Daniel D. Christensen. "Inside the Mind of a Savant." Scientificamerican.com. www.scientificamerican.com/article.cfm?id=inside-the-mind-of-a-sava. May 31, 2006. Accessed January 4, 2011.

Treffert, Darold A. and Gregory L. Wallace. "Islands of Genius." *Scientific American*. Sciam.com. http://lcn.salk.edu/press/uncommon_genius.pdf. June 2002: 76–85. Accessed January 4, 2011.

Trismegistus, Hermes. Walter Scott, ed. and trans. *Hermetica*. Boulder, CO: Hermes House; 1982.

Trotter, Wilfred. *Instincts of the Herd in Peace and War*. 4th edition. New York: Macmillan; 1919.

Trousseau, Armand. Wikipedia. http://en.wikipedia.org/wiki/Armand_Trousseau. Accessed January 20, 2012.

Troward, Thomas. *The Wisdom of Thomas Troward*. Volume I. Radford, VA: Wilder Publications; 2008.

Trump, Donald. "The Time 100. Heroes and Pioneers: Wesley Autrey." May 3, 2007. www.time.com/time/specials/2007/time100/article/0,28804,1595326_1615754_1615746,00.html. Accessed December 8, 2011.

Tucker, Jim B. *Life Before Life: Children's Memories of Previous Lives*. New York: St. Martin's; 2005.

Turner, Frederick. *Natural Religion.* New Brunswick, NJ: Transaction Publishers; 2006.

Twain, Mark. Quoted at Goodreads.com. www.goodreads.com/quotes/tag/cats. Accessed November 24, 2012.

———. Quoted at Goodreads.com. www.goodreads.com/quotes/tag/dogs. Accessed November 24, 2012.

Tzu, Lao. Derek Lin (trans.) *Tao Te Ching.* Taosim.net. http://www.taoism.net/ttc /chapters/chap01.htm. Accessed March 29, 2013.

Underhill, Evelyn. *Mysticism.* New York: Dutton; 1961.

Utley, Robert M. and Wilcomb E. Washburn. *Indian Wars.* New York: Mariner Books/ American Heritage Press; 2002.

Valletin, Antonina. E. W. Dickes (trans.). *Leonardo da Vinci: The Tragic Pursuit of Perfection.* New York: Viking; 1938.

Van de Castle, Robert L. *Our Dreaming Mind.* New York: Ballantine; 1994.

Van der Post, Sir Laurens. *Jung and the Story of Our Time.* New York: Vintage; 1977.

Van Lommel, Pim. *Consciousness Beyond Life: The Science of the Near-Death Experience.* Reprint edition. New York: HarperOne; 2011.

——— et al. "Near-Death Experience in Survivors of Cardiac Arrest: A Prospective Study in the Netherlands." *The Lancet.* 2001; 358: 2039–45.

Van Oss, Stefan. "Hunch Prompted Dutch Man to Cancel Flight on Air France 447." Seattlepi.com. June 1, 2009. Available at: http://blog.seattlepi.com/aerospace /archives/170003.asp. Accessed December 6, 2011.

Vanderbilt, Gloria and Thelma Furness. *Double Exposure: A Twin Autobiography.* London: Frederick Muller; 1959.

Vedral, Vlatko. "Living in a Quantum World." *Scientific American.* 2011; 304(6): 38–43.

Vernon, Mark. Philosophy and Life blog. http://www.markvernon.com /friendshiponline/dotclear. Accessed December 14, 2011.

Vivekananda. "Spiritual Practices: Silence." www.spiritualityandpractice.com/practices /practices.php?id=28&g=1. Accessed January 7, 2012.

Volk, Steve. *Fringe-ology: How I Tried to Explain Away the Unexplainable.* New York: HarperOne; 2011.

Voltaire. "La Princesse de Babylone." In *Romans et Contes.* Paris; Éditions Garnier Frères; 1960.

Von Franz, Marie-Louise. *Psyche and Matter.* Boston: Shambhala; 1992.

Wackerman J., C. Seiter, H. Keibel, and H. Walach. "Correlations Between Brain Electrical Activities of Two Spatially Separated Human Subjects." *Neuroscience Letters.* 2003; 336: 60–64.

Wagner-Pacifici, R. and H. J. Bershady. "Portents or Confessions: Authoritative Readings of a Dream Text." *Symbolic Interaction.* 1990; 16: 129–43.

Walach, Harald, and Rainer Schneider. Rainer Schneider and Ronald A. Chez (eds.). *Generalized Entanglement From a Multidisciplinary Perspective.* Proceedings of a conference in Freiberg, Germany, October 2003. Washington, DC: Samueli Institute; 2003.

Wales, Jimmy. Wikipedia. http://en.wikipedia.org/wiki/Jimmy_Wales#cite_note -roblimo-47. Accessed November 21, 2011.

Walker, Alice. *Anything We Love Can Be Saved.* New York: Ballantine; 1998.

Warcollier, R. "Un Cas de Changement de Personnalité avec Xénoglossie." *La Métapsychique 1940–1946;* Paris; 1946.

Watson, James D. *The Double Helix.* New York: Touchstone; 2001.

Watson, John B. Quoted in David G. Myers. *Psychology.* New York: Macmillan; 2004.

Watson, Lyall. *The Nature of Things: The Secret Life of Inanimate Objects.* Rochester, VT: Destiny Books; 1990.

————. "Natural Harmony: The Biology of Being Appropriate." Lecture delivered to The Isthmus Institute, Dallas, Texas, April 1989.

————. *Twins: An Investigation into the Strange Coincidences in the Lives of Separated Twins.* London: Sphere Books; 1984.

Watts, Alan. Quoted at Secondattention.com. www.secondattention.org/videos /alanwatts.aspx. Accessed July 17, 2010.

Weber, Renée. *Dialogues with Scientists and Sages.* New York: Routledge and Kegan Paul; 1986.

The Week Staff. "Should Yoga Be an Olympic Sport?" http://theweek.com/article /index/225075/should-yoga-be-an-olympic-sport. Accessed March 3, 2012.

Weil, Andrew. *Spontaneous Healing.* New York: Knopf; 1995.

Weller, Edward. *Hubble: A Journey Through Space and Time.* New York: Abrams; 2010.

West, Rebecca. *A Train of Powder.* Chicago: Ivan R. Dee; 2000.

White, Frank. *The Overview Effect.* Reston, VA: American Institute of Aeronautics and Astronautics; 1998.

Whitehead, Alfred North. *Essays in Science and Philosophy.* New York: Philosophical Library; 1948.

Whitman, Walt. *The Complete Poems.* New York: Penguin Classics; 2004.

————. *Leaves of Grass.* Bartleby.com. Great Books Online. www.bartleby.com/142 /86.html. Accessed November 22, 2011.

Whittier, John Greenleaf. "Telling the Bees." *The Complete Poetical Works of John Greenleaf Whittier.* Whitefish, MT: Kessinger Publishing; 2003.

Wigner, Eugene P. "Are We Machines?" *Proceedings of the American Philosophical Society.* 1969; 113(2): 95–101. Available at: Jstor.org. www.jstor.org/stable/985959. Accessed February 2, 2011.

Wilber, Ken. *A Brief History of Everything.* Boston: Shambhala; 1996.

————. *Eye to Eye: The Quest for the New Paradigm.* Revised edition. Boston: Shambhala; 2001.

————. *Integral Spirituality: A Startling New Role for Religion in the Modern and Postmodern World.* Boston: Shambhala; 2007.

———— (ed.). *Quantum Questions: The Mystical Writings of the World's Great Physicists.* Boston: Shambhala; 1984.

————. *Sex, Ecology, Spirituality: The Spirit of Evolution.* Second Edition. Boston: Shambhala; 2001.

————. *The Spectrum of Consciousness.* Wheaton, IL: Theosophical Publishing House; 1977.

Wilson, Colin. *The Occult.* London: Watkins Publishing; 2004.

Wilson, Woodrow. Quoted at GoodReads.com. www.goodreads.com/quotes/tag /dogs. Accessed November 23, 2012.

Winkler, Marilyn. Personal communication to the author. May 14, 2009. Used with permission.

Winter, Dylan. Starlings at Otmoor. www.youtube.com/watch?v=XH-groCeKbE. Accessed December 4, 2011.

Wiseman, Richard and Marilyn Schlitz. "Experimenter Effects and the Remote Detection of Staring." *Journal of Parapsychology.* 1997; 61: 197–208.

Wiseman, Richard, M. Smith, and J. Milton. "Can Animals Detect When Their Owners are Returning Home? An Experimental Test of the 'Psychic Pet' Phenomenon." *British Journal of Psychology.* 1998; 89(3): 453–62.

Wittgenstein, Ludwig. Propositions 6.4311 and 6.4312. *Tractatus Logico-Philosophicus.* Seattle, WA: CreateSpace; 2011: 93.

————. *Tractatus Logico-Philosophicus.* London: Routledge and Kegan Paul; 1961.

Wölfli, Adolf. Recited and set to music. Adolf Wölfli Foundation. www.adolfwoelfli.ch /index.php?c=e&level=5&sublevel=1. Accessed March 24, 2011.

Woodley, Sherrida. *Quick Fall of Light.* Spokane, WA: Gray Dog Press; 2010.

Wright, Lawrence. "Double Mystery." *The New Yorker.* August 7, 1996: 45–62.

————. *Twins.* New York: Wiley; 1997.

Yu, Beongcheon. *The Great Circle: American Writers and the Orient.* Detroit, MI: Wayne State University Press; 1983.

INDEX

J

K

L

O

ABOUT THE AUTHOR

Larry Dossey, M.D., is a leader in bringing scientific understanding to spirituality and rigorous proof to complementary/integrative medicine. He is an internal medicine physician and the former chief of staff of Medical City Dallas Hospital. Dr. Dossey is an international advocate for the role of the mind in health. He is the author of the *New York Times* bestseller *Healing Words,* the first in-depth look at how compassionate intentions and prayer affect healing. He has lectured at the nation's leading medical schools and hospitals and internationally. He has been featured several times by Oprah—her TV show, radio show, and magazine—and many other major radio and television programs. Dr. Dossey is the author of 12 books, which have been translated into languages around the world. He is the executive editor of the peer-reviewed journal *Explore: The Journal of Science and Healing.* Follow Dr. Dossey at www.dosseydossey.com.

Hay House Titles of Related Interest

YOU CAN HEAL YOUR LIFE, the movie, starring Louise L. Hay & Friends
(available as a 1-DVD program and an expanded 2-DVD set)
Watch the trailer at: **www.LouiseHayMovie.com**

THE SHIFT, the movie,
starring Dr. Wayne W. Dyer
(available as a 1-DVD program and an expanded 2-DVD set)
Watch the trailer at: **www.DyerMovie.com**

THE BIOLOGY OF BELIEF: Unleashing the Power of Consciousness, Matter & Miracles, by Bruce H. Lipton, Ph.D.

DEEP TRUTH: Igniting the Memory of Our Origin, History, Destiny, and Fate, by Gregg Braden

THE HONEYMOON EFFECT: The Science of Creating Heaven on Earth, by Bruce H. Lipton, Ph.D.

MIND OVER MEDICINE: Scientific Proof That You Can Heal Yourself, by Lissa Rankin, M.D.

RESONANCE: Nine Practices for Harmonious Health and Vitality, by Joyce Whiteley Hawkes, Ph.D.

SPONTANEOUS EVOLUTION: Our Positive Future and a Way to Get There From Here, by Bruce H. Lipton, Ph.D. and Steve Bhaerman

All of the above are available at your local bookstore,
or may be ordered by contacting Hay House (see next page).

We hope you enjoyed this Hay House book. If you'd like to receive our online catalog featuring additional information on Hay House books and products, or if you'd like to find out more about the Hay Foundation, please contact:

Hay House, Inc., P.O. Box 5100, Carlsbad, CA 92018-5100
(760) 431-7695 or (800) 654-5126
(760) 431-6948 (fax) or (800) 650-5115 (fax)
www.hayhouse.com® • **www.hayfoundation.org**

Published and distributed in Australia by: Hay House Australia Pty. Ltd.,
18/36 Ralph St., Alexandria NSW 2015 • *Phone:* 612-9669-4299
Fax: 612-9669-4144 • www.hayhouse.com.au

Published and distributed in the United Kingdom by: Hay House UK, Ltd.,
Astley House, 33 Notting Hill Gate, London W11 3JQ • *Phone:* 44-20-3675-2450
Fax: 44-20-3675-2451 • www.hayhouse.co.uk

Published and distributed in the Republic of South Africa by:
Hay House SA (Pty), Ltd., P.O. Box 990, Witkoppen 2068
Phone/Fax: 27-11-467-8904 • www.hayhouse.co.za

Published in India by: Hay House Publishers India, Muskaan Complex,
Plot No. 3, B-2, Vasant Kunj, New Delhi 110 070 • *Phone:* 91-11-4176-1620
Fax: 91-11-4176-1630 • www.hayhouse.co.in

Distributed in Canada by: Raincoast, 9050 Shaughnessy St., Vancouver, B.C. V6P 6E5
Phone: (604) 323-7100 • *Fax:* (604) 323-2600 • www.raincoast.com

Take Your Soul on a Vacation

Visit **www.HealYourLife.com®** to regroup, recharge,
and reconnect with your own magnificence.
Featuring blogs, mind-body-spirit news, and life-changing
wisdom from Louise Hay and friends.

Visit **www.HealYourLife.com** today!

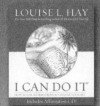